The Empowerment Solution

"We humans need this book now! Our thoughts and our minds have the ability to heal with this guidance. The greatest relationship you have is with yourself, and Dr. Schaub does an incredible job of teaching us to empower ourselves with the amazing information in this book."

DANA G. COHEN, M.D., COAUTHOR OF *QUENCH*

"So many of us are looking for answers to help with anxiety, poor self-esteem, lack of confidence, insomnia, and countless other issues. Many of these issues stem from stories never told or beliefs that are not founded in reality. Friedemann Schaub, M.D., Ph.D., has compiled in *The Empowerment Solution* all the tools that will bring freedom from anxiety and self-doubt and then enhanced personal empowerment, which we all strive for in life. It is a must-read for all of us on a quest for self-empowerment."

MARCELLE PICK, OB/GYN NP, AUTHOR OF
IS IT ME OR MY HORMONES?, *THE CORE BALANCE DIET*,
AND *IS IT ME OR MY ADRENALS?*

"Living in survival mode makes us feel anxious and powerless. Dr. Schaub's book will show you how to get through survival mode and come out on the other side. *The Empowerment Solution* puts you on a path of self-exploration to learn how to own your energy and life again. This very helpful guide not only provides practical and powerful steps for how to regain your power but also shares real-life examples from Dr. Schaub and his clients in stories that we can all identify with. Dive into this book, implement the exercises, and on the way discover how effortlessly you can become empowered."

DR. MAYA NOVAK, MINDFUL HEALING EXPERT AND
AUTHOR OF *HEAL BEYOND EXPECTATIONS*

"*The Empowerment Solution* is such an insightful book. A light went off inside when I learned about anxiety being an inner compass that alerts us when we're off our path. It makes perfect sense. I also found the chapter "Self-Compassion: The Key to Owning Your Hidden Gifts" very moving and profound. It truly helped me connect to the scared little boy in me. I lost my dad to cancer and that loss would've been much, much harder for me had I not connected those fears into strengths. Dr. Friedemann and this book helped me do that."

MAURICE BENARD, DAYTIME EMMY AWARD–WINNING ACTOR ON
GENERAL HOSPITAL, AUTHOR OF THE
NEW YORK TIMES BESTSELLER *NOTHING GENERAL ABOUT IT,*
AND HOST OF *STATE OF MIND* PODCAST

"In this insightful and helpful book, Dr. Schaub offers far more than the standard techniques for dealing with fear and anxiety. He goes deeper and gets at the real causes of our discontent. Most importantly, Schaub provides solutions that reconnect us with ourselves, our power, and our fundamental ground."

NANCY COLIER, AUTHOR OF *THE EMOTIONALLY EXHAUSTED
WOMAN* AND *CAN'T STOP THINKING*

THE EMPOWERMENT SOLUTION

Six Keys to Unlocking Your Full Potential with

the Subconscious Mind

Friedemann Schaub M.D., Ph.D.

Destiny Books

Rochester, Vermont

Destiny Books
One Park Street
Rochester, Vermont 05767
www.DestinyBooks.com

Text stock is SFI certified

Destiny Books is a division of Inner Traditions International

Cataloging-in-Publication Data for this title is available from the Library of Congress

ISBN 978-1-64411-641-8 (print)
ISBN 978-1-64411-642-5 (ebook)

Printed and bound in the United States by Lake Book Manufacturing, LLC
The text stock is SFI certified. The Sustainable Forestry Initiative® program
promotes sustainable forest management.

10 9 8 7 6 5 4 3 2 1

Text design and layout by Kenleigh Manseau
This book was typeset in Garamond Premier Pro with Sabon LT std and Roboto
used as display fonts

To send correspondence to the author of this book, mail a first-class letter to the
author c/o Inner Traditions • Bear & Company, One Park Street, Rochester, VT
05767, and we will forward the communication, or contact the author directly at
https://drfriedemann.com.

To my beloved wife, best friend, and home of my heart,
Danielle Rama Hoffman

CONTENTS

PART III

Taking a Stand

From Pleasing Others to Loving
Your Authentic Self

PART IV

Taking Charge
Integration through Implementation

• • • • • •

INTRODUCTION

When I was seventeen years old, my dad and I went on a short hiking vacation in the Italian Alps. Frankly, spending four days with my father wasn't something I was really looking forward to. Since I could remember, his intense and unpredictable angry outbursts and mood swings kept my mom, sister, and me on edge. So going on holiday with him felt like having a picnic in a minefield.

One day, as we were walking across a beautiful mountain meadow, he suddenly said, "You know, since I was seventeen, I've always been anxious." This took me by surprise. I knew that my dad was forced to fight in World War II when he'd just turned seventeen. He never talked about his certainly horrendous experiences on the battlefield. I just knew that he was captured at the end of the war and kept in a French prison camp, where he almost died from starvation. And when he and his best friend escaped, his buddy was shot and killed in the process, while my father just barely made it. He must have been dealing with survivor's guilt. Afterward, he surrendered to the US Forces because he knew he had a greater chance to survive in an American prisoner-of-war camp.

My father was fifty-five at the time of our hike. Was this traumatic past still haunting him after all these years? I wondered. Maybe because I hadn't said anything, he continued: "You know it isn't just what happened during the war. What makes me anxious is the fear of losing everything and ending up having nothing, just like I grew up." My dad was just a little boy when his father passed away from tuberculosis. His mom raised his three sisters and him on a minimal salary, and through arduous work she made ends meet. He had told me before how little his family had had to eat, and how after the war ended his older sisters took their cart and traveled—sometimes gone for weeks—far beyond their home in the Black Forest, to beg farmers for some vegetables or a little bit of flour.

As my father continued sharing his constant worry of being impoverished, it dawned on me that much of his anger and depression must have been fueled by his anxiety. Logically, there was no reason for him to be concerned. He was a successful countryside doctor with a thriving practice he'd built with my mom, who was also a physician. But, as he admitted during the hike, as soon as a patient switched to another colleague or he had to deal with an unexpected expense, his anxiety overwhelmed him, causing him to catastrophize and worry day and night. "And there is nothing I can do to make my anxiety go away," he said.

I guess seeing a counselor or psychiatrist would have been an option, but my dad was too proud and too scared to admit his struggles to anyone. I'm still not sure why my father chose that day as one of the rare moments he was willing to show me his vulnerable side. Nevertheless, what he confided in me affected me deeply. I knew how anxiety felt since I'd been dealing with it myself since I was ten years old. Like most of us, I wasn't encouraged to discover who I was as a child, trust in my inner wisdom, or follow the guidance of my heart. Instead, I was told that I was better off controlling my natural cheerfulness, to become more serious, conform to what others expected from me, and stay motivated to advance by competing and comparing myself with my peers. During the hike with my dad, I promised myself, as most seventeen-year-old teenagers do, that I would never become like him and end up stuck in a prison of doubt, worry, and powerlessness.

Well, never say never. Fast forward thirteen years, and I was on my way to getting trapped in the very same mindset. As a stressed-out resident in cardiology, I too had spent many days and sleepless nights agonizing about how everything could be taken away from me. By everything, I meant my career, in which I'd invested so much time and energy that it had become my identity. I constantly worried about how to please my boss, appear as motivated and competent as my colleagues, and avoid getting negative attention. Admittedly, the pressure to perform and fit in wasn't all in my head. My department head was highly ambitious and swift to write off those he deemed unsuited to help him reach his goals. Even though I felt like a victim of my circumstances at that time, it was still me who chose to combat my stress and anxiety with greasy food, too much wine, the occasional medication, and overcome my sense of powerlessness with hard work and gallons of coffee.

Five years of chronic stress and anxiety on this hamster-wheel-on-overdrive took a toll on me. After several middle-of-the-night panic attacks, I realized that the path I was on and the pace at which I traveled weren't sustainable. I felt lost. One day I walked into a church, somehow hoping that spending a bit of time in this quiet space would give me some answers. To my disappointment, I neither received any guidance nor did I feel any better. All I felt was a big emptiness in my heart that I had no clue how to fill or even reach, because it was surrounded by a wall of anxiety, insecurity, and confusion. Maybe it would have been wise to look for a counselor. Yet, I was already too far down the road my dad had laid out for me, so my pride and fear of showing vulnerability stopped me from looking in the yellow pages, picking up the phone, and making an appointment.

As I described in my first book, *The Fear and Anxiety Solution,* years later, I learned to understand and appreciate anxiety as an inner compass that alerts us when we're off track and out of alignment with ourselves. Although my experience as a resident was rough at times, I'm glad my anxiety didn't give up on me. It continued to push me to take an inventory of my life and ask myself important questions such as, Is that all that my life is supposed to be? Am I really happy with who I am and with what I am doing?

Again, for a long time, no answers. But at least these questions kept me wondering whether I should continue on this path of life or choose a different one, until one day fate smiled on me and nudged me to make a choice. This was when everything changed, which I will tell you more about in the last chapter of the book.

If you ask yourself these questions, Is my life all it is supposed to be? and Am I really happy with who I am and what I am doing? do you get any answers? Or do you tell yourself, as I did, that you need to suck it up buttercup and stop complaining, because it could be worse?

Not to sound uncaring, but if there was one positive aspect of the COVID-19 pandemic, it was that people took this frightening and challenging time as an opportunity to reflect on themselves and their lives. Many of my clients told me that, particularly during lockdowns, they realized how hectic, busy, and overwhelming their day-to-day lives had become. Once the pandemic restrictions took all the usual obligations, expectations, and distractions away, they felt a strange sense of relief and peace. As one of my clients put it, "Although I'm not able to leave the house and do what I want, I feel freer and lighter than I have in a long time. There's no pressure to perform or fit in, no fear of missing out or not measuring up, and nobody who can make me feel that I'm not good enough."

For many people, the old, autopilot way of living, which someone described as "nobody wants to die, but everybody is just killing time," appeared no longer acceptable. The break from a life that had become unmanageable and deprived of joy and meaning was more than a welcomed reprieve. It awoke a strong desire to break free from the old way of living, which is reflected in the Great

Resignation.[1] Although vaccines and new treatment options have somewhat reduced the dangers of COVID-19, many citizens haven't been willing to let their lives go back to "normal." According to the US Department of Labor, 4.3 million Americans left their jobs in August 2021, which equates to about 2.9 percent of the national workforce.[2] In an interview with the BBC, Professor Martha Maznevski of Western University in Ontario, Canada, explained that the number of people thinking about quitting their jobs may be much higher.[3] According to Professor Maznevski, two broad categories of people choose to participate in the Great Resignation. One is the people who make a good salary but feel uninspired by their jobs and are unwilling to exchange personal fulfillment for advancement in their careers. The other category is minimum wage workers, who are fed up with the toxic and unhealthy conditions they have to endure. I believe that no matter whether people quit a high-paying tech job or a "sweat-job" in retail, hospitality, or the supply chain, they all refuse to sacrifice any longer their health and wellbeing for work that causes them nothing but stress and anxiety. It's still uncertain if the Great Resignation is a new trend or a short-term phenomenon, but the COVID-19 pandemic has magnified for many what I experienced twenty-five years ago: a deep urge to quit the feeling of powerlessness from living in survival mode and start taking the reins of my life.

Since you were drawn to this book, you probably share the feelings of anxiety and powerlessness and the desire to become the empowered leader of your life. And while you may be satisfied with your job, your sense of stressful disempowerment may come from your relationships with others—and yourself. Do any of the following scenarios sound familiar to you?

- You feel trapped by the shadows of past trauma and abuse, and because you don't trust anyone, you keep everybody at arm's length.

- You're too afraid to draw attention to yourself, so you keep your life small and predictable instead of exploring what else is possible for you.
- You're afraid of failure and thus never complete what you started. You stare at an overwhelming mountain of unfinished tasks and overdue obligations.
- Due to insecurity and lack of self-worth, you constantly adjust to what others want you to do and be, or try to get their approval by taking care of their needs while never daring to express your own.
- You put all your energy and attention into finding true love, but instead of happiness and fulfillment, all you receive are countless rejections and disappointments.

If you've been dealing with stress and anxiety due to one or more of these challenges, you've been stuck in survival mode—at least in parts of your life. Chances are that, more often than not, you've wanted to quit much more than your job; you've wanted to quit yourself.

Looking back twenty-five years, my biggest struggle wasn't my job in the cardiology department. What made me feel powerless and lost was that I was disconnected from myself. As a result, I didn't know who I was, what I had to offer, and what I wanted from life. I was usually uncomfortable in my own skin, unable to make clear decisions based on what was right for me, and constantly floating like a feather in the wind looking for someone or something to give me a grounding sense of meaning, worthiness, and belonging. But no direction, instruction, and validation from the outside could soothe my troubled mind and fill my starving heart. It wasn't until I learned to understand my subconscious and consciously fostered a harmonious relationship with this deeper part of my mind, that I finally received answers from within.

You too may have been searching for yourself for quite some time, but you've kept on looking for answers from the outside due to the lack of inner guidance. Maybe you've tried other books, courses, meditations, and mindfulness practices to gain a sense of clarity and peace. And while you've made some progress, you may still feel somewhat empty-hearted, ungrounded, and uncertain about what it means to live as your true self. Wouldn't it be great if you could finally switch out of survival mode and into a more empowered and authentic version of yourself?

The good news is that *The Empowerment Solution* will help you get there by employing the best guide for this quest: your subconscious. I wrote this book based on my twenty years of experience helping people work with their subconscious minds to overcome anxiety and powerlessness and reconnect with themselves. *The Empowerment Solution* shows you step-by-step how to break free from the six most common survival patterns—victim, invisibility, procrastinator, chameleon, helper, and lover—and transform them into the six keys to self-empowerment, allowing you to take self-reliant ownership of your life. You will learn how to disentangle from the past and peel off the layers of false identities, limiting beliefs, and self-negating patterns that have prevented you from seeing and appreciating your inner brilliance. You'll reconnect with your essence, realign your thoughts, feelings, and actions with your authentic truth, and open your heart to reclaim the dormant gifts and powers that reside within.

Not all of the six survival patterns may, at first glance, resonate with you. As a confident extrovert or self-proclaimed go-getter and overachiever, you may be unable to relate to the invisibility pattern or the procrastinator pattern. Or you may tell yourself that the lover pattern doesn't pertain to you because you're a happy, commitment-hesitant single or in a harmonious long-term relationship. And who wants to be called a victim? But you might soon find that we all have these patterns in our survival repertoire. We may just use some in more subtle ways—or have tried to avoid and suppress them, even though they are parts of our subconscious mind.

Reconnecting with these patterns and turning them into their empowered versions will help you access dormant aspects of your potential that will deepen your relationship with yourself and enrich your life with greater joy, purpose, and fulfillment.

The Empowerment Solution is designed as an experiential self-discovery journey. Just as you would take your time to learn to know someone you could fall in love and spend the rest of your life with, pace yourself as you travel on this journey. Take time to process and solidify the new insights you gain about yourself. Practice the self-empowering tools you obtain in your daily life; and continue to appreciate how, with every chapter, you feel increasingly at home with yourself and confident in creating the reality you desire.

This book has all you need to rewrite your outdated owner's manual and become the authentically empowered leader of your life. My only regret is that I could not give my dad a copy during our hike in the Alps. I believe this book could have ended his struggles and transformed his inner world. That's my hope for you.

PART I

Taking Inventory

Why You Are Never Powerless

1
....
Survival and the Slow Loss of Self

For most of us, surviving isn't about staying alive but staying comfortable. Yet, what we should fear more than getting hurt, judged, or rejected, is the painful regret of never having ventured beyond our comfort zone—and never having lived with greater joy and purpose.

You are embarking on a journey of self-discovery and empowerment. With all expeditions, it's wise to define where we started, how we got there, and where we want to end up. Let's be honest, you didn't pick up this book because your life is going swimmingly and you wake up every day with a big smile on your face. Most likely, you're dealing with stress, anxiety, lack of confidence, a general sense of feeling powerless, or maybe even feeling depressed. Welcome to the club; you're not alone. As you will see in a moment, most of our society struggles with similar issues.

But feel good about yourself, that you chose not to throw your hands up in the air and accept your challenges with anxiety or insecurity as a weakness that you need to cope with for the rest of your life. Instead, you're reading this book because you believe enough in yourself to want to learn how to heal from within. Having dealt with anxiety and lack of self-worth myself, I know how much courage and commitment it takes to explore how and why our mind has been making our lives so difficult. But the reward of better understanding our mind is that we also figure out how we can use its power to uncreate these challenges.

In *The Fear and Anxiety Solution,* I described a step-by-step process to overcome fear and anxiety by finding and resolving their subconscious root causes. This was just the beginning. After helping thousands of people worldwide overcome anxiety, lack of self-esteem, and chronic stress, I've found that the key to profound and lasting change is to establish an authentically empowered relationship with ourselves. How we get there is what this journey is all about.

Let me ask you, how often do you feel powerless in just one day—overwhelmed by obligations and unrealistic expectations, stuck in situations that feel impossible to change, or victimized by people you can't control or even by your own emotions? You're stuck in traffic and worry that you'll end up late for work. Your boss pushes an unreasonable deadline on you, which means less time with your loved ones during the weekend. At home, you have to walk on eggshells because your partner is again cranky and shut off but unwilling to talk or do anything about it. And as soon as you wake up in the morning, you wonder when your anxiety may attack you again. The more life appears overwhelming and out of our control, the more powerless we feel.

Yet, we're born with sheer unlimited potential to grow, adapt, and succeed, which makes us innately powerful. Just the fact that we learned how to crawl and then walk, that we figured out how to use our mouths and vocal cords to form words others can understand, and that we developed skills to relate to the world around us proves that we are innately powerful. So when and how do we end up losing our power?

There are undoubtedly many reasons why for many of us life seems overwhelming and unmanageable. Our world faces unprecedented challenges, such as climate change, racial injustice, mass shootings, and political divisiveness. Since the beginning of the COVID-19 pandemic, the level of stress and anxiety has only escalated. The fear of getting ill or losing a loved one, the loss of freedom, financial stability, and normalcy, as well as inflation and a looming recession, are just some of the additional concerns most of us are dealing with right now. A study from June 2020 found that more than three times as many US adults reported symptoms of severe psychological stress in April as they did in 2018.[1] According to a report from the American Psychological Association, more than 80 percent of US adults cite worries about the country's future as a significant source of stress.[2]

Even if we were to put aside the fallout of the pandemic and other challenges, there are four reasons why life has become increasingly stressful during the last two decades.

- To keep up with the increasing demands of our daily lives, we've become busier than ever before. Whether we're pushing ourselves for job security, to maintain a particular lifestyle, to prove our worthiness, or just to make ends meet while also caring for the kids, there remains little time to relax, reflect, and recuperate. Yet no matter how fast we rush through our days and how much we cross off our long to-do lists, we still regularly fail to meet the high expectations of ourselves or others, leaving us feeling defeated, deflated, and not good enough.
- With the omnipresence of smartphones and tablets, we are inundated 24/7 with an enormous amount of data. To compute and sift through this vast external input, our minds work overtime. The combination of busy lives and busy minds means for many a lack of rest. Data from the National Health Institute showed that 35 percent of working adults are not get-

ting adequate sleep, which is defined as seven hours or more per night.[3]

- Paradoxically, while the digital age allows us to be connected to everyone, it prevents us from connecting with ourselves. With the ever-expanding influence of social media and its blurred lines of reality and virtuality, we struggle with the fear of missing out, not fitting in, or not being unique enough. The need for individuality and authenticity is replaced by the need to impress and be liked. Rather than turning inward to discover and embrace our gifts, talents, and desires, we focus on living up to increasingly unattainable standards.

- Unlike our computers, our minds haven't been able to update to calmly sift through the endless amount of information we're flooded with. Being already overloaded, we tend to pay attention to only the fear-mongering messages that promise to tell us the truth, no matter how ludicrous it appears. As extreme views, misinformation, and conspiracy theories erode our trust in fundamental institutions of society, such as government, science, education, and even democracy, absurd movements such as QAnon, the lizard people conspiracy, and flat-earthers gain more followers. It appears that we're dealing with a growing crisis in faith, desperately looking for something or someone to believe in and hold onto.

It all sounds pretty overwhelming, right? That's what our subconscious thinks as well, which is why it's rushing to the rescue. To help us cope with life's challenges, this deeper part of our mind employs two survival modes, avoiding and pleasing, to protect us from what it considers dangerous threats, such as hurt, criticism, ridicule, rejection, failure, and abandonment.

The avoider and pleaser modes consist of six distinct survival patterns—victim, invisibility, procrastinator, chameleon, helper, and lover. There's nothing wrong per se with any of these survival patterns. Most of us use them in various aspects of our lives. But survival patterns, triggered by chronic stress and anxiety, become a problem when they turn into our default ways of being and make us approach life in constant self-defense. Considering the high prevalence of anxiety and stress, it's fair to assume that a large percentage of our society lives in perpetual survival mode.

WHERE DO SURVIVAL PATTERNS COME FROM?

Let me start with a broad overview before we go into details. Our subconscious mind developed survival patterns early in our lives when we depended entirely on the adults around us. Whether we were dealing with instability or volatility in our home, or were repeatedly neglected, judged, made fun of, or punished, our subconscious carefully registered and analyzed negative messages and events to determine whether we were safe, could trust in others, and deserved to be taken care of. It didn't take significant trauma and abuse for the subconscious protector to doubt our safety. We may have had a completely ordinary upbringing on paper, and our siblings may still reminisce about the good old days, but because some of us are more sensitive, a relentlessly teasing brother, our parents' disappointed look when we didn't receive straight A's, or the time when our best friend ditched us for somebody else, signified that life is scary and we need to watch out to avoid getting hurt.

Our subconscious uses these emotionally charged memories as reference points for the future by condensing them into beliefs that define our perspective of ourselves and the world around us (see page 17). An extreme example of this process is a phobia. One day when I was six years old, I heard my mom screaming bloody murder. I ran to the kitchen to find out what had happened to her. I had never seen my mother as frightened before, as she stared at an enormous spider on the floor that just moments before had been crawling on her. Watching my mom with so much angst created a new belief that I needed to steer clear of spiders because they are ter-rifying and dangerous. I am not proud to admit that even into my early thirties, the sight of a hairy eight-legged creature with beady eyes made me run out of the room and ask my wife Danielle to take the monster out of the house.

In contrast to phobias, survival beliefs are more general and wide-reaching. The most common ones are, "I am not safe, I am not good enough, I don't belong, I am not loveable, and the world isn't a good/safe place." Beliefs are powerful filters that distort, general-ize, and omit the external input we are receiving. Suppose that you had been ostracized in school and so you assumed that you don't fit in with others. As an adult, the filter of this limiting belief would make you always remember when your colleagues at work grabbed a coffee without asking you to join. And you would completely for-get that they only went without you because they were planning to throw you a birthday lunch. Limiting beliefs also become self-fulfilling prophecies, as they make us act in ways that confirm their premise. A classic example is when we believe that we are not love-able, and though we are with an adoring partner, we either become so needy or so jealous and suspicious that we eventually push them away, proving to ourselves that nobody can ever love us.

Due to the chronic stress we are living with, our subconscious is on continuous high alert, scanning for any potential danger that may be similar to what we've experienced in the past. Once the sur-vival loop gets triggered, let's say by our mom criticizing that we never stop by, a friend not returning our calls, or an overwhelm-ing amount of work, our subconscious cross-references the current experiences with memories of similar events. With a "See, I knew that I needed to take over, because nothing has changed since our past," the subconscious inner protector launches into survival mode by pulling out the old limiting belief filters to highlight what is "really" going on. These filters distort our perception and make the potential threat bigger and more imminent, and the consequences more severe. Through these filters it is evident that Mom will never approve of us, our friend is mad at us, or that we will inevitably get fired because we can never get on top of the mountain of work that only grows bigger by the minute. The distorted view on reality then activates negative self-talk, anxiety, stress, insecurity, guilt, or shame. If we don't consciously challenge this knee-jerk self-defense reaction, which we'll get into later, the mental-emotional response sets in motion one or several of the six already mentioned survival patterns. Caught in this survival loop, we shift from being competent adults to behaving like we did when we were children.

We shrink like kids when we feel criticized, overextend ourselves to get approval, and want to hide under a blanket to avoid uncomfortable tasks. Even though rationally, we know that we should shrug off other people's opinions and face potential challenges calmly and level-headed, the subconscious survival patterns continue to override any logic and reasoning.

Short-term survival patterns of making ourselves small and invisible, over-giving and over-pleasing, or putting off the tasks at hand can give us a sense of safety or belonging. Yet letting these patterns dominate our lives has two significant downsides:

1. We lose our power because we believe that our safety and well-being depend on others, instead of finding peace, strength, and validation from within. As we feel more and more powerless, we get more easily triggered, which reinforces the beliefs of not being safe, good enough, or belonging, and fuels our struggles with stress, anxiety, and insecurity. Life becomes an endless survival loop just to make it through another day.

2. The second downside of making surviving our primary focus is that we no longer slow down to listen to our thoughts, face our emotions, or ask deep questions such as, What do I really want? What is my purpose? or What is the meaning of life? Since we never developed strong self-awareness, self-acceptance, and self-

worth, we eventually become more than powerless—we become disconnected from ourselves.

Depression and hopelessness set in when we realize that no matter how many people or situations we avoid and how much approval

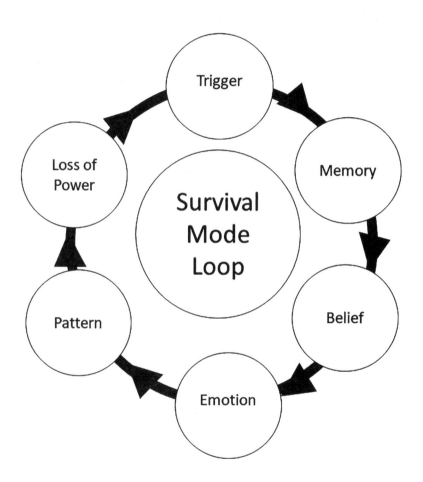

Survival Mode Loop
An emotionally charged memory consolidates into a belief that shapes our perception of reality and activates emotions and behaviors. This survival pattern overrides logic and reasoning. As a result, we lose our power and become disconnected from ourselves. Then a trigger kicks off the memory, and round and round we go.

we receive, we still end up stuck, powerless, and unsure of who we are and whether we matter.

SELF-EMPOWERMENT AND THE ILLUSION OF BEING POWERLESS

Now for the good news: you can switch out of the survival loop for good. You are not powerless, and you can't give your power away. Let's take a look at these common examples of how you might feel you give your power away:

- You consider outside opinions more seriously than your own.
- You follow others' advice, even though you don't want to.
- You prefer to stay quiet and unnoticed.
- You let people talk down to you without pushing back.
- You never say "no" to what others want you to do.

Sounds pretty disempowering, right? But as you look more closely, ask yourself, "Am I giving my power away, or am I not asserting my power?" If you believe more in what others say, it's because you haven't figured out what you choose to believe in. If you prefer to stay invisible and voiceless, it's because you haven't fully embraced the gifts and qualities that make you unique and precious. And if you don't respect your boundaries, it's because you haven't become your own source of safety and validation. In none of these everyday examples have you given anything away. What makes you feel powerless is that your subconscious keeps relying on the familiar survival patterns because it assumes you're still small and helpless. And since your subconscious believes you're powerless, your conscious self does too.

Before you rush to blame your subconscious, remember that it keeps on treating you like an overprotective nanny because the only reference points it has are the memories and limiting beliefs from your childhood. But like using a map from 1965 to find your way around New York City, navigating through life with outdated beliefs will not get you to a place of happiness and fulfillment. In addition, these old limiting beliefs usually aren't based on who you are but on how you've been treated by others, which generally says more about them than it does about you. Therefore, the solution to empowerment isn't to take your power back, because you can't give it away, but to make accessing and harnessing your innate power your default way of being. For this, you need to update your belief system so that your subconscious no longer merely reacts to people and circumstances in self-defense. In other words, to get out of survival mode and become empowered, you need to learn to know, appreciate, and eventually love what is authentically you and yours.

Now that you know where you started from and how you got here, and you have some idea of the destination of this journey, how do you know that you've arrived and have become the empowered self? Some people describe being empowered as being able to take charge of the circumstances and direction of our lives. Others believe that empowerment allows us to influence, direct, and even control everyone around us. However, self-empowerment goes far beyond forcing our will onto our reality or other people.

You are self-empowered when you:

- trust in your wisdom and capabilities to learn and grow from anything life brings you
- accept that your source of safety, self-worth, and belonging is within
- confidently take ownership of your life
- know with every fiber of your being that your authentic self and the gifts that you carry inside matter to the world
- consider yourself an integral part of the web of life and thus treat yourself and all the beings around you with appreciation, compassion, and respect

• commit to taking care of your health and well-being with kindness and love

Of course, this list could go on and on. Feel free to add to it. I can imagine that you're already thinking of other aspects you associate with self-empowerment. If you ask me, I find being empowered means creating a joy- and meaning-filled life by choosing freedom over safety, integrity over invisibility, and purpose over comfort.

Accepting your power and approaching life with a sense of responsibility, self-reliance, and a deep desire to grow and evolve is an ongoing process. It takes awareness, time, and commitment to connect to your authentic self and harness your full potential. But in the end, no matter how you want to define empowerment, you know that you've reached your destination when you feel you've come back home to yourself. That is where this book will take you.

So the next question is, how do we become self-empowered? This is where the subconscious mind holds the keys.

2

THE SUBCONSCIOUS MIND

Your Agent of Change

Without directions, even the most loyal and competent helper becomes helpless.

If you're like most people, the relationship to your subconscious may be fraught with suspicion, incomprehension, and a sense of disenfranchisement. You may associate nightmares, bad habits, and self-sabotaging behaviors with your subconscious. Let's say, consciously, you're clear that becoming healthy and fit is a priority for you. But somehow, you find yourself binging on chips and chocolate each night, and you usually don't wake up in time to work out. Unless, of course, you're torn from sleep by the same horrible dream, where you're at work and suddenly realize you forgot to put clothes on before leaving the house. But then again since you're still feeling flustered and vulnerable from this nightmare, going to the gym and "parading" your extra pounds is the last thing you want to do. This is just an example of how your subconscious can keep you stuck in anxiety-producing self-defeating loops. So what's there to like?

I get it. I also trusted my conscious, rational mind more and believed that the best way to relate to the subconscious was to ignore it, hoping it would eventually stop causing trouble. But since I learned about the multiple ways this deeper part of the mind supports us every day, I consider the subconscious our most powerful and loyal ally. Here are its major functions and the reasons why researchers believe that our subconscious runs at least 70 percent of our daily life.[1]

Did you know that our subconscious is responsible for our emotions? This explains why our feelings can appear so irrational, ill-suited, and uncontrollable. The subconscious also creates, files, and stores all our memories. Because our conscious mind's abilities to process data are limited, the subconscious keeps most of our memories securely locked until it seems appropriate for our conscious mind to retrieve them. This deeper part of our mind also ensures that our body's trillions of cells work harmoniously together. The vast majority of our physiology, such as breathing, digesting, and the beating of our heart, are out of our conscious control. Even when we consciously choose, for example, to sit down and grab a cup of coffee, our subconscious takes charge by translating our decision into the more intricate details of its execution, such as flexing, relaxing, and extending the necessary muscles. Thanks to our subconscious control of daily automatic behaviors, we can drive, shave, or eat with a fork and knife without paying much attention—and still, nobody gets hurt.

Yet, for the journey from survival to self-empowerment, the most relevant task of the subconscious is how it filters and condenses the vast amount of information we're constantly exposed to. To prevent our conscious mind from overloading, our subconscious provides only the small amounts of details it considers essential. At the same time, it keeps tabs on our environment by registering any clues and subtle hints relevant to us. Chemistry, intuition, first impressions, or the famous gut feeling stem from this input of our subconscious mind.

Some of the most powerful subconscious filters are our beliefs, as they shape and distort our perception of reality. For example, you wake up in a good mood. The sun is shining, and summer feels as though it's right around the corner. You're enjoying the aroma of freshly brewed coffee and warm toast. Your streaming service is playing only your favorite songs, and on your way to work, all lights are green. You feel in the zone and are confident that your date tonight will be exciting and even better than the two times you've already gone out. But in the evening, as you leave work, you wonder if you've anything new to talk about. As you worry that your love-interest will think less of you if you're not as funny and upbeat as you were the last time, your confidence starts to waver. But despite your uneasiness, dinner went well and you both had a wonderful time. You would think you'd be content.

However, your mind is occupied by one nagging question: "Why did he/she/they look twice at the phone during dinner?" The concern that you're just not interesting enough for anybody to want to commit erases all the moments your date showed affection and adoration. On top of that, back home you get a message from your sibling, complaining that you never visit your parents, and then you discover that you're out of coffee for the next morning. Why did a day that started so well turn into such a nightmare?

Sound familiar? Such drastic changes in our perception and, consequently, our emotions can make us feel like the victims of our own reality. But as you can see in the preceding example, our concept of reality doesn't depend on facts, but on how our subconscious interprets them based on its belief filters. The belief of not being interesting enough could be rooted in your relationship with a critical parent who never had anything good to say about you. This imprint may have created a fear of rejection, causing you to either avoid close relationships or overcompensate by pleasing others. Due to this limiting belief, your doubt that you have anything worthwhile to share seems confirmed when your date glances at the phone. All the contradicting positive and uplifting input and feedback you've enjoyed during your dinner becomes irrelevant. Since our perception of the world and ourselves is all created by our subconscious (depending on which of its filters we are looking through), we need to continuously question whether how we think, feel, and act, and navigate through life, is based on assumptions or actualities.

CONSCIOUS-SUBCONSCIOUS COLLABORATION: THE PATH FROM SURVIVING TO THRIVING

We may not be victims of our circumstances, but are we victims of our subconscious beliefs and patterns, thus forced to live on survival autopilot? Or can we consciously switch these awareness filters and behaviors—and break out of survival mode into thriving mode? Although it may appear that our subconscious only cares about our safety, it has another prime mission—to make us happy. Again, depending on our early imprints and beliefs, our subconscious may place a stronger emphasis on either safety or fulfillment. However, when our security is no longer in question, the subconscious naturally focuses on supporting us in creating more joy and satisfaction.

So, can we proactively make our subconscious shift gears? Yes, by consciously collaborating with our subconscious mind, which is what the processes in this book are all about. Here's a brief overview of why conscious-subconscious collaboration is so effective and how it works.

The Subconscious Needs Conscious Guidance to Change and Evolve

With all its powers and possibilities, our subconscious has one shortfall: it needs our conscious input to stay up-to-date and to serve us in the best possible way. Like a child that requires the support of a caring adult to grow and reach its full potential, our subconscious remains stuck in its old programming unless the conscious mind teaches it new perspectives and strategies. I know, to collaborate with a relatively obscure part of your mind may sound like a daunting task, but becoming the leader of your subconscious is not only effective and rewarding, it's, as you'll find out, also not as difficult as you may think.

The Conscious Leader Needs to Be Trustworthy

Consider your subconscious as your inner protector, who, until now, was entirely dedicated to ensuring your survival. Convincing this part of your mind to let you, the conscious adult, take control is a big ask. After all, since you may have been fluctuating between either ignoring, fighting, or giving in to your inner protector's survival patterns, your subconscious probably doesn't have a lot of trust and confidence in your conscious leadership. For your subconscious to feel reassured that it no longer has to stay in its safety-above-all mode, you need to show that you can treat yourself with the reliability, care, and kindness you wished you had received when you were little. This means responding to anxiety and insecurity with patience and compassion, redirecting negative thoughts toward positive and empowering perspectives, and most importantly, practicing conscious-subconscious collaboration with daily consistency and commitment. Of course, easier said than done. But rest assured that each chapter of this book will provide you with the insights and tools to help you grow into this leadership role and thus gain the trust of your subconscious.

Communicating with the Subconscious Mind Is Straightforward

Did you know that you can't enjoy a novel or a film without your subconscious being involved? This part of your mind transforms a page or a screen into a gateway to another world. As you let your imagination carry you from the present moment into a fictional reality, you become a participant in the exciting tale you're reading or watching.

When it comes to consciously working with your subconscious mind, all you need to do is let your imagination lead you gently from your rational thoughts to your emotional and sensory aware-ness, from your head to your heart. For example, suppose you want to revisit a specific event from your childhood. Start with thinking about the situation, where it happened, when it took place, and who was involved. Then replay the memory on your inner screen. The subconscious language consists of images, sensations, and feelings—just like in your dreams. Thus, you know that your subconscious communicates with you when you gradually remember what you saw, heard, felt, smelled, and maybe even tasted during that event. And you can respond by using emotion and sensory-rich visualiza-tion to convey any healing messages or new instructions. This form of conscious-subconscious communication makes the deeper pro-cesses in this book so compelling.

The Emotions Create the Memory for the Subconscious

Your subconscious files and stores most of your memories according to their emotional relevance, which often results in an inevitable loss of accuracy. Generally, we remember events with a strong emotional charge—positive or negative—more vividly.[2] Just like beliefs, strong emotions are also filters of the subconscious mind, leading to distor-tions or deletions of what actually happened during the events. So the stronger you feel during a situation, the more likely you will remem-ber it—but the less likely you will recall its details accurately.[3]

The Subconscious Is a Time Machine

As soon as you fully immerse yourself in thoughts and emotions about the past or the future, for your subconscious, you're experi-encing whatever happened or will happen right now in the present moment. Whether you're agonizing about having made an inappro-priate joke to your in-laws six months ago, or are fantasizing about the cruise on the Mediterranean you booked for next summer, your subconscious perceives that you're in that particular event: flushed with embarrassment over the lousy punchline or relaxing with a

Mai Tai on the lido deck. This way, you can revisit a memory with a fresh mindset, choose how you want to relate differently to whatever happened there, and already experience what a new approach to a formerly disempowering situation will feel like in the future.

The Subconscious Lets You Rewrite History

We all know about the "time heals" phenomenon, where traumatic or difficult events reexamined after several months or years appear smaller and less challenging than they once did. But what if you could learn to accelerate the time it takes to heal the past by actively reshaping how you want to perceive and relate to your memories?

Let's recap. Your subconscious wants to listen to and follow the guidance of your conscious mind; its concept of time is fluid, and it evaluates memories according to what you feel about them rather than what happened in them. Together this leads to one powerful conclusion: for your subconscious mind, memories aren't facts chiseled in stone. They're more like Play-Doh that can be stretched, condensed, and shaped in any way possible. As you will soon experience, this flexibility of your subconscious allows you to address and resolve the events that are at the root of your survival patterns and thus create a clean slate.

As I mentioned before, traumas such as abuse, neglect, rejection, and abandonment are often the reasons why our subconscious shifts into survival mode. However, most of us also suffered from distorted memories that led to limiting beliefs and non-supportive self-defense patterns. Depending on our mindset and emotional backdrop, our subconscious can make mountains out of molehills and life-changing disasters out of minor episodes others didn't take seriously. When I was in high school, a handful of my classmates thought it would be funny to start a collection to pay for a nose job for me. This joke seriously dented my self-esteem, even though my girlfriend at that time insisted my schnoz was one of my best features. I became extremely self-conscious and wondered if I should chip into the noselift fund. Several years later, I changed my story and told myself that these kids made fun of me because they were jealous that I had better grades and more success with girls than them. With this new narrative, I could let go of the stinging embarrassment the memory of this event had routinely brought up for me.

Rewriting your history doesn't mean you need to erase the traumas or injustices that established your belief that you should take cover, hide out, or care more for others than yourself. But the past will no longer wield power over you once you update your story and determine that the reasons your subconscious sent you into avoidance or pleasing mode are no longer relevant in your current life.

Beliefs Can't Be Erased Unless They're Replaced

Healing your history isn't enough to get you out of survival mode. Even if you no longer feel triggered by or attached to difficult events from your childhood, as long as your subconscious filters and behaviors stay the same, nothing changes. An example would be someone who had been abused by a parent but, through working on themselves, let go of the traumas and even forgave the abuser. This part of their life may be healed. Yet the beliefs of being unsafe, unable to trust others, or being flawed and broken will continue to distort their perspective of themselves as somebody who needs to stay quiet, small, and ideally invisible. Even though they no longer suffer from nightmares about their past, their day-to-day life is still overshadowed by the protective beliefs and behaviors their inner protector implemented in response to what had happened.

But just erasing old beliefs isn't enough either. Imagine that you could wake up one day and all the limiting beliefs that held you back went poof! Gone. No more, "I am not safe," "I'm not good enough," or "I need to please others to be accepted by them." But now what? From the perspective of your subconscious, you're dealing with an identity vacuum, which needs to be filled as soon as possible. No identity means you don't exist. So unless you come up with a new set of beliefs, your subconscious will quickly slip back into old, familiar grooves.

The good news is that as the conscious leader, you can choose to update your beliefs so that they more accurately represent the authentic and empowered person you grow into and the way you want to perceive the world around you. And once you've expressed and enjoyed this new version of yourself for a while, you may want to go to the next level of your personal evolution and grow beyond that. What you'll find is that there's always more for you to discover and more untapped inner resources to harness.

Survival Patterns Can't Be Erased Unless They're Replaced

If you grew up in northern Alaska and then moved to Florida as an adult, you'd probably want to remove the long underwear, wool sweater, heavy pants, thick coat, gloves, and boots that protected you from the biting cold before walking onto the beach in 95 degrees Fahrenheit weather. But to avoid being arrested for indecent exposure, you need to find something else to put on. The final step to switching out of survival mode is to replace its patterns with new approaches. The most effective way to introduce new empowering habits is to upgrade those you want to replace.

THE SIX KEYS TO SELF-EMPOWERMENT

On this journey, you will obtain six keys that unlock the hidden strengths of each survival pattern to transform them into new self-empowering strategies.

The keys and strengths are:

- Self-responsibility: Own your past by learning and growing from all that life brings.

- Self-compassion: Own your hidden gifts by cherishing and comforting your innocent self.
- Self-reliance: Own your actions by balancing purpose and pleasure.
- Self-reflection: Own your truth by aligning with your essence.
- Self-commitment: Own your time and energy by stewarding your resources.
- Self-love: Own all aspects of yourself by caring from your heart.

Together, these keys, strengths, and self-empowering strategies provide you with all you need to become the leader of your mind and take ownership of your life.

This may sound a bit abstract, so here's an example. Blake told me in our first session about one of his childhood's pivotal, life-changing experiences. When he was seven, he and his older brother were rough-housing in the living room. Their mother told them several times to tone it down, but her words had no effect on the boys. Suddenly, she stormed into the room and screamed, "I've had it with you. I'm leaving, and I'm not coming back!" She grabbed her hat and coat, threw open the door, and ran from the house. The kids, who'd never seen their mom that angry and exasperated, were stunned. "What just happened?" They looked at their dad, who had come down from his home office to get some answers, but all he said was, "Now you've done it. Mother is gone for good."

As time ticked by, the children's confusion turned into concern and then sheer panic. After what was probably only thirty minutes but seemed to them like hours, they started begging their father to somehow make their mother come back. Blake recounted with tears in his eyes how they kneeled in front of their dad, pleading and crying that they were sorry and would never again do anything to upset their mom. At first, their father remained stoic and unmoved, insisting that it was all their fault and they had to get used to living without their mother. Then finally, knowing that his wife had just gone to her sister's to vent, he called to deliver the message that the boys had repented and asked that she please reconsider her decision and give her sons one more chance. A short while later, when the door opened and my client's mom returned, the kids ran up to her and told her how sorry they were and how grateful they were she'd come back.

While this entire event occurred over two or three hours, its ripple effects lasted several decades. Blake told me that from that day on, he never dared do anything that might annoy his mother. Not that he hadn't been a pretty good kid before, but after the threat of being abandoned by her, his invisibility pattern stepped in to ensure he never expressed any needs, desires, or concerns to his parents. Blake figured being quiet and unnoticeable would certainly please them more than the way he'd been when he was so naïve to believe he could just be himself.

Looking back, Blake was sure it wasn't his mother's intention to stifle his emotional expression for the rest of his life. Yet her theatrics with the intent to shock her boys into submission resulted in at least one of her sons feeling he no longer could trust his parents to love and accept him for who he was. And for Blake, that belief of not being fundamentally good enough and loveable remained a major deterrent to creating healthy friendships or romantic relationships. "I know this tiny event during my childhood shouldn't have been such a big deal for me, but it seems that whenever I'm dating someone, this memory comes rushing back and makes me immediately insecure and tongue-tied. You can imagine how much fun these dates turn out to be."

Blake felt exhausted and utterly disappointed with himself as he reflected on all the abandoned endeavors. He realized how often he had held himself back with thoughts such as, "If they really listen to me play music, they'll know I'm not all that good. If I really try to do X job seriously, I'll fail in front of everyone. If I really get close to someone who's stable and caring, they'll realize what a loser I am, so I'd better just stay away."

Blake's life completely changed when he started to implement the six keys of empowerment. With the key of self-responsibility, he stopped blaming his parents for his insecurity and instead reclaimed his birthright to express himself and have fun. Through self-compassion, he no longer surrendered to his anxiety and shyness but kindly reassured the scared little boy inside of his heart that it was safe to be seen and heard. Self-reliance allowed Blake to stop procrastinating. He kept his room in order, opened the mail every day, and, for the first time, finished his taxes on time. Once Blake became aware of this true essence and realized that he was innately worthy and loveable, he committed his time and energy to making his life reflect his truth. He consistently practiced his Saz, a traditional Turkish instrument, to finally follow through with his dream to organize a concert to share his music with others. And he moved from a small, utilitarian apartment to a new, peaceful home with a beautiful garden. As Blake found love for himself, he let go of the draining, one-sided relationships he had desperately held on to and opened up to meeting new people who appreciated him for who he was and not for what he did for them.

In one of our last sessions, Blake said, "I'm so grateful that my conscious and subconscious mind get along. I always relied on my intellect, but now I also value the subconscious voice that doesn't speak in logic and words but through emotions. I can hear its messages and respond to them in the language it can understand. Yes, my subconscious harbored fear and held me back to keep me safe, but as the seat of emotions, it also gives depth and meaning to everything in my life. If my life were a garden, I was afraid to enter it for the first thirty years of my life because my subconscious believed it wasn't safe. Now I know that it's up to me to create the Eden I want, and I've become a skilled gardener who understands the function of plants and how to take care of them. But only because my subconscious feels safe with me can I appreciate my garden's magic and beauty."

Are you ready to grow out of self-protection mode and become the leader of your mind and the creator of your reality? Let's get started.

PART II

Taking Responsibility

From Anxiously Avoiding
Discomfort to Confidently Creating
Your Reality

3

·········

The Victim Pattern
and the Illusion of
Powerlessness

Becoming a victim wasn't your choice. Remaining it is.

Let's take a look at the first pattern of the avoider survival mode—the victim. Empowering the victim, which this chapter is about, will get you already in touch with one of the most essential self-empowerment keys—self-responsibility.

Since no one likes to be called a victim or looked at as one, your initial impulse may be to skip this chapter. However, as you'll discover, the inner victim is not only a fundamental aspect of our psyche but also one of the most powerful. Pretending that this part doesn't exist would be like ignoring basic sensations such as hunger, tiredness, or pain. You may get away with it for a time, but eventually, you'll pay the price for your neglect. Helping the victim evolve beyond its limitations by respecting, understanding, and addressing its needs is a crucial step in your empowerment journey.

You could argue that there are two kinds of victimizations—real and imagined. Although, this distinction doesn't seem to matter when you feel you're a victim. The first type, the real victim, would be someone who's experienced hardship or abuse, either at the hand of others or through traumatic ordeals. For example, children who are molested, bullied at school, or neglected by their parents. Victims of crimes, domestic violence, and severe accidents. Those who've lost their loved ones or their homes in a natural disaster. And, of course, the millions of refugees who are desperately seeking a safe place to exist, like victims of wars or brutal regimes that have no regard for human life.

The second type, the imagined victim, is as ancient as the story of Adam and Eve. When a serpent persuaded Eve to eat from the forbidden tree of knowledge, Eve also gave Adam a piece of that fruit. When God questioned the two, Adam blamed Eve, and even God, since the woman was given to him by the creator. Eve accused the serpent of being the real offender. Both Adam and Eve were unwilling to take responsibility for their actions. Instead, they saw themselves as innocent victims, ultimately getting themselves expelled from the Garden of Eden.

The imagined victim type could also be called the victim of our perceived limitations because it gets triggered when we feel out of control and unable to change the situation we're in. It's this type of victim most of us are familiar with. Let's be honest, how many times a week do you feel like a victim? As our lives are overtaken by busyness and obligations, and our to-do lists grow longer and longer, the mountain of unfinished tasks seems to overshadow each moment increasingly. At some point, everything becomes too much and too difficult to handle, and we don't know where to begin or what to do. Feeling completely overwhelmed, we can quickly become victims of our circumstances. We interpret small mishaps and incidents—spilling a glass of milk, misplacing a bill, being ignored by the barista in the coffee shop—as personal attacks by humanity, life, or the universe that push us over the edge into the abyss of despair and powerlessness. We can also feel victimized by our job, the economy, the government, the dog next door, our parents, or our kids. Even our own emotions or our body, if they don't comply and change the way we imagine, can become perpetrators who assault and imprison us.

Whether real or imagined, the problem with staying in the victim role is that it can ultimately lead to self-victimization. As we continue to identify ourselves with the past, the circumstances we are in, or those who did us wrong, we stay stuck in the notion that we can't have the life we want and are bound to get hurt and let down again. We become frustrated and ashamed for being weak and unable to take control. We become rigid and righteous toward others and ourselves and eventually shut down because we lose trust and hope for the future.

As with all survival patterns, when you approach life from the mindset of the inner victim, you ultimately lose your power and, with that, a sense of confidence, joy, and purpose.

HOW DO YOU KNOW YOU'RE IN VICTIM MODE?

You may still sit on the fence about whether you have an inner victim and whether this part of you has kept you in survival mode. So let's take a closer look at the typical signs of living in the victim pattern.

You're Stuck in the Past

Like most people, you may have gone through some hardship, traumas, and accidents. You may have been hurt, insulted, betrayed, or disappointed by others. But while those who have treated you poorly may have forgotten all about you and moved on, your inner victim continues to suffer from the pain they caused you. Any time a situation arises that makes you feel similarly disrespected or mistreated, you replay in classic "poor me" fashion this and all the other injustices that occurred to you, trying to find answers for plaguing questions such as "why?" and "why always me?"

As a child, Patricia had felt that her parents didn't care about her. Her workaholic father was rarely around, and when he was, he appeared mostly grumpy and short-tempered. Her mother seemed more interested in meeting her friends or improving her bridge game than spending time with her daughter. Being a rather sensitive kid, Patricia suffered from the neglect and lack of warmth and love in her home. When she started school, she found out that scoring good marks was the only sure way to get a little bit of positive attention from her parents. Naturally, her sense of self became highly dependent on her achievements and the approval of others.

As an adult, Patricia created a stellar career as a lawyer and was well-liked and respected by her peers and friends. However, it didn't take much for Patricia to feel hurt and abandoned again. A friend not calling her back right away, her boss not acknowledging her excellent report, the neighbor not saying "hello" as she rushed out of the house to get to work—events like this could easily trigger Patricia's inner victim and pull her into a dark hole of pain, loneliness, and despair. To make matters worse, Patricia's victim usually added a heavy dose of self-loathing to the already painful mixture of shame, insecurity, and resentment, keeping her glued to the past and the notion that she was fundamentally flawed and unlikeable.

As I mentioned, the past, especially our early years, is the reference book for our subconscious mind and its survival patterns. This is why, like in Patricia's case, relatively harmless situations that an adult mindset could easily disregard can trigger a full-blown victim response, making you feel as small and powerless as a child. But don't get frustrated with yourself for reacting in such a disempowering and immature way. Try to appreciate that your subconscious hasn't learned yet how to respond to these triggering situations in a more self-assured manner.

You Justify Your Misery

A client told me about how her sister goes into the victim role whenever her age comes up. She's single and has convinced herself that women over fifty are inevitably invisible to the rest of society. The more her friends try to convince her that she shouldn't buy into ageism but should appreciate how healthy, vibrant, and beautiful she is, the more defiant she becomes. "She is so adamant that her point of view is correct," my client said, "that I sometimes wonder if she's more comfortable in the victim role."

When you're in victim mode, you may become righteous and even entitled to feel sorry for yourself. You tell yourself and anyone who stays around to listen to you that you genuinely don't have choices, that the unfortunate circumstances you're in are bigger than you, and that how people treat you is neither your fault nor anything you can change. When a well-meaning friend challenges your bleak assessment, you dismiss their advice and support, even though deep inside you know they may be right. Instead, you angrily defend your victimhood and insist that you've tried everything to improve your situation, without success. Hence, there's no hope for betterment. Although this reaction mode may appear rather stubborn and short-sighted, have compassion for your inner victim. For it, the idea of stepping out of powerlessness and taking responsibility is often too scary to even consider.

Your Body or Your Emotions Become the Enemy

People who feel assaulted and held hostage by their anxiety or depression, an uncontrollable barrage of intrusive thoughts, or by a chronic physical illness, often struggle the most because there's no place for them to escape from their perpetrator.

Lindsay, a high-functioning entrepreneur and pillar of her community, started in her mid-fifties to struggle suddenly with anxiety and panic attacks. It all began with some hair loss, which prompted her to schedule a visit with a highly recommended dermatologist. Although this doctor may have been very competent, he entirely lacked warmth or compassion. When he told Lindsay flat out that she may just have to deal with female baldness, it felt like a death sentence. The rush of anxiety made her dizzy and she almost passed out. When she reached out to her doctor to steady herself, he backed away as if he was afraid or disgusted by her. This lack of support and empathy from someone whom she was supposed to be able to trust, affected her deeply. Lindsay, who was used to being respected and in control, felt for the first time in decades completely rejected, alone, and powerless. This was when her odyssey with anxiety started.

At first, it was more a sense of restlessness that she felt during meetings in the office. She noticed that she didn't like it when people talked "at" her and tried to convince her of their views. In those moments, she felt trapped and just wanted to run away. Over the next few months, she became more uncomfortable and anxious in big crowds, on busy streets, and in grocery stores. As her comfort zone shrank, she began to avoid traveling, going out on the weekends, and even driving. Desperately seeking a solution, she went through a number of psychiatrists and therapists without finding any sense of relief. After four years of dealing with a constant undercurrent of anxiety and frequent spikes of panic, she was able to function only with the help of anti-anxiety medication, which she didn't like to take. Still, more and more frequently this seemed to be the only option for her to make it through the day.

Anxiety became Lindsay's tormentor. From the moment she woke up, she looked over her shoulder, worried that the anxiety would attack her again. "This is no way to live; I'm held captive by this awful feeling. I don't know how to get away from it, because as soon as I relax, the anxiety rears its ugly head again." Feeling victimized by her own emotions, Lindsay focused most of her energy on anticipating and enduring the onslaught of fear and anxiety. She no longer expected to have a pleasant day but braced herself for the abuser to once again beat her down.

At some point, she became so scared of the anxiety that she considered escaping the pain by ending her own life. When she realized that suicide suddenly seemed a viable option for her, she decided to stop running away from her anxiety and instead face her emotions and take responsibility for them. That was when Lindsay and I started to work together.

You Need a Villain and Become the Perpetrator—of Both Others and Yourself

For the inner victim to justify its worldview and ultimately its existence, it depends on finding its counterforce—the villain. The need for a villain often leads to distorting and misinterpreting normal relationships as unsafe, unfair, or abusive. You may feel victimized by the expectations of your spouse and your kids. Or you may turn your friends, family members, or counselors into culprits, because, as their well-intended advice "clearly proves," they don't understand or care about you. In the victim role, you take everyone and everything personally. Any perceived wrongdoing is an indication that you've pulled the short end of the stick in life and that the entire universe is against you, and you aren't destined to be happy.

You could assume that being in victim mode makes you kinder and more compassionate toward yourself. However, as you've probably experienced many times, your inner victim can be quite judgmental and attack you with self-loathing and disdain. From its perspective, the world is categorized into black and white, good and bad, and powerful and powerless (like yourself).

Since she was a teenager, Jenny struggled with insecurity around other people. Being smart and getting good grades didn't help boost her popularity among her peers. Some of her classmates teased her relentlessly by calling her a nerd, an unattractive wallflower, a future spinster, and other hurtful names. Although plenty of kids liked her, Jenny only remembered those few she associated with feeling unworthy, ugly, and unlikeable. During her twenties and thirties, she dated either emotionally unavailable men or flat-out cheaters who took advantage of her naiveté and insecurity. Every time she found out that she'd been betrayed once again, her anger and rage turned inward rather than to the men who hurt her. Her daily affirmations included "People don't like me. There's something wrong with me. I'm not lovable. I deserve to be mistreated. If I were different, men would stay with me. . ." This constant self-bashing, combined with a general distrust of people, increased her sensitivity and self-consciousness. Thus her perceptions of abuse went beyond situations with the men she dated. Whether at work, on vacation, or in her neighborhood, everybody seemed to reject her as soon as they learned to know her better. She constantly wondered what she'd done wrong to make people dislike her so much. Or was she just cursed?

Jenny became more and more depressed and isolated. She even tended to push away the few friends who remained loyal to her. In one of our sessions, she shared with me that a friend had reached out with a simple email to check on her. When she responded that she didn't feel that well, her friend wrote a brief message back, letting her know that he was sorry and hoped things would improve for her soon. Jenny told me that this email made her even sadder and demonstrated that her friend didn't care about her at all. She wrote back to him, complaining that she was disappointed in his curt reply and that he obviously didn't want her in his life. When he tried to explain that reaching out to her in the first place was a sign that she mattered to him, Jenny got irritated and called her friend defensive and unable to accept criticism. The correspondence went downhill from there.

Jenny admitted that what she wanted from her friend was an apology for the pain and sadness he'd caused her with his initial email. Being in the victim pattern, she couldn't accept that his intentions were good and that there was nothing to fault him for. Jenny told me that she frequently accused people of either not supporting her or deliberately wanting to hurt her. "I don't take responsibility for how I'm treating them. It is as if I want to prove to myself that people don't like me. I spent days in bed ruminating on everything they did or said to me. I'm angry with them, but I'm even angrier with myself. I automatically blame myself for how people treat me because I believe I'm broken."

I can imagine that at times when your inner victim takes the reins, you've also found yourself trapped in a self-defeating paradox. On the one hand, you have the anger-fueled desire to lash out or push away those who hurt and disrespect you. On the other hand, you attack yourself for all the flaws and faults that explain why people mistreat you in the first place. The question is, does your inner victim know that it prolongs the cycle of abuse by villainizing others and battering itself?

HOW THE VICTIM PATTERN KEEPS YOU SAFE: EVASION, DEFLECTION, AND AGGRESSION

Some people feel ashamed and frustrated with themselves for stumbling into the victim mode. "Why should I feel sorry for myself when compared to others, my life is pretty good? I need just to stop whining and be more grateful." While a heavy dose of self-chastising may quiet the inner victim for a little while, denying and suppressing our feelings can ultimately lead to self-victimization. Remember, our minds have evolved to serve us; thus, the inner victim must also serve some purpose. The fact is that no matter how easy or difficult, safe or traumatic our lives have been, the victim's role in the subconscious survival team has only one concern: our protection. However, with its patterns ranging from hiding out to lashing out, our inner victim is probably the most creative when it comes to defending us.

Dan, a young man in his late twenties, was known by his friends to always complain either about his job or his girlfriends. Usually, he felt underappreciated by both, which is why he changed his relationships and jobs at least every six months. Although he couldn't change how people treated him, leaving employers and girlfriends behind still gave him a sense of power and control. Yet when he was fired (for the first time ever) from his work and ditched by his girlfriend on top of that, his inner victim took over his life and he became very depressed and withdrawn. The hurt and shame were so overwhelming that he didn't want to interact with anyone. After a couple of weeks his loyal friends started to worry about him and showed up on his doorstep. When Dan saw them, he broke down and started crying. He told them all the details of how unfairly he'd been treated, how neither his employer nor his ex had given him a chance, how they were only interested in themselves . . .

His friends supported him and told him how much his situation sucked and how sorry they were for what he'd gone through. They encouraged him to believe that something better, in both love and career, would come his way, but their assurances just opened up another layer of victimhood for Dan to wallow in. "No, that will never happen," he told his friends. "People just don't understand who I really am and what I have to offer. I'll always be alone and probably never find a job I can be passionate about." And then the crying would start again.

One of Dan's friends tried to switch tactics, encouraging him by saying he was giving the people who'd dumped him way too much power, and he should forget about them. Unfortunately, that opened Dan's floodgates even more. "I know I'm a pathetic loser. I'm just not as strong and cool as you guys. Obviously, you'll all stop hanging out with me soon." For the rest of the evening Dan's buddies tiptoed around him, trying to be as supportive as possible without making him sink deeper into self-pity.

Another two weeks passed, and Dan had still barely left his house, let alone applied for another job. His friends grew more concerned about him and encouraged him to start taking control of his life. Dan became angry and screamed, "How dare you say this to me? I've tried everything in the past and nothing's worked. You have no idea how frustrating it is when, despite all your efforts, nothing ever pans out for you. Why don't you just go f#?k yourselves and leave me alone." Realizing that Dan wasn't ready to listen or get help, his friends gave him more space, which of course whipped Dan's inner victim into even more of a frenzy.

Honestly, haven't you ever felt the way Dan did: spinning out on an emotional roller-coaster you can't seem to get off? The inner victim can avoid danger by either making you hide from the world or roll on your back like a small puppy that shows its belly, hoping this gesture of submission will stop the aggressor from harming it.

Being overly suspicious, your inner victim keeps others at arm's length through defensiveness, blame, and accusations, even if they intend to help you. Just as in Dan's and Jenny's case, your subconscious mind highlights and enlarges any potential sign of judgment or disrespect from others so that you can't be blindsided. Of course, this creates a rather distorted view of reality. Similar to a phobia of dogs, where even the smallest Chihuahua becomes a bloodthirsty beast, while in victim mode your perception is that, in one way or another, everybody is against you.

In victim mode, you can also become a judging and punishing prosecutor, fueled by hurt and rage, attacking anyone who doesn't seem to agree with you. We've all enjoyed books and movies such as *The Girl with the Dragon Tattoo, Thelma and Louise,* or *Kill Bill,* where the victim transforms into a badass. Who doesn't like to root for the underdog when it comes to teaching the bullies a lesson? You could argue that many revolutions and civil rights movements were driven by people who channeled their victimization into an angry uproar against the status quo.

Unfortunately, whether it's on a personal or global level, the victim's uprising is often driven more by aggression, righteousness, and the need for payback than the desire to create positive change. When victims try to free and empower themselves by passing their shackles of pain to those they blame for their misery, the destructive victim-perpetrator cycle only continues. The pattern of turning the tables from powerlessness to controlling others is one of the most unhealthy ways people respond to their inner victim. Unlike the heroes of novels and movies, most victims don't directly confront those they feel victimized by. Instead, they either unleash their bottled-up anger and frustration on innocent bystanders, or they try to get back at the perpetrators in more covert ways by using their victim status to justify misconduct. Consider the employee who proclaims that financial pressure or stress at work causes them to kick their dog or to yell at all the terrible drivers making their life deliberately miserable. The parent who, after a divorce, constantly bad-mouths their ex to their kids to make sure that they'll distance themselves from them. Or the disgruntled citizen who rationalizes committing tax fraud because they don't feel that the government cares about them. Although it may appear more powerful to be in the role of the judge, the punisher, or the rebel, eventually, the victim needs to recognize that their wounds don't heal faster by inflicting hurt on others.

WHY THE VICTIM AVOIDS CHANGE AND RESPONSIBILITY

In contrast to the two other patterns in the avoider mode—the invisibility and the procrastinator—the victim pattern usually doesn't result in a feeling of security, control, or the sense of having dodged a bullet. In the victim role, you continue to suffer the consequences of your past. Every insult, letdown, or deception is securely stored in your memory and kept in the forefront as a cross-reference for any current interaction or situation in which you may find yourself.

The problem is that each time you feel you've been wronged and you vow never to forget what happened to you, you are so focused on the past hurt that you become unaware of your present responsibility to heal your wounds and improve your life. By holding on to the notion that your suffering affords you the right to be angry, anxious, depressed, hurt, and ultimately stuck, your inner victim gives you permission to stay the same—and in the extreme, never grow beyond the status of a powerless child.

The victim's attachment to misery serves three purposes.

One: By refusing to outgrow the disempowering patterns of the past, you can avoid a more proactive, self-determined, and mature role in your life. In the mind of the inner victim, taking responsibility comes with an inherently greater risk of failure, judgment, and pain.

Two: The avoidance of change serves as a sort of entitlement to be treated by others with a soothing mixture of support, sympathy, and lack of expectations. Your inner victim yearns for acknowledgment for its suffering and ultimately hopes that someone will come to the rescue. Anyone who doesn't want to buy into their victimhood is declared a villain who can't be trusted and needs to be avoided. In this regard, the victim can be quite effective in controlling others. Some try to get the attention they want by relentlessly beating the drum of their hardship, nagging, throwing temper tantrums, or making ultimatums and threats. The secondary victims of such campaigns are often perturbed friends and family members, who discard their own reasonable boundaries in the desperate effort to appease the moaning victim.

Others are more manipulative and passive-aggressive. A client of mine told me that his mother, who had always appeared the victim of his raging and alcoholic father, confided in him one day that she often deliberately created fights with her spouse. His mother said that every time he apologized to her after the effects of the alcohol had worn off, she at least knew that she still mattered to him in some way. After all, in her mind, some attention was better than being completely ignored.

Three: The last reason why the inner victim wants you to stay in a self-made cocoon of hurt, resentment, blame, and imagined impotence may be the most disempowering and difficult to admit. The victim avoids taking responsibility because it assumes that the villain would get off the hook this way. Some of my clients admitted they didn't want to change, heal, and feel better because if they did, their abusive or neglectful parents could convince themselves they'd done an excellent job raising their child. Others realized they were clinging on to the slim but persistent hope that one day the people who'd hurt them would miraculously admit their guilt and repent for their wrongdoings. Since they'd never received an acknowledgment or apology from their perpetrators, their inner victim refused to heal the wounds of the past until the debt was paid. In a similar vein, some of my clients who'd been betrayed, mistreated, or dumped by their partners held on to their pain because they didn't want to abandon the dream that their misery could soften the hearts of their exes and lead them back to them.

To let go of their victim survival patterns, all these clients needed first to accept a simple but hard-to-swallow truth. The only certain outcome they would get from waiting for a magical turnaround was that they would continue to put their future and their opportunities for more peace, joy, and fulfillment into the hands of those who didn't seem to care about them in the first place.

Despite its protective intentions, the self-destructive downward spiral of the victim pattern is pretty obvious: you continue to identify yourself with the past and those who did you wrong. You stay stuck believing that you have been dealt a rotten hand, that life is not fair, and that you're bound to get hurt, abused, and betrayed again. So you treat others with suspicion, ready to push anybody away at the first inkling of disappointment. In the end, the limiting beliefs of the victim become a self-fulfilling prophecy, and you find yourself isolated, misunderstood, and powerless.

So how can you heal and outgrow the victim patterns? And how do you get to the empowered version of your inner victim?

4

....

SELF-RESPONSIBILITY

The Key to Owning Your Past

If you want to be as big as you can be, you need to let go of those who make you feel smaller.

Although you may know you're a good person who has something to offer the world, when your victim pattern runs your life, you inevitably feel stifled and trapped by people you've encountered in the past or are dealing with now. A parent who hurt, abused, or neglected you during your childhood. A teacher who made fun of you in front of the class. An ex who betrayed and disappointed you, or your current spouse who's becoming increasingly critical and angry. Or you may feel held hostage by circumstances—your job, your financial situation, the government, or even by your own mind.

It makes sense that one of the essential steps to self-empowerment is to take your power back from the people and events of your past. But how do you reclaim your power? Isn't the damage already done? Well, as I explained before, A. you never lost your power in the first place, and B. for your subconscious the past isn't chiseled in stone. Research shows that every time you recall a memory, it organically changes.[1] You could say as you grow and change, so does your past.

For example, Dan, a high school friend, struggled for years with how our German teacher ridiculed him for his atrocious writing skills. Even after we graduated, the thought of the fear of embarrassment caused his stomach to twist into knots. However, his poor grades hadn't extinguished his desire to write and express his vivid imagination. Fast forward twenty years, my friend became a celebrated German author of several award-winning books. Now, when we tease him about his sharpest critic, he only shares his gratitude for our teacher. "I think the fact that she didn't believe in me forced me to believe twice as much in myself—and work infinitely harder on my craft. Without her making fun of me, I may have never had the 'I'll show you' attitude to go after my dream."

My friend unknowingly used the self-responsibility key to take back his power. Self-responsibility is not an invitation to find excuses for those who hurt you and turn the blame game on yourself. When you take self-responsibility, you don't wonder who is at fault for whatever happened to you in the past. Instead, you start with letting go of the anger, pain, fear, or shame that used to chain you to it. Then you accept that no matter what happened or what was done to you, you always have the power to choose how you want to interpret and respond to your experiences. This way, you no longer perceive your life as a string of random events but as an extension of your thoughts, feelings, beliefs, and actions. Finally, you vow to create your reality to the best of your abilities, even if things don't always go according to plan.

In other words, by taking self-responsibility, you are making four empowering choices:

- To commit to your wholeness and well-being, regardless of whether others made you believe you don't deserve to be treated with kindness and care.

- To take charge of your thoughts, feelings, beliefs, and actions.
- To be curious and open to how you can learn and grow from the past.
- To take ownership of your present and future and become the creator of your reality.

Self-responsibility is the key to self-empowerment and personal freedom. Eleanor Roosevelt said "Freedom makes a huge requirement of every human being. With freedom comes responsibility. For the person who is unwilling to grow up, the person who does not want to carry his own weight, this is a frightening prospect."[2] To be free to be your empowered self, you need to grow beyond the self-defensive beliefs and survival patterns that are rooted in your past. The authentically empowered you is a competent, mature, and caring adult who takes responsibility for all aspects of your life—even those that made you feel victimized and powerless.

Remember Lindsay, who was afraid of her anxiety? Because she was used to being confident and in control of her life, the intensity and unpredictability of her anxiety and panic attacks left her feeling trapped by her own emotions. When we started working together, Lindsay said that even before her anxiety attacks, she often was uncomfortable during business meetings, in large crowds, or on long plane rides. Somehow, she'd always pushed through her discomfort by telling herself, "I just need to get it over with." However, when her anxiety and panic seemed to take over her life, just "getting it over with" was no longer an option. Instead, she coped by avoiding anxiety-triggering situations as much as possible. Or, as a last resort, she'd take fast-acting anti-anxiety medication, which she hated to do because it made her feel drowsy and out of control.

During our first session, Lindsay described the difficult circumstances of her childhood. Her mother and father divorced when she was just four years old. Her father was given custody, and the two of them moved in with his parents and sister. The rare times Lindsay visited her mom, she was ignored or treated with cruelty and disdain. Lindsay's mom frequently told her she was worthless and stupid and seemed to enjoy embarrassing her in front of other kids. While from the outside, Lindsay's life with her father, aunt, and grandparents appeared safer and more stable, this image couldn't be further from the truth. When Lindsay was just five years old, her father started regularly sexually abusing and raping her for many years. Feeling trapped, with nowhere to go, the little girl decided that the best way to survive the horrific pain her father was causing her was to "get it over with."

Lindsay remembered that when she was sixteen years old and, potentially, could have left her home and started her own life, an inner voice told her, "You're not ready to be out in the world. Yes, your father's doing horrible things to you, but this is the pain you know. You can endure it for two more years and then go to college, make a fortune, and never have to rely on anyone again."

It's hard to imagine how difficult it must have been for Lindsay to postpone freedom from abuse and the opportunity to set herself up for a bright and prosperous future. But the same strong will and determination forged from her terrible circumstances enabled her to endure, maintaining a vision for a better life until it became a reality.

The strategy of ignoring her feelings and almost stoically suffering through the horrendous abuse allowed Lindsay to escape her home eventually, seemingly unscathed. She went to college with the commitment to becoming so successful and financially independent that no one could ever take advantage of her again. With her sharp mind, creative talent, strong drive, and unwavering tenacity, Lindsay built a thriving publishing company. This allowed her to create and own the safe and comfortable home she'd always dreamed of.

However, Lindsay had never given herself permission to look back and acknowledge that she'd been a victim of severe abuse and neglect. She was so busy pushing forward and achieving increasingly higher goals that there was no time to address the wounds of her childhood or even acknowledge they existed. It wasn't until her shocking encounter with the rude dermatologist, who scared her about potentially having to live with female baldness, that she became aware of her deep-seated vulnerability. The uncaring doctor triggered her subconscious belief from childhood that the people she was supposed to trust and rely on would inevitably hurt and mistreat her. From that point on, her get-it-over-with strategy was replaced by an anxiety-driven let's-get-out-of-here response that she'd suppressed since she was five.

For several years, Lindsay fought her anxiety with her usual vigor and tenacity, with only one goal in mind: to return to the confident and powerful businesswoman she'd identified herself with. However, neither psychiatrists, counselors, nor alternative healers could help her, because all she focused on was battling and conquering her emotions. As a last-ditch attempt, she reached out to me, and by that point, she was willing to go beyond her resistance to addressing her past.

During our work, Lindsay came to understand that her anxiety didn't intend to torture or entrap her. While she had felt victimized by her anxiety, all her emotions did was make her aware of the unattended wounds her parents had inflicted on her. The victim part of her subconscious, which she had tried to ignore for many years, was still reeling from childhood traumas. The visit with "Dr. Frankenstein," as she called the dermatologist, was so triggering that from that point on, the life of the adult no longer appeared to be safe. Once Lindsay began to see the world through the eyes of her child-like inner victim, she felt trapped, threatened, and overwhelmed by other people.

As we began our work together, Lindsay recognized that even though she had perceived herself as empowered and liberated from her parents' abuse, she was still living in survival mode. She'd been running away from her childhood because, subconsciously, she still felt held hostage by her father.

When this realization hit her, Lindsay looked at me with desperation. "So I tried to escape my father's prison by running away from myself. What is the key to set me free?"

"Are you ready to forgive your parents?" I asked.

She inhaled sharply but remained silent.

"Don't worry," I said, "forgiveness isn't doing your parents any favors or letting them off the hook. Forgiveness is all about you taking charge of your healing by liberating yourself from the past."

Like Lindsay, you may have believed that by refusing to think about those who've hurt you, your pain will go away. Although this method may work for a while, in the end, it's like avoiding a stack of bills hoping they will eventually pay themselves. Usually, your inner victim doesn't forget what's happened to you. While you may successfully bury the villains of your past in oblivion, the injuries they caused don't heal on a deeper subconscious level. Chances are that others are re-triggering and potentially worsening these wounds. You can run from those who've hurt you, but you can't hide from the pain they created. Eventually, it will catch up to you.

FORGIVENESS: WHAT IT IS, AND WHAT IT IS NOT

Before we move into the healing power of forgiveness and how it relates to self-responsibility, remember to be patient with yourself as you get ready to forgive. Let's say you were freshly hurt or blindsided by somebody and are still in shock and disbelief about what has happened. Forgiveness doesn't have to be the first thing on your mind. You may want first to let the dizziness of confusion pass and become grounded within yourself again. Then you may need to acknowledge and attend to your bruised heart and give yourself space and time to grieve and heal. If you jump too quickly into forgiving the person who caused you all this suffering, you may skip the critical step of acknowledging your wounds and honoring your birthright of having others treat you with dignity, respect, and kindness.

If you're not ready to forgive just yet, don't pressure yourself. There's nothing wrong with you. We all know that forgiving those who've caused us pain or treated us poorly can be hard. Yet when you think about it, there comes a time when you are starting to hurt yourself by not forgiving. At that point, fury and blame act like emotional superglue between you, the past, and those who wronged you. The burden of hurt, anxiety, and shame leave you feeling drained, powerless, and trapped. You continue to reopen old wounds by ruminating on questions such as "Why me?" or "How could they do this to me?" while giving your time, energy, and power to those who didn't or still don't respect and care about your well-being. At that moment, forgiveness is the next crucial step to healing and moving forward.

Even then, when you know that forgiving, letting go, and moving on is the most sensible choice, you might wonder why it still seems so difficult to follow through. What probably holds you back, besides not knowing how to go about forgiving someone, is that you have questions and confusion about forgiveness. Let's get those resolved.

Does Forgiveness Mean Letting the Perpetrators off the Hook?

Let's say your mind is like a drinking glass that contains your memories, emotions, beliefs, and thoughts. Early in life, everything in your world may have appeared as clear and straightforward as pristinely pure water. Then outside influences introduced insult, rejection, or abuse, and in turn, you reacted with hurt, disappointment, and resentment. The resulting mixture clouded and darkened your mind to the point that you're now unable to see through and beyond the murkiness of the past. The lack of perspective can trigger the inner victim to step into the role of your protector. This is when you recount all the injuries and injustices in your life, expect the past to repeat itself, and perceive everyone as a potential perpetrator.

In the glass-of-water analogy, you would ideally pour out the muck of the past that's clouding your mind and replace it with fresh, clear content. Unfortunately, your inner victim usually prefers to wait, albeit usually in vain, for those it deems responsible to clean up the mess they created. I've already mentioned several reasons why the victim doesn't want to take responsibility: (1) to get attention and be taken care of, (2) to avoid failure and judgment, and (3) to not let the villains off the hook. To make you feel less impotent, the victim often tries to cover up the hurt and pain by holding on to resentment and outrage.

Not forgiving is like playing a tug of war with the past. While those you may have struggled with have already left the playing field, you're still standing with the rope in your hand, waiting for someone to apologize so you can finally get off the turf. The victim doesn't realize that you're wasting precious time by stagnating in the mud of the past instead of kindly and compassionately attending to your wounds.

So forgiving someone doesn't mean you agree with or condone their hurtful behavior. Instead, forgiveness is essentially an act of self-care, because you're accepting responsibility for your life by turning your focus away from those that mistreated you and toward your healing and growth.

Does Forgiveness Mean Forgetting and Opening to More Hurt?

Some people see forgiveness as a naive or foolish choice because they believe those who forgive also forget and that forgetting means remaining open to more hurt, abuse, or betrayal. In reality, when you're holding on to grudges, blame, and pain, you continue to identify with the shadow others cast on you, unable to appreciate the light within you. You keep your heart small, tight, and walled off to protect yourself from getting burned again. While this approach may appear safer than forgiving, you don't often realize that you also deny yourself access to the powerful resources that reside in your heart, such as love, kindness, compassion, and intuition. If you're closing your heart to protect yourself, you're pretending that you can only exist as a smaller version of yourself. Like a little kitten who needs to hide under a chair because it's afraid to get stepped on. The truth is that when you open your heart and access your inner resources, you're much safer and more capable of dealing with any challenges because you're approaching them from a more expanded and authentic place.

Forgiveness is restoring trust within yourself. And as you learn to trust yourself more, you'll gain clarity about what it takes for someone to earn your trust. That way, forgiveness opens the door to those who prove they have your best interest in mind. At the same time, you maintain a healthy, self-empowered boundary against those who've hurt you.

Forgiveness works best when you're willing to perceive the past as an opportunity to learn more about yourself, life, and those who hurt you. As you're learning, you're not dismissing or forgetting the injustices that occurred to you, you're just no longer willing to stay emotionally attached or identified with them. Instead, you're determined to grow beyond them.

Is Forgiveness a Sign of Weakness?

Mahatma Gandhi expressed the opposite opinion when he said, "The weak can never forgive. Forgiveness is the attribute of the strong."[3] Considering the tremendous personal hardship as he fought with only nonviolent means for India's independence from the British Empire, I can imagine that Gandhi was confronted with the temptation to resort to retaliation and revenge. But, he resisted the urge to answer aggression with aggression and remained stead-fast in his resolve that India could be liberated through peaceful, civil resistance. People such as Gandhi, Martin Luther King Jr., Rosa Parks, and Nelson Mandela have exemplified how forgiveness isn't a sign of weakness but requires strength, courage, and the conviction that hating does not lead to healing.

Can Forgiveness Only Be Accomplished by Someone Who's Extraordinarily Kind and Evolved?

You don't have to be a Mahatma Gandhi or Mother Teresa to forgive. Although, in some cases, it may appear that forgiveness requires the open and enlightened mind of a yogi and the kind and pure heart of a saint, letting go of the victim role is ultimately a *selfish* act—in the most positive sense of the word. You're making the decision that you'd rather be free than furious, rather at peace than at war, rather happy than self-righteous. When you choose to forgive, you're nudging the inner victim out of the driver's seat and claiming the responsibility for your happiness and well-being. And isn't taking responsibility for yourself what being an adult is all about?

Forgiveness is an organic healing process that addresses the wounds of the past and allows you to disentangle from unhealthy and unequal relationship patterns. The key to forgiveness is compassion, one of the most powerful inner healing resources. In *The Art of Happiness,* the Dalai Lama said, "Love and compassion are necessities and not luxuries. Without them humanity cannot survive." Compassion is the great equalizer of our emotions. When we are compassionate with those who caused us anguish and pain, we are no longer powerless.

No matter how badly someone treated you, compassion allows you to acknowledge that whatever they did wasn't a reflection on you, but stemmed from their own confusion, hurt, self-loathing, or despair. With compassion in your heart, you can understand

and maybe even relate to the culprit's struggles, but you no longer identify with how they chose to see and treat you. Or as Martin Luther King Jr. said in *A Gift of Love,* "There is some good in the worst of us and some evil in the best of us. When we discover this, we are less prone to hate our enemies." In this regard, compassion can become a protective barrier that shields you from others' negativity and from your own righteous anger and resentment toward them. I will share more about the protective nature of compassion in chapter 6.

The following forgiveness process, which I call the Disentanglement Process, is an opportunity to learn from and grow beyond unhealthy relationships of your past or present while strengthening your connection to the power of self-responsibility.

So I invite you to stop wondering whether you're kind, strong, or wise enough to forgive. You don't need to be evolved to start to forgive—you evolve through forgiveness.

• • • • • •

DEEP EXERCISE

DISENTANGLEMENT: PEACE AND FREEDOM THROUGH SELF-RESPONSIBILITY AND FORGIVENESS

Having supported many clients through the Disentanglement Process below, I know how challenging it can be to take the reins from the inner victim by forgiving and letting go of hurt, anger, and the need for payback or at least an apology. Yet the rewards are numerous. To quote Marianne Williamson, "Forgiveness is not always easy. At times, it feels more painful than the wound we suffered, to forgive the one that inflicted it. And yet, there is no peace without forgiveness."[4]

I believe that the peace we gain when we learn to forgive is the reason why studies have found that the act of forgiveness can reduce depression, anxiety, and anger, lower blood pressure and cholesterol, boost the immune system, and improve relationships and outlook.[5]

The Disentanglement Process allows you to free yourself step-by-step from the relationships where you felt victimized and disempowered. During this exercise, you'll consciously work with your subconscious. You'll clearly instruct this deeper part of the mind of your choice to let go and outgrow certain people from your past or present.

Here is a summary of the following five steps:

Step 1: Preparation. In this first step, you determine which person you want to forgive and disentangle from and get your subconscious ready for this process.

Step 2: Setting the Stage. Here you bring the person who had hurt and victimized you onto an imaginary stage.

Step 3: Lessons Learned—and Taught. Given that on the journey of life, we are all teachers and students for each other, you can now access the insights and growth opportunities from the relationship with the individual on the stage.

Step 4: Freedom through Forgiveness. You complete the old victim-perpetrator dynamic by releasing all the negativity you've taken on, and reclaiming the personal power you've given to that individual.

Step 5: Disentanglement. In this final step of the process, you're freeing yourself from any residual attachments to the person on the stage.

As you already know, the language your subconscious understands consists of images, sensations, and emotions, which you'll utilize in this process. So while going through the steps of forgiveness, keep in mind that the visualizations are more than just pleasant imagery. They provide your subconscious with a new understanding and framework for moving beyond the victim pattern into the doorway to greater freedom and self-empowerment. In other words, don't overthink this process, but approach it with an open mind and heart.

Step 1: Preparation

The goal of this first step is to get your inner victim on board with this forgiveness process. You may have previously tried to move beyond the victim role and leave the past behind. But as soon as you did, you noticed negative thoughts flooding your mind, such as, "You only set yourself up for getting hurt again. It's not safe." Or "You can't just let those who still owe you an apology off the hook. If you do, they'll always see you as weak and pathetic." Or maybe "There's something wrong with you. This is why people treat you badly."

We already talked about how, in its effort to protect you, the inner victim can take on the role of the villain by scaring, judging, or beating you down before anyone else can do the same. This part of your subconscious may interpret forgiving and letting go as a completely ludicrous and dangerous proposition, which it strongly resists. Thus, the barrage of negative self-talk aims to make you hopefully ditch the idea. Rather than ignoring these thoughts, acknowledge them and allow the inner victim to express itself. Then patiently answer and counterbalance its concerns with strong reasons why you choose to forgive.

When you're ready to begin, choose a person from the past or present who you feel victimized, betrayed, or unfairly treated by. The first time you go through this process, you don't want to focus on the most challenging or traumatizing relationships. Pick someone you feel has done you wrong but doesn't send you into a major anxiety attack when you think about them. If you see yourself more as a victim of your circumstances, choose someone you've previously blamed for keeping you stuck, small, and without hope for change.

When you've selected this person, notice if there's an emotional charge connected with them. Let's say you've chosen your brother, who used to relentlessly tease you during your childhood. You may find there's no negative emotional attachment, even if you recall some of those upsetting events from when you were little. If there's no tension, pressure, anger, hurt, or anxiety, chances are that your subconscious mind has already healed and released you from this relationship.

Then again, maybe someone comes to mind from high school, who you used to be friends with until they ditched you to hang with the more popular kids. You may not have thought about this betrayal for many years, but now that the image of this individual has popped into your mind, you realize how much emotional baggage you're still carrying from that time. This would be an excellent person to forgive, let go of, and disentangle from.

Giving the Inner Victim a Voice

Now that you've decided which person you want to forgive and detach from first, write out the story of how you felt when you got hurt and how you still feel about this individual. Acknowledge the wounds, the agony, the anxiety, the sadness, and the shame you may still associate with this relationship. Express your frustrations, anger, or disappointments to give your inner victim the attention it needs and deserves.

Instead of getting sucked into the negative emotions these memories trigger, visualize the source of these feelings—your inner victim—as a smaller part of you, like a little sub-personality that resides in your mind or heart. You may imagine the victim as a hurt child, a younger self who still feels unsafe and powerless in the face of the villain. You can also see your inner victim at the age you were when you were initially hurt by the person you want to disentangle from.

Have compassion and understanding for this part of yourself, but also recognize that it's not all of who you are or want to be. As I mentioned, compassion can function as a buffer, allowing you to understand and relate to others' struggles without becoming enmeshed in them. In this case, your compassion creates a healthy internal boundary between you and your inner victim. You can acknowledge the pain this part of you feels, but you don't fully associate yourself with it any longer. This boundary of compassion is the first step to de-identifying yourself with this survival pattern and moving forward toward empowerment.

How Did the Victim Role Affect Your Life?

As your inner victim tries to protect you from being mistreated again, it's crucial to convince this part of your subconscious that staying attached to the one who caused you pain isn't safe either. To do this, consider how much the victim survival pattern has cost you. For example, to avoid conflict and stay out of harm's way, you may have tried to become invisible, put yourself on mute, and suppressed your natural desire to speak up for yourself. To avoid being judged and rejected, you may have bought into the idea that you're flawed and incapable, and consequently, given up on pursuing your dreams and desires. Or to please and appease the figure on stage, you may have spent an enormous amount of energy playing the role of caretaker and peacemaker, while denying yourself the right to attend to your own needs.

So ask yourself, how much time and energy have you lost by rehashing the traumas and injustices this person inflicted on you while they may have forgotten all about you? How much has the relationship to yourself and others suffered because your inner victim doesn't trust anyone? To what extent has your inner victim stopped you from growing and expanding by keeping you and your life small and predictable to avoid attracting negative attention? How often have you blamed yourself for the pain others have caused?

Take an inventory, ideally in writing, of all the negative consequences being in victim mode has had on your life.

What Will Happen if You Forgive and Move On?

Some of the greatest motivators for change can be found in the answers to the simple question: "What's in it for me?" In other words, what will be the positive consequences of forgiving and disentangling from this unhealthy relationship? To discover the benefits of forgiveness, write about how you'll feel when you no longer attach your sense of self to the hurtful actions of this person. The freedom you gain when you stop waiting for an apology or some kind of reparation. And how much stronger you'll feel when you turn the tables, take your power back, and commit to taking responsibility for yourself.

Imagine how forgiveness through compassion will bring calmness and peace to your heart and mind, so you can eventually open them again. How your open heart and mind will enhance your capacity for love, hope, and joy, and thus allow you to establish more harmonious, respectful, and fulfilling relationships with yourself and others.

The more excited and motivated you feel about the positive outcomes of forgiveness, the less resistance you can expect from your inner victim. Contemplating the benefits of letting go is like installing a window in the thick wall of the victim's self-created imprisonment, an opening that permits this part of your subconscious mind to get a glance at life beyond survival mode.

Step 2: Setting the Stage

Close your eyes, take a couple of deep breaths, and remind yourself that you're safe here and now. No matter where your mind takes you, you can always return to the safety of the present moment by simply opening your eyes. Then imagine you're sitting by yourself on the balcony of a beautiful theater. Your chair is cushy and comfortable, and you're looking down with anticipation on the warmly lit stage. Bring the person you've chosen to forgive and disentangle from onto the stage. Notice whether you picture the individual as they were when you first met or at the age that person is now. From your vantage point on the balcony, they may appear smaller and possibly less threatening than in your memory. How do you feel? Do you sense an emotional charge, such as rage, anxiety, or hurt? Or do you feel relatively neutral and even eager to let go and move on? Once you've pictured this person on your stage, you can open your eyes again.

Step 3: Lessons Learned—and Taught

Evolution has taught us that the purpose of all life is not just to survive, but to grow, learn, and evolve from our experiences to become the best versions of ourselves. Thus a more empowering perspective of the victim-perpetrator paradigm is that we're all just students and teachers for one another. It's our responsibility to take advantage of the growth and learning opportunities every relationship presents, no matter how dysfunctional they may be.

In this vein, ask yourself: "What have I learned or can I still learn from this person on the stage?" It may be a bit challenging at first to consider the villain as your teacher. That person may have never expressed kindness toward you or supported you in any way, and they may not seem particularly skilled or evolved. So what, for crying out loud, could they potentially teach you? The truth is that sometimes you can learn the most from those who hurt you the worst and made the gravest mistakes. It has been often quoted, though the originator is anonymous, "Learn from the mistakes of others. You can't live long enough to make them all yourself." Here are a few questions that can help you discover the wisdom of what this relationship can teach you, both about yourself and about the person on the stage:

Why Was This Individual Able to Get Under Your Skin?

It may be tough to swallow, but you're much more likely to take other people's judgments or mistreatment personally if you believe that, on some level, they're right. Here's an example. Let's say you're six feet eight inches tall and weigh 250 pounds. If someone called you "teensy-weensy," you'd probably take this comment as a joke rather than an insult. Or if being honest and truthful is one of your highest moral values, and someone accused you of always lying, chances are you'd quickly shrug off this criticism because you knew the comment wasn't valid. However, suppose you already wrestle with self-limiting beliefs such as not being good enough or not being loveable. In that case, you're much more susceptible to taking other people's judgy remarks to heart.

When I was in my twenties, I convinced myself that I couldn't rely on anyone because people were usually selfish and disinterested in supporting others. Sure, there were reasons rooted in my childhood that fostered such a bleak and dim view of humanity. But all this belief did was set me up to feel continuously disappointed and let down. Looking back, this outlook was not fair to others or to myself, because no matter how hard anyone tried, my inner victim could only perceive their flaws and lapses. I couldn't appreciate that most of my coworkers, friends, and family members just did their best. Instead, I anticipated that everyone would fall short of my expectations and confirm the notion that nobody could be trusted.

When you think about the mistreatment you experienced in your relationship with the person you're about to disentangle from, can you appreciate that there's a connection between that pain and any of your pre-existing wounds and self-limiting beliefs? Whether you've told yourself that you're flawed or different from others, you're not worthy of speaking up and defending yourself, or you're simply not safe in the world, such limiting beliefs make you much more vulnerable to getting hurt by others.

The perspective that it's not just the individual on stage that caused you pain and anxiety, but also your own limiting beliefs, is empowering and liberating because it places the power and responsibility to heal and change back into your hands. And it may point toward other, earlier relationships that may be important to disentangle from as well.

Do You Need Better Boundaries?

The answer to this question may be an obvious "yes, of course" to you, but the need for better boundaries is still worth pointing out. Reflecting on how you've allowed others to behave can teach you the importance of establishing or reinforcing solid external boundaries, such as asserting your needs or avoiding people who don't treat you as you deserve. Such reflection may also remind you that it's time to enforce better internal boundaries by unburdening yourself from what other people may have thought, felt, said, or done to you. Why? Because *most perception is projection.*

You're already aware that our subconscious filters, such as memories, emotions, and beliefs, distort whatever we perceive into a subjective version of reality. Suppose you have always been overly concerned with your body weight or struggled with self-esteem. As a result, you may harshly judge strangers for being overweight or dismiss people's confidence as arrogant and condescending. As I just mentioned, these filters also determine whether you feel victimized or misunderstood by other people's behavior.

Of course, the reverse is also true. The behaviors and judgments of those who mistreated you are based on the fabric of their subconscious filters and, therefore, say much more about them than you. This is why we can't take other people's opinions, good or bad, personally. We'll discuss this liberating concept in more detail later in the book. For now, take as potential learning that to establish a healthy inner boundary, you want to value your opinion about yourself more than that of other people.

What Strengths and Positive Qualities Did You Exhibit in Response to This Relationship?

Coming from the victim's perspective, you may have perceived yourself as anything but strong or positive. However, what about your resilience? The mere fact that you haven't given up but are working on yourself right now proves that your spirit has prevailed. And did you give into the temptation to take on the negativity of those who mistreated you? To dominate and harm others when you felt the most hurt and powerless? To take your anger and frustration out on those who may appear even "weaker" than yourself? Sure, it's possible you may have lashed out occasionally when you felt pushed to the brink. But, again, your willingness to take responsibility for your growth and healing demonstrates that your values of right and wrong, your compassion for others, and your fundamental goodness remain intact. Otherwise, you would have already skipped this chapter altogether. A force inside has kept you on the path to creating a more joyful, purposeful, and self-empowered way of living. So embrace your inner strengths and gifts, no matter if others ignored you or labeled you as weak and unworthy.

Considering the Hardship This Person on Stage Caused You, What Is There to Learn about How You Want to Be Treated by Others and How You Want to Treat Others?

Rejection, neglect, abuse, betrayal, disrespect, inconsideration—these are just a few examples of how you may describe what the person you're about to forgive did to you. Many times, you may have mulled over the injustice you've experienced, repeatedly reliving situations that made you feel victimized. For your inner protector, dwelling on this negativity may feel familiar, safer, and even strangely comforting. Yet, to move beyond the dysfunctional patterns of this relationship, you need to provide your inner victim with a new direction, a focus on what you truly want to receive from and share with others.

Think about the words that best describe how this person treated you, and then choose the opposite as a new point of reference regarding how you want to relate to others. Opposite qualities could be *awareness, acceptance, kindness, tenderness, consideration, support, patience, respect, loyalty, trust, compassion, love*—all essential aspects of empowered living. Stepping out of the victim pattern into self-responsibility means you're committed to being the friend, parent, spouse, coworker, or boss you wished you'd had yourself.

You may have already vowed that you won't pass on what's been inflicted on you and thus treat other relationships with more tolerance, care, and compassion. However, you may have forgotten to include the most important relationship in your life—the one with yourself. So think about it, how can you support yourself in filling the void and healing the wounds others caused you? How can you rebuild a foundation of trust and self-worth from the rubble of the past? If you're drawing a blank, don't worry. Like many of us, you may not have spent much time wondering how you can be kinder and more supportive of yourself. But you're on the right path. As you move through this book, you'll gain ample insights and work through many processes that will lead you to a more profound appreciation for the magnificent truth of who you are. And as you learn to value yourself more, you'll naturally become aware of your needs and desires and find ways to fulfill them.

Discovering and owning the learnings you can gain from this challenging relationship demonstrates to your inner victim that you're no longer passive and powerless. Even though you can't control people and their behavior, you can always take self-responsibility and choose the meaning and value you want to give to their behavior. When you do so, the mud of dysfunction, betrayal, neglect, or abuse that kept you stuck becomes the fertile ground for your growth, self-acceptance, and empowerment.

Since we all act as teachers and students for each other, the question of what can be learned from the relationship applies to both parties— you and those that hurt you. So last but not least:

What Could the Person on the Stage Have Learned from You?

It's probably fair to assume that who you are and what you stand for differs vastly from the person on stage. So maybe you were the one who brought light into the darkness of their life. Or you demonstrated loyalty, commitment, and integrity, even though you didn't receive the same in return. Maybe your innocence and vulnerability could have inspired this individual to open their heart and honor their sensitivity. Or at least, your hurt and disappointment alone could have prompted them to reflect on their actions and choose to treat others with greater respect, kindness, and care.

Whether this person was a good student and appreciated what you had to offer or they neither noticed nor cared about who you truly are, it wasn't and isn't your responsibility to change that. All that matters is that your presence provided them an opportunity to learn and grow.

Now that you've retrieved the learnings from this relationship, you're ready to complete and resolve it on a conscious and subconscious level.

Step 4: Freedom through Forgiveness

What keeps your inner victim bound to the perpetrator besides your emotional attachments is the sticky mixture of negative emotions and beliefs you've taken on from this person and the personal power you've surrendered to them.

Let me explain. To protect you, the victim survival pattern makes you keenly aware of what the people you interact with are thinking and feeling, even if they don't openly express themselves. In this survival pattern, your subconscious mind not only registers their negativity, but it also takes everything personally and thus absorbs, in a sponge-like fashion, all their judgments, criticism, insults, and perceptions. Other people's negativity, anger, or insecurities become yours. Their critical and distorted perceptions about who you are, which again are often rooted in their struggles with themselves, become the suffocating framework for your own identity.

In this step of the Disentanglement Process, you'll be able to release all the negativity you've taken on and reclaim the personal power you've given to that individual.

Now, close your eyes and imagine you're once again looking down from the balcony at the person on the stage. Notice that you may already feel less emotionally charged and attached than when you first visualized this scenario. Then take a deep breath in and declare to yourself that **you're no longer willing to**:

- Base your sense of self on the negativity this person projected onto you.
- Give your power away and hold yourself back from personal growth and empowerment.
- Cling to the list of debts this person has accumulated with you.

- Wait for an apology or compensation for the pain this person caused you.
- Hold on to resentment, anger, or the need for retribution.

Instead, you choose to release this person and yourself from all hurtful, negative, and dysfunctional attachments. You choose freedom over the false comfort of hiding behind your inner victim. You choose forgiveness over the self-destructive desire for revenge. Kindness over the need to be right.

Now, in your mind's eye, share with the individual all you've gained and learned from the relationship, and anything that you still want to express before you disentangle. Then, when you are ready, declare out loud or to yourself three times, "I forgive you. I release you. I let go of the past."

Imagine that as you say these words, you're sending forgiveness, compassion, and healing energy from your heart to the stage. You can visualize this energy as a beam of white or golden light emanating from your heart and starting to envelop and permeate the person you're forgiving. After a few moments, pour the soot of all the negativity you've absorbed from this person into the healing light. All criticism, insults, or abuse that has been projected onto you. All anger, disregard or neglect you have taken personally. All limiting beliefs, distorted perceptions, and self-sabotaging patterns you've acquired in response to this relationship. Drain all the waste of the past into the warm and powerful ray of compassion and forgiveness, and then send it back to its origin.

Once you feel complete, take a deep breath in and state again, "I forgive you. I release you. I let go of the past." Now, add to this healing light of compassion and forgiveness all the anger, resentment, pain, anxiety, guilt, and shame you've felt as a result of this relationship. Let go of the need to receive acknowledgment of your suffering, an apology for the injustice, or some sort of redemption for the hardship this person caused you. Release the blame and self-loathing you may have used to punish yourself for something that wasn't your fault in the first place. Commit to completely letting go of all the negativity that tied you to the person on the stage.

As you release all the negative energy toward this individual, you free up space inside yourself to be filled with the personal power you had given away. Take another deep breath and confirm once again, "I forgive you. I release you. I let go of the past." Then choose to reclaim all the power you surrendered to the person you're disentangling from. You can imagine this power like a wave of energy that swooshes toward you, or like spheres of light in different sizes and colors floating out of the person on stage and heading in your direction. Continue to send from your heart forgiveness, compassion, and healing rays, while you let your power gently re-enter your core.

As you absorb your personal power, you may sense your entire being becoming lighter and more expansive. At the same time, the individual on the stage appears to deflate and become increasingly smaller. You're outgrowing the limiting dynamics of this relationship by letting go of the energies, emotions, and imprints that don't belong to you, and taking back your power, which allows you to be your authentic, unbridled self.

Again, say or think three times, "I forgive you. I release you. I let go of the past," and watch the person on the stage becoming more and more infused with your healing light of compassion and forgiveness. At some point, they are nothing but a shiny white or golden silhouette, without any trace of the negative energy you've returned to them. This is the sign from your subconscious mind that the slate is wiped clean, and that you are ready to take the final step to complete and resolve this relationship in its old form.

Step 5: Disentanglement

Notice the invisible—but for you right now detectable—one, two, or several energy bonds, cords, or tethers that attach you to the person on the stage. These connections represent the chains that kept you trapped and tied to that person, the bonds that have felt as though they were not only a part of your history, but also your identity. In the past, whenever you thought about this individual, you may have felt tension in your chest, pressure in your stomach, or heaviness in your forehead. Imagine these energetic connections as though they're ropes that have been somehow attached to your chest, your belly, or your head. Or you can picture strings that are tied around your ankles, wrists, or neck. Since you have created a clean slate between you and the person on the stage, now is the time for you to sever these ties.

Once again, say three times, "I forgive you. I release you. I let go of the past." Free yourself from these attachments by untying the knots, unplugging the cords, or slicing through the tethers. This isn't a violent or forceful act but a powerful symbol of your liberation from the past. Notice that each time you sever a rope, you have a bit more room to breathe, more space to grow and expand, and more energy residing inside you. As you free yourself from these old connections, imagine they are also automatically falling off the person on the stage.

Once all the attachments are severed, see the silhouette of the person you have forgiven and released leaving the stage, moving forward on their own path—which is entirely separate from yours—and becoming smaller and smaller until there is nothing but a dot on the horizon, which soon completely disappears.

Enjoy the freedom and expansion this disentanglement provides. Breathe and relax, letting your mind continue to process and integrate the healing effects of this work. You have given your subconscious clear instructions to abandon the self-limiting victim patterns it tried to protect you with. Now you have space to discover, explore, and express more and more who you are—and enjoy every bit of it. To complete the exercise, deeply inhale and exhale as you let yourself float back into this present moment and open your eyes.

......

INTEGRATION

Letters to and from the Past

Suppose you struggle to finish this process in one sitting or feel somewhat incomplete. In that case, you can of course repeat the steps several times until you feel you've concluded the disentanglement.

Once you are convinced that you have completely disconnected from this relationship, you can deepen and expand on these healing changes by writing two letters. The first one is to the person you have just forgiven and let go of. Summarize the learnings and insights you have gained, and why you chose to replace hurt or anger with compassion, confidence, and inner peace. Since you have let go of any expectations for this person to change or apologize, there's obviously no need to send the letter. For your inner victim though, your letter is a powerful confirmation that you've outgrown the relationship's victim-perpetrator paradigm.

The second letter you write to yourself in the voice of the individual you have disentangled from. In this letter, express everything you would have liked to have heard from this person but never did. This can be a heartfelt apology, an explanation of why they couldn't appreciate you more and treat you better, or a reflection on the pain, fear, or self-loathing this individual had been struggling with. I know you have just let go of the need for an apology, but it will be soothing for your inner victim to hear this person make amends.

You probably wonder whether you're not just deceiving yourself by crafting a letter and pretending it comes from someone else. Still, as we already discussed, to your subconscious mind, it doesn't matter whether something is real or imagined. Your subconscious takes whatever you think and feel at face value. So as you're creating this letter of atonement, know that for your inner victim it may be the finishing touch in this process of healing and completion.

Common Questions about
Forgiving and Letting Go

The Disentanglement Process has helped countless of my clients to liberate themselves finally from disempowering relationships, and set the space for further growth and self-empowerment. Yet there are some common questions and concerns they've expressed that are worth addressing here.

Q: What if I have a hard time forgiving someone?

A: With certain people you might find it difficult to send the energy of compassion and forgiveness their way and release them from the past. The difficulty could mean that you have more to learn from these individuals, or that you haven't fully committed to letting go of all the debt they had racked up over the years. Either way, take your time to contemplate how these people were teachers for you, and how they have or could have grown from the relationship. Then remind yourself that your intention for this process isn't to be right or to be compensated for others' wrongdoings. Your intention is to be free—free to grow into the empowered leader of your life.

Q: How am I supposed to relate to people who are still a part of my daily life after I've disentangled from them?

A: This is one of the most common concerns. Keep in mind that disentanglement doesn't mean you must cease all interactions with those you've forgiven and released. Of course, with some of the people you've disentangled from, you may have a sense of completion, and thus no need or desire to reconnect with them. You can leave such relationships behind you in the past. With others—perhaps a spouse, your parents, or your boss, you may naturally wonder what you'll feel about them once you've disentangled. Let's say you've let go of your parents. Will you still care about them, or will they no longer matter to you? Will you go right back into victim mode when they act in ways that trigger those feelings of powerlessness? Will you notice a difference or will you feel the same, and if so, does this mean you failed?

When I disentangled myself from the often challenging and insecurity-triggering relationship with my father, I asked myself: What will happen when I visit my parents? Well, before I saw them again, I prepared myself. I just thought about some of the ways my father used to push my buttons: questioning my choices, worrying about my future, criticizing my driving, or arguing with my mother. When I recalled such situations, I noticed, to my surprise, that I didn't react with the familiar mix of disappointment, self-doubt, and anger. Instead, I felt a refreshing level of detachment.

Then I reminded myself of all I had learned from and about him during the Disentanglement Process. I could appreciate how much insecurity and fear my dad carried in his heart. How the loss of his father when he was just six years old, his experiences during World War II, and his time as a prisoner of war had trapped him in his survival patterns. Through this more compassionate lens, it became apparent that even though my dad appeared controlling and judgmental, all he wanted was to feel safe and loved. Voicing his doubts about my decisions didn't mean he thought he knew what was right for me. He just wanted me to reassure him that I would be okay. His critical remarks about my driving weren't a reflection of how I handled traffic, but more about how difficult it was for him to trust and let go of control. Even his angry outbursts with my mother, upon looking back, appeared just like the temper tantrum of a little boy who pushes people away when he needs them the most.

Admittedly, the way my father treated his family wasn't always the most mature and evolved. However, the Disentanglement Process allowed me to create a healthy and compassionate distance from his energy and projections. And afterward, I felt closer to him than ever. I no longer took any of his behaviors personally. Instead, I could accept his shortcomings and love and appreciate him for who he was.

I can imagine you'll experience similar shifts with some of the people you will disentangle from. Having learned from and grown beyond the victim survival pattern, you'll no longer absorb their negativity or feel responsible for their beliefs, feelings, and behaviors. Instead, you'll find it easier to set clear boundaries and push back or remove yourself when you're treated unjustly—a topic I will cover in the *helper pattern* chapter. And just as I discovered with my father, you may also find a greater openness and softness in your heart for those you once felt victimized by, accepting them and their shortcomings with more compassion and understanding.

Q: Can I also use this process to forgive myself?

A: Absolutely, in a slightly modified form. As I mentioned, shame, guilt, and self-blame are common reactions of the inner victim. "I should have done something different," "I'm weaker or less than others," or "There's something wrong with me that people choose to hurt me," may have been some of your self-critical narratives. Therefore, imagine yourself on the stage, ideally at the age when the shame and guilt started. Point out to that younger self that you have made the choice to reclaim your power by learning and growing from the past and letting go of all negativity that kept you bound to it.

Then, in the spirit of self-responsibility, ask yourself these questions:

- What can I learn from how that younger version of myself acted and responded to the events of the past?
- Why were my younger me's actions the best they could do at that time?
- How would I now respond differently should a similar situation arise?

Once you've answered these questions, pour compassion, forgiveness, and healing light from your heart into the version of yourself on the stage, dissolving and releasing all guilt, shame, and self-loathing that part of you had held on to. Imagine the emotional burden disintegrating, and like smoke or little dust specks, rising up and out of the body of your younger self, which becomes increasingly light, pure, and whole again. Then, instead of disentangling, gently bring that part of you into your heart, integrating it into the wholeness of your being. This way, you're communicating to your subconscious mind that you truly accept and appreciate who you were and what you did or didn't do.

Q: I feel victimized by life and by God. How do I forgive and disentangle from *them?*

A: The short answer is, you can't. Just as we can't blame the rain for getting us wet, gravity for keeping us fastened to the earth, and our parents for bringing us into this world, it's futile to blame life, the universe, or a higher power for the hardships we may encounter on our journey. Don't get me wrong, I have strong spiritual beliefs and don't perceive life as just a random sequence of events. However, I also believe that we can't control all our circumstances, no matter how hard we try. Yet what we can control is how we respond to whatever happens to us. And if you find that in the past you've reacted to challenges in your life in ways that make you feel ashamed and frustrated with yourself, now that you know how, it may be the best time to forgive yourself.

When choosing how to respond to circumstances outside our control, Aimee Copeland is a true inspiration. Aimee, a twenty-four-year-old student from Snellville, Georgia, hadn't a care in the world when she went zip-lining with her friends on a hot summer day. Yet sometime during this exciting outing, she became infected by a rare flesh-eating bacteria and lost both hands, one foot, and one leg—indeed a devastating tragedy for such a young woman. However, according to Aimee, her life became more meaningful and precious. "I don't take for granted anymore how beautiful [life] is . . . Everything smells better; colors are more vibrant than ever before. Instead of saying I'm disabled, I say I have different abilities." This young woman understands that there are no limitations—and that we can make a choice to be either the victim or the creator of our reality.

······

Taking self-responsibility is a huge step toward self-empowerment. After Lindsay forgave and disentangled from her parents, a massive weight lifted from her heart. She no longer had nightmares about her father abusing her and felt a sense of resolution with her past. Yet she continued to struggle with her anxiety and the urge to run away from any uncomfortable situations. She still preferred staying safely tucked away at home rather than going to her busy office or leaving the house. Everything changed for her when she started to address and resolve the invisibility pattern, which is what this next chapter is about.

5

THE INVISIBILITY PATTERN
Living Under the Radar

*May all that is unforgiven in you be released; may your
fears yield their deepest tranquilities; may all that is
unlived in you blossom into a future graced with love.*
—JOHN O'DONOHUE

If you've been living in the *avoider* pattern of making yourself
invisible, a typical weekday morning could look something like
this: As soon as you wake up, you're overcome with a feeling of
dread. Leaving the safety of your warm bed and getting ready for
the day already seems too much for you. Just the thought of having to go to the office and deal with your colleagues and your customers makes you feel uneasy. In the kitchen, you feel attacked
by a barrage of bad news announced by an annoyingly perky TV
anchor, which increases your desire to go back to bed and pull the
covers over your head.

You keep the conversations with your spouse and kids to a
minimum and try to leave the house quickly before anyone can ask
you to do something for them. Then, as you sit in traffic or on a
commuter train, you become over-stimulated by horns honking,

truck exhaust, or the woman across the aisle snapping her chewing gum. To distract yourself, you think about work, which throws you into a shame spiral, because you remind yourself that you've had the same job for almost ten years without ever getting a promotion or raise. Yes, flying under the radar is your preferred way of traveling through life, but what if everyone is making fun of you and talking behind your back? And what if your boss realizes that you are not doing such a great job and will want to get rid of you? Thoughts like this quickly morph into what-if scenarios of losing your job, house and family, and living under a bridge. You feel anxious, alone, misunderstood, and unable to turn your life around.

The worry and anxiety stay with you throughout the remainder of the day. As usual, you keep your head down and try not to make waves. And when one of your colleagues pushes work they don't want to deal with onto your desk, you just silently nod with a forced smile, because you hate confrontations. During lunch, when all the others are out to eat, you're actually glad you can nibble your sandwich by yourself in front of your computer. Being ignored feels so much better than having to deal with potential judgment.

Once you're back at home and everyone has gone to bed, you finally start to relax. The best time of day is when you can lose yourself in your favorite TV shows or enjoy spending a couple of hours in the much more empowering virtual reality of video games. There you can be someone else and show your true potential as a fearless leader, a hero, or a monster slayer. In that world behind your TV or computer screen, you feel more alive and engaged than when you have to face real-life situations. As you often do, you go to bed long after midnight because you can't pull yourself away from your alternate life. The following day, when your alarm rips you from your dreams, you're faced with going through the motions of another *Groundhog Day* without any hope for change.

THE GREAT DISAPPEARING ACT

The invisibility pattern is based on the assumption that any form of unwanted attention, judgment, or criticism needs to be evaded at all costs. As you see yourself as different and not fitting in, other people become potential threats, which is why loneliness and isolation are your comfort zone. And yet, deep inside, you crave nothing more than love, connection, and a sense of belonging.

Agoraphobia and social anxiety are extreme forms of this survival pattern. When the invisibility pattern takes control of your entire life, just being in the world appears scary and overwhelming. In these cases, the inner protector (the subconscious part that runs this pattern) reduces the purpose of your existence just to make it through another day without getting harmed or annihilated. Most people held hostage by this pattern suffer in silence, stuck in the seemingly unresolvable inner battle of needing help, yet being too afraid to reach out to others.

However, living with the invisibility pattern doesn't necessarily mean that you constantly struggle. Many people who choose to remain unnoticed would tell you they're content with their lives as long as they can stay within the strict boundaries of their comfort zone. The problem with comfort zones is that they tend to become smaller and smaller. I often hear from clients about how their world shrank through the years. Yet, they continue to settle for a diminished version of their lives, as they are convinced that predictability and safety are the best they can hope for—no matter how tiny, suffocating, and pointless their existence may have become.

All living beings aim to grow and expand. Suppressing this natural desire to keep ourselves and our life small and safe takes enormous effort, which is why invisible avoiders often end up suffering from low energy and depression.

You may be surprised to hear that there is another form of the invisibility pattern that is common in people that perceive themselves as outgoing, confident, successful, and adventurous. Let's say you've felt comfortable being the over-achiever and in control of your life, but you avoid acknowledging to others and yourself how hard it is for you always to have to perform, compete, be on, or be in charge. Or you like to show up for others as the solid rock they can lean on, but you don't dare to let anyone see your vulnerable side.

Andrew was perceived by his friends and colleagues as a fearless go-getter who never shied away from risks or obstacles. Although he was plagued by anxiety, Andrew wasn't willing to show it, or even give any attention to his emotions. One night, when he took his daughter to bed, he noticed that she seemed sad and troubled. When he asked her if there was anything on her mind, she said, "No thanks. I talk about my problems with the school counselor. You and Mom are more like robots. You function perfectly but don't seem to have any feelings."

This was when Andrew realized that he hadn't only run away from his anxiety, he also avoided being close to anyone. For example, when his wife was dealing with a mysterious illness, which turned out to be Lyme disease, it was difficult for Andrew to be around her.

"It was as if my wife, who used to be the safest person for me, suddenly scared me. At first, I tried to help her find answers, but nothing I suggested seemed to make a difference. The harder I tried without success, the more frustrated and anxious I became. At some point I started to blame my wife for her illness, when in reality, I just felt helpless and like a failure. I escaped by focusing all my attention on work so I didn't have to be around her, because her suffering was unbearable for me to watch."

You can imagine that Andrew's wife wasn't too pleased by her husband avoiding her at a time when she needed him most. However, she knew intuitively that his behavior wasn't about her and their marriage but had more to do with Andrew's childhood.

When he was a little boy, Andrew's mom fell ill with breast cancer. For years, he watched her going in and out of hospitals and spending weeks at a time in bed because she was too weak to get up. Throughout this time, his mother changed physically and became increasingly withdrawn. Her son couldn't understand what his mother was going through and why she didn't want to spend more time with him.

In the beginning, Andrew tried to make his mother feel better by telling her stories and making her laugh. But as she grew weaker and had barely the energy to get out of bed, he kept away from her. It was too difficult for him to watch her suffer when he couldn't do anything about it. Andrew told me that when his mom passed away, he didn't feel anything; he couldn't even cry. For a long time, he judged himself for not grieving her death more. He believed he must be a cold and heartless person who didn't care about anyone.

However, during our work together, Andrew realized the opposite was true. As a boy, Andrew was so sensitive and caring that all he wanted was for his ill parent to get well again. When that little boy had to face the reality that his mother was going to die, his own fear and sadness, combined with the pain and suffering he imagined she was going through, became too much to handle. To protect himself, Andrew's subconscious mind chose to avoid any form of strong emotions. As a result, he not only hid his own feelings from himself and others but also became numb to what those around him were feeling, no matter how much they struggled. Decades later, Andrew became a highly accomplished adult and a pillar of his community. Yet, since the invisibility pattern continued to hide the most sensitive and vulnerable aspects of himself, he often felt alone and isolated, without a real sense of belonging.

Sounds familiar? This form of "partial" invisibility, which I will discuss later, is much more common than living in complete hiding. The goal of this chapter—and the entire book—is for you to get back in touch with the aspects of your personality that you usually avoid or struggle with. Because once you've healed, integrated, and transformed these parts into their empowered versions, your life will become a more joyful, meaningful, and fulfilling expression of your authentic self.

HOW DO YOU KNOW WHEN YOU'RE DEALING WITH THE INVISIBILITY PATTERN?

Overall, you could say that the invisibility pattern operates with the same slogan as Southwest Airlines: "Wanna get away?" As I just mentioned, in its most intense and all-encompassing form, this pattern can lead to chronic anxiety and the inability to have a meaningful social life. But it's more common that the invisibility pattern makes us conceal the facets of ourselves that feel the most vulnerable, insecure, or ashamed.

Here are some common examples of how this survival pattern may have taken charge of your entire life or certain aspects of it.

You Make Yourself Unnoticeable
You try not to draw attention to yourself. You dress unobtrusively, preferably in beige or black, speak quietly, hunch your shoulders a bit, and usually avoid eye contact. You feel uncomfortable when you're asked questions about yourself and prefer to keep conversations to a minimum. You don't talk about your talents, strengths, and successes, because you don't want to make someone feel bad or envious. You don't allow yourself to buy a new car, because the neighbors might think you're too flashy or suffering from a midlife crisis.

You Avoid Being Vulnerable
As with all the survival patterns, the invisibility pattern may only show up in some areas of your life, which you already know as partial invisibility. Like Andrew, you portray yourself as easy-going and

self-assured, while making sure that nobody knows how you feel. All you care about is keeping everyone at a safe distance, because if you were to open up and start sharing your thoughts and emotions, you'd only expose yourself to potential hurt, criticism, and the pain of the inevitable rejection and abandonment.

Whether you're avoiding expressing your ideas, desires, needs, or discontents, or are afraid of revealing your sexuality, sensitivity, or uniqueness, the invisibility pattern protects the aspects of your personality it deems too fragile and vulnerable to expose to potential ridicule and rejection.

You Avoid Intimacy, Deeper Connection, and Commitment

Besides hiding from the critical gaze of others, your invisibility pattern tries to keep you safe by preventing you from building closer relationships with others. You long for love, friendship, and a sense of belonging, but as soon as you let someone get closer, you become more and more uncomfortable. Your inner critic spirals into narratives such as, "Others can't be trusted, because they either want to hurt me or, if they pretend to be friendly, they only want to take advantage of me." You become increasingly suspicious, frustrated, and disappointed with your relationships. Eventually, you find a reason to get out of them and retreat into the safety of your hermit's cave, feeling relieved that you don't have to bother with "these people" any longer. But even though you live by the creed "better be safe and lonely," at times, you can't completely shake off the painful sting of isolation.

You Have Difficulties Making Decisions

You agonize about what to wear for work, what to write on a birthday card for your sibling, or what to order in a restaurant as if your life depends on it. And once you make a decision, you second-guess yourself on whether it was the right one. For you, choices are scary because they're statements about your likes and dislikes, and thus, reveal more of who you are, which makes you more vulnerable to opinions from others.

You Feel Easily Criticized and Rejected

Since the invisibility pattern's goal is to evade negative attention, you become immediately defensive and deeply hurt whenever you notice someone doesn't agree with you. You can't just let other people's opinions roll off your back or consider that their points of view may be an opportunity for you to learn and grow. You even feel so sensitive and self-conscious that you take the most harmless banter or playful teasing as a crushing blow. When a stranger accidentally pushes you as he's rushing up the escalator, or a waitress takes longer to spot you sitting by yourself in the restaurant, you convince yourself that this is once again proof that people don't like or respect you.

You Feel Sensitive, Anxious, and Easily Overwhelmed Around Other People

When your invisibility pattern runs your life, socializing isn't your idea of a good time. In a small group, you vigilantly scan and evaluate how people communicate—their facial expressions, body language, and energy—so that you can quickly detect and ideally avoid or deflect any potential negativity directed toward you.

Being around larger numbers of people, such as in a mall or in a movie theater, makes you feel tired and foggy-headed. You don't only register other people's behavior, you also seem to sponge up their feelings and energies. This can leave you confused about whether you're feeling your own emotions or someone else's. The time to recuperate and feel fully restored from being out in the world takes longer and longer until it seems you're all the time emotionally and physically exhausted. Being highly sensitive in a competitive and demanding world with little patience for emotions and vulnerabilities makes you feel flawed, weak, and consequently, even less motivated to engage with others.

You Put Yourself Down

Your inner critic, which can be the voice of the invisibility pattern, works overtime. The gist of these critical comments is that there's something wrong with you and that you don't fit in, so you need to keep your head down, avoid being a target or making a fool of yourself, and in this way, make it through another twenty-four hours.

You Avoid Yourself

You don't look into the mirror because you detest what you see. You don't acknowledge or attend to your feelings because you believe that you're broken. You don't pay attention to your needs and wants because self-care is a luxury you can't afford; instead, you treat yourself with neglect and disdain.

You Struggle with Lack of Energy or Chronic Physical Problems

It's a well-known fact that long-standing anxiety can lead to chronic pain, high blood pressure, auto-immune diseases, and other physical illnesses. While some of these challenges can be explained by the wear and tear of running on adrenaline, cortisol, and other stress hormones, there may be another explanation about why the body seems to pull the brakes on our lives. Many of my clients who have been struggling with joint and muscle pain, chronic fatigue and inflammation, or auto-immune diseases, admitted that before they got sick, they used to push themselves extremely hard not to let their anxiety and sensitivity hold them back.

Paula is a good example. Her only agenda during her childhood was to escape her violent and abusive mother, who regularly expressed her anger and frustration with life by whipping her little girl until she could barely walk. Feeling usually small and insignificant, hitting her daughter probably gave her some sense of power and control. Needless to say, Paula's survival instincts were on high alert 24/7. Until she was eighteen years old, hiding under the staircase or in the nearby forest were her best bets to escape being punished for just existing. As soon as she was old enough, she left her parents and never looked back.

Paula's thirst for freedom and independence sent her traveling around the world, restlessly seeking new adventures and thrills. Photography became her passion and source of income; a backpack and a pair of comfortable hiking boots were all she needed for her personal comfort. Whether she crossed a desert in Africa, or fought her way through the forbidding terrain of the Amazon jungle, she felt the most alive, secure, and at home with herself in the midst of the wilderness. For years, this nomadic lifestyle with all its challenges and potential dangers seemed to build Paula's confidence and sense of self.

One day, somewhere in Peru, Paula and a woman she'd been traveling with for a few weeks met two men at a market who offered them a ride to the next town. Having had only good experiences with strangers so far, Paula and her friend gladly accepted the offer. However, the men didn't drive them straight to the neighboring village. Instead, they told the women they had to pick up a buddy at a nearby farm. As soon as they arrived at the remote farmhouse, their demeanor changed radically. The men yanked the women out of the car and told them that if they wouldn't comply they'd shoot them. Guns pulled, the thugs shoved Paula and her friend down the stairs into a dark and musty-smelling basement, where they locked them in. This was the first time since she'd left her childhood home that Paula felt terror again. Yet, while her companion remained frozen in shock and disbelief, Paula's survival instincts kicked in, prompting her to fervently search for any potential escape route.

To this day, Paula can't explain why the only small window in that room wasn't locked or barricaded. Maybe the men hadn't expected to take hostages, or they'd counted on the women being too frightened to attempt a breakout. Or as Paula told me, "Maybe it was just my guardian angels showing up for us."

The women had to suppress the urge to quickly scramble through the opening and run for help. Instead, they waited until it was dark outside to carefully climb out and slowly crawl away from the farmhouse. Only when they felt certain they were out of sight did they start running, hoping they would stumble upon a road or a house. Luckily, they reached the road and were able to stop a car, which brought them back to safety.

Yet Paula's ordeal had only begun. Happy to be alive, she quit her trip and returned to New York, to the apartment she shared with a close friend. At first, considering the trauma she'd gone through, she didn't think much of the fact that all she wanted was to sleep and recuperate. However, a few days in bed turned into several weeks. No matter how long she rested, for some reason she couldn't find the energy to get dressed and leave her place. Concerned that she may have caught some bug during her travels, she consulted several doctors, but nobody could find a plausible explanation for her complete lack of energy.

Paula stayed house-bound for more than a year, and only very slowly started gaining back a little bit of her energy. Once an enthusiastic globetrotter, her life had shrunk to the size of her two-bedroom apartment. Eventually, she started working again, yet it was impossible for her to drive or fly anywhere outside the city. The mere thought of going on a trip could cause a panic attack followed by utter exhaustion.

From a clinical perspective, Paula most likely suffered from post-traumatic stress disorder and chronic fatigue syndrome. Yet from the subconscious mind's point of view, another explanation for her mysterious illness and inability to travel could be that her invisibility pattern pulled the emergency brake to keep her safe. After her terrible experiences with her violent and abusive mother, part of her subconscious already considered the world a hostile and unsafe place. Only when she finally got away from her family was Paula able to override the protective pattern and discover and embrace her adventurous nature.

At first, her subconscious protector may have been reluctant to let go of control, wondering whether she was truly safe roaming around in the big wide world. Then, as Paula became more adept at navigating around some of the more exotic and remote parts of the planet, the inner protector gradually relaxed and let the adult Paula be in charge. But as soon as she was in serious trouble again, the invisibility pattern, which had kept her alive throughout her childhood, kicked right back in.

It always amazes me how quickly and forcefully the old survival patterns can get reactivated, even if they seem to have retired from their jobs years ago. Paula's physical symptoms, which kept her tucked away in a small apartment, and her subsequent inability to travel more than a few miles beyond her home, were all part of the invisibility pattern. When we started to work together, more than fifteen years after the incident in Peru, she still could only drive on small roads and hadn't traveled by plane at all.

Yet once Paula acknowledged, addressed, and resolved her childhood trauma and the root causes of her invisibility pattern, she was able to expand her life again. Six months into our work together she sent me a postcard from Switzerland. "I did it," she wrote. "The world is my home again. And, thanks to our work, now I am also more at home with myself than ever before."

Of course, not all lack of energy or chronic physical problems are caused by an inner protector on overdrive. Nevertheless, for many of my clients, the concept of their chronic illness being a form of subconscious emergency brake was an eye-opening revelation, which, when looking back on their history, they wholeheartedly agreed with.

......

Do any of these expressions of the invisibility pattern appear familiar to you? Let's face it, most of us have an innate fear of standing out, being criticized or rejected, and thus losing the connection to the tribe. Our need to blend in and not draw any negative attention to ourselves outweighs our desire to express ourselves authentically. We hold ourselves back from sharing our thoughts and feelings to ensure we don't reveal anything that could potentially be used against us in the future. We don't address hurtful comments and misunderstandings because we want to avoid conflict at all costs. Yet, these patterns may be so familiar to us that we don't realize how they create a constant undercurrent of stress, anxiety, and defensiveness. And as you focus on how to be unnoticeable to others, you become increasingly unaware of yourself. This is why the invisibility pattern is potentially your biggest blind spot—and why resolving it can be your greatest opportunity to gain a deeper understanding and appreciation of who you truly are.

WHERE DOES THE INVISIBILITY PATTERN COME FROM?

The invisibility pattern is probably developmentally the earliest and the most instinctual of all survival patterns. It's usually established during our childhood when we felt the most powerless and dependent on others. Since our ability to keep us safe was very limited at a young age, hiding out and becoming invisible appeared to the subconscious as the best option, especially if we were dealing with confusing and unstable circumstances.

Looking back, you may have always told yourself that you had an ideal childhood, and that you'd been well loved and taken care of. Yet maybe a teacher made fun of you in school, or one of your friends suddenly didn't want to play with you anymore, or your parents went through a phase during which they fought a lot about money issues, or you'd just heard about that kid in your neighborhood who was killed in a hit-and-run accident. Any of these situations could be a reason for your subconscious to shift its invisibility survival pattern into gear.

Donna, a successful designer, had a difficult upbringing. Her father was a domineering patriarch who frequently criticized and belittled her mother, whom Donna described as very anxious and neurotic. Donna's older brother, who was extremely popular due to his good looks and cool cockiness, completely ignored Donna at best, but more often, treated her with an air of disgust, as if her mere existence was a complete inconvenience for him. While her brother simply left the house to hang out with his pals when their parents were fighting, Donna, who didn't have many friends, hid in her bedroom closet with fingers stuck in her ears to avoid hearing the shouting and crying. At fourteen, Donna realized she wasn't interested in boys but had a massive crush on her girlfriend, one of the few who seemed to like her for some reason. Terrified that this abomination would be found out, Donna made sure to hide her feelings so that no one could ever reject her for who she was.

Donna's only escape from a hostile world that didn't want or accept her was her art. She would sit for hours in her small bedroom, drawing landscapes and villages filled with happy families, children, and pets, who got along and enjoyed playing together. There was harmony, love, happiness, and butterflies in her imaginary world. Since Donna was the only one who had access to that little paradise, it was the one place she felt safe to be herself.

Once an adult, her talent, hard work, and ability to listen and understand people's ideas, helped Donna to become a successful graphic designer in a leading advertising agency. Although she would describe herself as rather shy and introverted, she delved headfirst into her fast-paced and highly demanding career. She loved her work because she felt the most peaceful and purposeful when, through her art, she could bring more color and beauty into the world. However, it also took a lot out of her to expose herself daily to the judgment and scrutiny of her colleagues and clients. At the end of the day, all she wanted was to retreat to her tastefully decorated sanctuary and hide out with cookies and a glass of milk.

While many people valued and admired Donna's professional persona, hardly anyone knew her privately. "I believe that people see me as an asexual being," she told me, "who lives only for her job and has no interest in anything else." Her double life as a top designer and a frightened hermit amplified her childhood's shame, fears, and insecurities. The more attention and approval she received for her craft, the greater her need to hide her sensitive, anxious, and vulnerable side, which she was certain no one would ever want to know.

Throughout the years, it became increasingly difficult for Donna to push her anxiety aside and put on the mask of the cool, brilliant artist who, unfazed by the pressure, deadlines, and high expectations, was continuously able to awe her clients and colleagues. But as soon as she left the office, Donna's inner avoider pulled her right back into the safety of invisibility, relieved that once again, nobody had found the ugly truth behind her mask.

Finally, when Donna was in her early fifties, the pain of loneliness and lack of self-love outweighed her fundamental need for safety, comfort, and control. It was then that she was willing to face the fears, insecurities, and limiting beliefs that had controlled her life since she was a little girl.

......

Have you ever thought about what your inner protector might look like? If you did, considering that this part of your subconscious frequently employs anxiety, worry, and shame to usher you into the shadows of obscurity, the image probably wasn't very friendly. Perhaps a nasty little devil or a yellow-toothed monster inside you—nothing you'd want to get close to or associate with. But, what if you imagined the inner protector as a much younger version of yourself who, early in your life, started to believe the world isn't a friendly place and people can't be trusted, just as you've seen with Andrew, Paula, and Donna? Would you still try to ignore or even get rid of this part of yourself? Or would you at least be more curious and open to discovering why it is trying so hard to keep you safe?

THE MISSION OF THE INVISIBILITY PATTERN

You're probably familiar with this phenomenon. Whenever you've stepped out of your comfort zone by speaking up or trying out something new, a voice in your head tells you that you're either putting yourself in danger of being judged or ridiculed, or that you should feel ashamed of yourself because you have surely behaved like a fool. The depleting and deflating effects of shame are astounding. Probably more than any other emotion, shame can make you feel small, inadequate, and even completely worthless.

But why does your inner protector deem feeling ashamed and worthless safer than feeling confident and self-assured? By shaming you, doesn't the invisibility pattern fulfill precisely the sentiment it tries so hard to avoid—to be judged and rejected? There is a two-fold explanation for this apparent paradox. First, your inner protector is a strong proponent of the "reject-yourself-first-before-others-can" paradigm, which is based on the assumption that you, the adult, are still as helpless and small as you were when the invisibility pattern kicked in for the first time. Controlled self-inflicted put-downs and hurts prevent you from sticking your head out and getting your hopes up, right before both get clobbered by the unpredictable but *inevitable* acrimony of your fellow earthlings.

The second reason the inner protector is willing to trade self-worth and self-expression for a sense of security is less apparent but even more meaningful. The question is, what is this part of you trying to protect? Of course, by definition, a guardian intends to keep you alive and unharmed—physically and emotionally. Yet you're usually not in grave danger when your inner protector promotes worry and panic before work Monday morning. And there is no reason to feel overwhelmed and anxious in the checkout line at a shopping center, or embarrassed and unworthy when you're at a neighbor's birthday party. So why such strong reactions to such relatively harmless day-to-day situations?

Let's remember that the invisibility pattern has its roots in a time during your childhood when you were not only the frailest but also still in touch with all the delicate and precious aspects of your true nature. These innate qualities may have been your vivid imagination and creative spark, your complete openness and unconditional trust in people's goodness, or your connection to the *unseen* world and unshakable conviction that your deepest desires and wildest dreams are bound to come true. Yet once you experienced hurtful judgment and rejection and realized that you were not unconditionally accepted and embraced, your subconscious decided it was no longer safe to be your unbridled authentic self. And since some aspects of your personality didn't appear desirable or welcome by those around you, they must be locked away and hidden before they could get you into further trouble.

This was when your invisibility pattern emerged, not only to protect you from the judgment of others, but also to safeguard the facets of your true self that were deemed too fragile and vulnerable to be kept in plain sight. It may sound paradoxical, but shame, which is the belief that something is wrong with you, serves as the shield that conceals these inner treasures. As long as you feel ashamed and unsafe, you won't dare to reveal these gems of your truth.

However, the intention was not to keep these parts of your authentic self hidden for the rest of your life. As a kid you may have told yourself, "When I'm a grown-up, I'll play and sing as much as I want," or "As soon as I'm eighteen years old, I'll have my own place, where I can finally be myself." Like a flower bulb buried under a thick layer of ice and snow, you always had the hope that one day the dark and cold winter would end, and you'd have the opportunity to let your precious gifts and dreams come back to life and flourish again. But as the years passed, invisibility became your reality, and the familiar toned-down version of yourself, your identity.

I was a happy-go-lucky child with blond hair, blue eyes, and a constant smile on my little face. Life appeared magical, with unlimited possibilities to dream, play, and have fun. I felt naturally connected with all living beings, and often spent hours watching the leaves dance in the sunlight, or saving the little bugs that fell into our pool from drowning. At that time, not only did plants and animals appear alive, but everything seemed to contain a kind of life force energy. I often saw the walls of my bedroom move at night, as if they consisted of thousands of little particles—like ants—that constantly shuffled around and reorganized themselves. A bit like in the *Matrix* movies. My mom said I probably had a fever, even though my temperature was completely normal. I still don't know whether what I saw was just a concoction of a developing brain, or whether I was truly able to perceive energy in motion.

When I was about eleven years old, my world of energy, rainbows, and unicorn horns came crashing down. It wasn't necessarily one event that activated my inner protector. First, my parents started to argue more, usually about money or my mother's parents, whom my dad disliked for some reason. Then my mom "turned on me" when I received my first D in high school. I can still feel my heart crumble with pain, shame, and disbelief at her endless barrage of threats and insults. But curiously enough, it was in response to the words of a stranger, that I lost—or hid—my innocence and trust.

One day, my parents hired a piano tuner, probably in the hope of making my abysmal playing sound a little bit better. He was a middle-aged man with a quiet but friendly demeanor who didn't mind that I inquisitively watched him adjusting the tension of each string. After each adjustment, he tenderly hit the piano key and listened carefully to its tone, eyes closed, head tilted slightly toward the instrument.

He told me he had perfect pitch and could recognize every single note without having to use a tuning fork as a reference. This thoroughly impressed me, and I became even more curious about this unusual man. We chatted about music, school, and his work. Then out of the blue he asked me, "Do you believe in God?"

I thought I knew the *correct* answer and told him happily, "Yes."

He smiled and said, "That's good. You know, one day God will test you to see whether you truly have faith in him."

Oh, my God, this little remark scared the bejesus out of me. Maybe it was the word "test" that triggered my already heightened fear of failure. Or it was the sudden possibility that God might not be friendly and unconditionally loving after all, but just like my parents, wanting me to perform and meet his expectations. From that day on, my trust in the love and support of a higher power vanished like a rabbit from a magician's hat.

Quickly, several subconscious protectors emerged, convened, and concluded that my lightness, openness, and faith in the goodness of life were naïve, no longer appreciated by others—including God—and needed to be replaced by seriousness, hard work, and a good deal of vigilance.

Consciously, I told myself that all I could do now was to be so good that God wouldn't test me or, even better, wouldn't notice me. Feeling often scared that my trial would soon approach in the form of World War III, my parents divorcing, or somehow losing my intelligence (which I didn't believe was that abundant in the first place), I developed obsessive-compulsive behaviors. You could say that my OCD was a compensatory mechanism during a time when I felt utterly powerless and out of control.

My hope was that if I would keep all the carpets in the house nice and straight, and pray at least one hundred times per day, I could prevent any unforeseeable catastrophes. Somehow, I must have believed that God cared about interior design and really wanted to hear from me one hundred times per day. Since my parents collected carpets of all shapes and sizes, my new job to keep my family safe and God at bay kept me quite busy. If you've ever suffered from OCD, you know how consuming and exhausting this behavior can be. Granted, once you've completed an obsessive-compulsive loop, you enjoy a brief moment of relief and an illusion of control. Yet when it comes to gaining peace of mind and greater trust in life, these methods are about as effective as trying to heat your home in the dead of winter one matchstick at a time.

While my OCD was driven by the subconscious pattern to vigilantly control the divine forces to keep myself and my family safe, another pattern fueled my need to be the best in my class, under the assumption that only through success would I be worthy of love and approval. You could say that my invisibility pattern wasn't the most dominant force, because my protective strategies focused more on pleasing God and my folks than on being small and unnoticeable.

I took on the role of the "good kid" who didn't cause any trouble, exceeded expectations, and volunteered to be the peacemaker in the family (my name, Friedemann, which means "man of peace," apparently predisposed me to this job). Yet I carefully hid my anger and frustration with my father, and my desire to get more comfort, love, and reassurance from my overly busy and often stressed-out mom. Behind my charming personality of an overachiever, micro-manager, and nervous wreck, I also concealed many precious and delicate aspects of that little happy-go-lucky boy I once was.

When you're living in an invisibility pattern you don't consider that, as you wall your heart off to protect yourself from others, you also obstruct your access to some of your most unique, valuable, and powerful aspects. You don't realize that the more you're pointing your sensitive inner radar to the external world, the less you're in touch with yourself. And you don't understand that long-term, the pain of being in this survival pattern is far worse than the pain other people's judgment or rejection can inflict upon you. Being in chronic invisibility mode is painful because you're stuck like a chick in an egg, always scared that someone will break the shell, and too afraid to break it yourself. Never connecting to the truth that resides within you, never living up to your potential, never experiencing your empowered authenticity—this is why living in survival mode is so detrimental and why anxiety and depression are the epidemics of the twenty-first century.

Don't get me wrong, I am not judging or criticizing anyone who has been living in survival mode. I've been there for many years. I just want to remind you how vitally important it is to shift your awareness inward and get back in touch with the forgotten facets of your authentic self. Being either stubborn or slow on the uptake, or most likely both, it took me several decades to finally realize that no matter how successful I was and how well I was masking my more vulnerable aspects, I couldn't find lasting peace, worthiness, and security outside of myself. The only way to truly feel safe and comfortable was to come home to me. To get there, I needed to unearth the gifts and magic of my youth, such as trust, spontaneity, curiosity, and the unrestricted excitement for the wonders of life.

Finding and reclaiming the hidden gifts of your authentic self isn't as easy as opening a refrigerator and grabbing a sandwich and a cold one. But by choosing to embark on this journey, as you've done by reading this book, you've already proven to yourself that you have the awareness, courage, and strength this path of growth and self-empowerment requires.

The next step is to convince your subconscious protector that you're safer when you have access to your true potential, and that you'll enjoy each moment with greater wholeness, purpose, and unconditional appreciation for yourself and the life you're creating.

Are you ready?

6

SELF-COMPASSION

The Key to Owning Your Hidden Gifts

If you want to be at peace with yourself, have compassion with the part of you that is afraid to be seen and judged—and the part of you that is afraid of never being seen and valued.

Compassion is defined as the feeling that arises when we are confronted with another's suffering and feel motivated to relieve it. Compassion motivates us to go out of our way to offer physical, emotional, or spiritual support. According to the Dalai Lama, our collective survival hinges on how much love and compassion we can muster for each other, not on how much we can control or avoid each other. Yet your inner protector may vehemently contradict the Dalai Lama by viewing compassion not as a necessity, but as a luxury you can't afford, just like a pint of chocolate ice cream for the man with two heart attacks who still doesn't fit into his pants. This part of your subconscious may equate being compassionate with being unnecessarily mushy, and therefore, more susceptible to hurtful judgment and rejection.

The truth is, compassion is an instinct humans and animals share. A study with rats showed that when given a choice between saving a friend from drowning or savoring a delicious piece of chocolate, they chose to aid their fellow rodent. Interestingly, those rats who had previously suffered a traumatic experience with water were even more likely to rush to help a distressed pal.[1]

The human capacity to feel compassion instinctually is undoubtedly no less developed. Researchers at the Max Planck Institute in Germany found that even toddlers as young as eighteen months were eager to help adults by reaching for a marker they accidentally dropped, or opening a cabinet door when they saw that the grown-up's hands were full.[2]

Whenever a region of the world is hit by a tragic event, such as a devastating storm, wildfire, or earthquake, thousands of volunteers spontaneously answer the call to help their compatriots in need. I always admire the helpers that come out in droves with trucks, boats, or by foot—whether to set up shelters, search for neighbors in need, or donate clothes and food. They put their own safety at risk to rescue those who can't help themselves. Countless people around the world owe their lives to this form of extraordinary selfless compassion. Examples like this show that no matter with how much suspicion and cynicism we regard one another, at the core of us humans resides goodness, compassion, and love. So maybe the most powerful reason to step out of the invisibility pattern and dismantle the guards around our hearts is that it allows us to access our natural tendency to support each other. Considering the myriad of severe global challenges, there may have never been a more critical time in history for humanity to have each other's backs.

"Sounds all well and good," you may think, "if I could only access compassion to help myself. How do I access compassion if I am too scared to be seen, let alone vulnerable?" As you will find out in this chapter, compassion is not only the treasure in your heart but also the key that will help you unlock it. But first, as I mentioned, you need to convince your subconscious that it is safe to let go of the invisibility pattern.

A SAFE NEW WORLD

Don't ignore your inner child. It holds your deepest pains, fears, and insecurities, and it guards your dreams, gifts, and desires.

The loss of our innocence and the emergence of the invisibility pattern go hand in hand. As you already know, both usually occur during our childhood, when we have to deal with confusing and overwhelming situations, unexpected changes, painful judgment, or rejection.

Some common examples of how we may lose our innocence are:

- Being bullied by siblings or kids in school
- Being emotionally, physically, or sexually abused
- Witnessing parents fighting, an accident, a natural disaster, a shooting, or other traumatic events
- Experiencing the loss of a parent, another family member, a friend, or an animal through divorce, moving, or death
- Being betrayed by a close friend
- Feeling neglected, lost, or abandoned by parents, siblings, or friends
- Dealing with illness or an injury

The more hurt, threatened, and powerless we feel as we face such challenges, the more likely our subconscious mind will kick into self-protection mode. Since it appears that we're not safe or unconditionally loved and protected, the subconscious concludes that the only way to escape any further hostility is to conceal ourselves—until further notice. This is a difficult and desperate decision because it means that to stay safe and survive, we must suppress and deny ourselves the natural desire to express all of who we are.

After I shut down and locked away my carefree buoyancy at the tender age of eleven—because it seemed only to get me in trouble—I secretly looked forward to the day when I could be that light and joyful again. I told myself that I would be free to be myself as soon as I graduated from high school. My goal was to become an actor, as I couldn't imagine anything more exciting than immersing myself in the minds and hearts of different characters. Being sensitive and empathetic, I was sure I could be successful. But my parents, both physicians, had other plans for me. They insisted I first go to medical school to try following in their footsteps. They assured me, "If you still want to become an actor afterward, you can always pursue this career. Look at Marianne Koch (a German actress known for her roles in spaghetti western and adventure films); she was a doctor before she became an actress."

My parents figured that after six years of college and cramming an unfathomable amount of data into my brain, I would have laid my silly childhood dream to rest and most likely stick with medicine. And they were right—at least for a while. Yet when panic attacks tore me from sleep during my residency in cardiology, I began to wonder whether this was the life I wanted to live for the next twenty-five years. Something inside me was ready to bust out of the safe space I'd built from accomplishments and external validation. Although it didn't make logical sense—and would probably cause my parents headaches and stress ulcers—I instinctively knew that limiting my identity to a white coat and a stethoscope was no longer enough for me. This was when my quest to find more meaning and purpose in my life began. I didn't know then that what I was really looking for was my authentic self—and with that, the aspects of my truth I had been hiding from the world and myself since I was eleven years old.

You may wonder which part of me created the panic attacks during my residency. My achiever and my avoider were probably content with the status quo of playing it safe by hiding behind my accomplishments. So there must have been another aspect of my subconscious mind that was less concerned about my safety and more worried that I wasn't living in alignment with my truth. Remember, the subconscious has two primary intentions: to protect us and to make us happy. Since my life as a physician was more or less stable and secure, I believe the part of my subconscious whose job it is to ensure happiness and fulfillment triggered the red alert panic button. This goes to show that anxiety isn't always about avoiding external danger and the possibility of injury. Anxiety can also make us aware that we—and our lives—aren't on track to create as much happiness and contentment as we're capable of.

But back to the invisibility pattern. You could say that each chapter of this book provides you with the awareness and insights to rewrite your personal owner's manual for a more fulfilling and empowered way of engaging in and creating your life. A life that reflects your true potential and not the muted version of yourself that has been run by survival patterns. It's worth noting that, in some ways, the invisibility pattern is more challenging to overcome than other survival patterns because its "duck and cover" approach makes any form of change or personal growth a scary and almost inconceivable proposition.

You may have heard of Hiroo Onoda, the lone Japanese soldier who kept fighting World War II on a Philippine island twenty-nine years after the Japanese surrendered because he didn't believe the war was over. Your inner protector probably has a similar conviction and dedication as this loyal soldier. And just like Hiroo Onoda, this part of your subconscious may assume that the threats and dangers of your childhood are still real and imminent.

Since the invisibility pattern and its innate avoidance of change can be the biggest roadblock on your journey to self-empowerment, it's crucial to spend some time convincing your subconscious that it is safe to be seen. But how can you inform and persuade your subconscious that you've changed and evolved since childhood, that you've grown into the adult who can handle life—and that the battle is over?

FIVE PRINCIPLES TO ENJOYING LIFE IN THE OPEN

Let's ease the fears and anxieties of your subconscious by explaining to this inner protector that holding on to the invisibility pattern is no longer necessary, and in fact, at this stage of your life, is more harmful than helpful.

1. Safety through Invisibility Is an Illusion

William, a client of mine, told me in our first meeting how he never felt that he fit in or belonged as a child. Growing up with cold and emotionless parents, Will always dreamed of being a part of a group of friends who cared about him. Yet being shy and awkward, his attempts to bond with others usually failed. "No matter where I was, at home or school, I always felt like the one looking from the outside in," he sighed. "But then one day, I turned it around," he told me proudly. "I created a wall around me that forced everyone to stay on the outside. This made such a difference to me. Finally, I felt safe and in control."

I don't like to burst bubbles, but when we talked more about how his life had evolved since this decision, Will realized he'd completely isolated and disconnected himself from the world around him. Not even his wife really knew who he was. Eventually Will admitted, "I guess I felt safe behind my walls but didn't recognize I'd condemned myself to a self-created imprisonment." The imaginary protective barrier that he'd built to stay unnoticed and to keep others at arm's length may have prevented him from getting disappointed, but it also prevented him from making his childhood dream of belonging somewhere come true.

"Security is mostly a superstition. It does not exist in nature, nor do the children of men as a whole experience it. . . . Avoiding danger is no safer in the long run than outright exposure. . . . Life is either a daring adventure or nothing."[3] These powerful words don't stem from a battle-proven warrior or a daring adventurer. These words from the 1940 book *Let Us Have Faith* were written by a person who, considering her challenges, would have had every reason to hide out. But Helen Keller—who, due to her deafness and blindness, was in many ways utterly defenseless—wasn't afraid of being heard and seen. She refused to identify herself with her disabilities or with the degrading mixture of pity and bewilderment with which most people treated her. Instead, she held onto the belief that her life mattered and that she was gifted with the strength, courage, and wisdom to make significant contributions to the world. Against all odds, she became a world-famous author and speaker, advocating passionately for women's and workers' rights. Helen Keller's story inspires and encourages all of us to avoid getting stuck in our perceived limitations, to make every day count, and to live with optimism and confidence. Or as she's reputed to have said, "Your success and happiness lies in you. Resolve to keep happy, and your joy and you shall form an invincible host against difficulties."

"Happiness, schmappiness—whatever." You can imagine your inner protector rolling its eyes, defiantly insisting that the avoidance of hurt and rejection is far more important than airy-fairy joy and happiness. At first glance, this dismissal may appear just and reasonable to you. However, the longer you stay in the invisibility pattern the greater the risk of getting hurt. Why? From this chapter, you already know that as you wall off your heart toward others, you also block your access to all the gifts and powers that reside within. By doing so, you don't only become invisible to others, you also become invisible to yourself. Not accessing your inner resources makes you react defensively to others and most of life's everyday challenges, rather than approaching them from a place of calm and centered competency. As you continue to feel small and powerless, like a child trying to survive in a harsh, unpredictable world, the likelihood of feeling threatened, hurt, and victimized again increases. So it begs the question, are you better off when your sense of safety depends on avoiding others, or on trusting in your gifts and strengths?

2. Whose Life Is It Anyway?

Okay, this may sound more like a rhetorical question than a life principle. "Of course, it's my life," you're probably thinking. Yet whenever your invisibility pattern is triggered and takes control, do you truly feel in charge of your life? Are you consciously choosing how you think, feel, and act in response to these triggers? Or do worry, anxiety, and insecurity make you automatically react in self-defense to the external threats your subconscious detects, expects, and most often probably just imagines? In these moments, is your life in your hands, or do the situations or people you feel the urge to hide from seem to have all the power? Going through life assuming you need to be invisible to survive is like going on vacation and trying to have as little fun as possible, so that it won't hurt so much when the vacation ends. While you gain a sense of control and security, you lose any chance for joy, meaning, and fulfillment.

In a study conducted by Karl Pillemer, professor of human development at Cornell University, 1,200 older Americans aged 70 to 100 plus were asked about their advice to the younger generations on how to lead happier and better lives.[4] One of the questions he asked was, "What do you regret when you look back at your life?" To his surprise, the most common answer wasn't about loss, failure, or hurt. Professor Pillemer most frequently heard from the elders about their regret at having spent too much time worrying. The overwhelming consensus was that reducing or eliminating worry altogether could have been the most powerful step toward greater happiness and contentment. One participant, eighty-seven-year-old James Huang, suggested: "Turn yourself from frittering away the day worrying about what comes next and let everything else that you love and enjoy move in. When I realized that my worries made no difference at all, I experienced a freedom that is hard to describe."

Life is an organic and ever-changing energy current of countless twists and turns, highs and lows, expansions and contractions. Just as it isn't compatible with life to stay forever in the mother's womb, or linger in the safety of a cocoon, resisting life's natural flow by avoiding the changes and risks that come with pursuing our dreams will inevitably lead to the painful regret that we've wasted precious and irredeemable time. And according to the older generation's wisdom, the pain of denying ourselves to lead an authentic life, rich in experiences, learning, and growth, is more severe than the pain that judgment, disappointment, or rejection could inflict on us.

3. The Meaning of Life Is Bigger than Just Making It to the End

It's been said that "The two most important days in your life are the day you are born and the day you find out why." Yet no matter which of your protective patterns is running the show, when you're in survival mode, the meaning of life tilts heavily toward just getting through. But is that really all there is to life—survival? Whether we're at school, work, or the gym, whether we cook at home or meet friends in a restaurant, whether we watch TV or shop in the mall, most of our daily activities have some intrinsic purpose. But when it comes to pondering the bigger question about the meaning of why we're here, most of us are either dumbfounded or too busy to contemplate this topic at all.

Throughout the history of humankind, great thinkers, philosophers, theologians, metaphysicians, and scientists have attempted to find the ultimate answer to why we're here. The answers they are coming up with are "doing good, being of service, pursuing happiness, leaving a legacy, living life to the fullest." These ideas are valid and make sense. However, since we are, at least biologically, creations of Mother Nature and not just inventions of our own minds, I'd like to turn to nature to address this question. Of course, survival is a major driving force in the wild. But beyond that basic objective, all animals and plants have the innate desire and instinctual determination to unfold and express their true potential.

Unlike humans, a tree doesn't wonder how high it may be allowed to grow, a tulip doesn't envy a rose, and a lion doesn't feel ashamed of its roar. Although being of service, finding happiness, and leaving a mark in the world are all worthy life purposes, they become hollow pursuits if we're carrying them out while being strangers to ourselves. How can we serve others when we don't know who we are and what we have to offer? And how can we find happiness and fulfillment when our hearts are blocked off to others and ourselves?

If we want to find the meaning of our lives, we need to move beyond survival consciousness and let go of the notion that life is a battle, a competition, or a series of benchmarks that must be achieved. Instead, we need to embrace that each of us is on a journey that starts at birth and ends at our expiration date. The purpose of this journey isn't to reach any external destination. It's a pilgrimage within, which, when we stay open and curious, leads us step-by-step closer to the vast and magnificent truth that resides in all of us.

I can imagine your inner protector is in dry heaves as you're contemplating abandoning your survival mode to discover your truth and potential. The notion of growing into your authentic self as the meaning of life is the complete opposite of the invisibility pattern's major objective, which is to make you contract to the size of a sand pebble so that nobody can know who you truly are. But before your inner protector makes you shove this book into the shredder, take a moment to consider the following principle and reason why it's safe and desirable to switch out of the invisibility pattern.

4. Reality Is Relative

This principle could have been called "perception is projection" or "don't take anything personally, because it isn't personal." As I already alluded to in the Self-Responsibility chapter, the fact is, there's probably nothing more distorted in the world than our perception of other people and ourselves. Here's an example. For more than twenty years, yoga has been a wonderful practice to regenerate my energy and balance my mind, body, and spirit. For a while I was into Bikram, or Hot Yoga, which is practiced in a room heated to 95–108 °F (35–42 °C). I have to admit, before each class I wrestled with a little inner voice that pointed out the insanity of bending myself into a pretzel in a Death Valley–like environment. But as soon as I remembered a friend's advice to focus on how accomplished I'd feel once the class was over, I found the motivation to pack my mat and towel and head to the Sweat Box (a fitting name for this kind of yoga studio).

One day, during a particularly challenging class, my quest for inner strength, peace, and harmony was significantly disturbed by an incredibly annoying fellow student I hadn't seen before. For starters, the woman, who was probably in her mid-thirties, chose to sit perpendicular to the teacher instead of facing her as the rest of the class did. On top of that, each time the instructor explained a posture, the Yogini asked for more clarifications, which she then promptly ignored as she moved into her own version of the pose. With angel-like patience, the teacher often repeated her explanations of the proper body position, but the student didn't even look at her.

I guess that the heat, dehydration, and refusal of my body to twist as far as everyone else's had already stretched my nervous system to the max. Yet rather than getting annoyed with myself that I couldn't relax, my mind chose to blame this *obnoxious* woman and her audacity for holding the entire class hostage with her questions and unwillingness to follow instructions. Who did she think she was? And why didn't the teacher tell her to shut her pie hole? You can tell that I really needed that yoga class, because obviously my attitude was anything but Zen.

I'm pretty sure I wasn't the only one who was relieved when the ninety-minute session was over. However, the real lesson for all of us who had projected our frustrations and negativity on this woman came as we were about to leave the room. It was when another student gently took the woman's arm, carefully helped her to stand up, and slowly walked her out of the studio that I finally understood. She was blind. It felt like an entire humble pie was smashed in my face. How could I not have realized what was going on with her? As a physician, should I not have figured that out? How could I have been so uncompassionate and judgmental just because I felt a bit uncomfortable?

It was a sobering experience to realize that I had just mentally chastised a person who had the admirable courage and strength to keep up with a rather demanding yoga practice despite her challenges. And it was a good reminder that what we perceive as reality is usually just our interpretation based on how we feel, think, and believe at any given moment.

Our thoughts, emotions, and beliefs serve as subconscious filters that delete, distort, and generalize the endless amount of information surrounding us. The purpose of these filters is to prevent our mind from suffering data-overload, which would make it impossible for us to function in the world. The downside of these filters is that, for example on a bad hair day, they make us ignore anything positive and uplifting, and instead just highlight the people and events that confirm the certitude that this will be one of those days we can't get through fast enough.

Now, the good news is that once we accept that our mind is full of funny mirrors that disfigure the facts and misinterpret reality, we can come to the liberating conclusion that everybody lives in their version of reality. Thus, nobody needs to take anyone's judgment personally. Or, as one of my teachers was fond of saying, "What other people think of you is none of your business."

5. *The Best Protection Is Compassion*

I just talked about how we all create our personal rendition of reality. Therefore, how others perceive us says more about them than about us. This realization may not yet fully convince your subconscious to drop the invisibility pattern and be ready to show up in the world. Especially if you've difficulties trusting others because you've been hurt and disappointed in the past, your inner protector may have operated by the creed to "be unnoticeable and notice everything." As I've already discussed, your invisibility pattern consists of two elements, hiding and scanning. To keep you safe, your subconscious uses your sensitivity as a fine-tuned radar system to diligently screen other people's behavior, emotions, and energies for any potential threat.

Yet the catch twenty-two with this form of amped-up sensitivity is that as you pick up emotions and energies from everyone around you, you also absorb and internalize them. As your protective sensitivity increasingly floods you with external information, it can become difficult for you to discern between your own feelings and those you have sponged up from others. Consequently, you don't feel safer but instead become more nervous, stressed, and overwhelmed.

You may have had an experience similar to this one: You walk into a meeting at work and immediately feel uneasy and tense. Although you're tempted to turn on your heels and leave, you force yourself to stay, but not without scolding yourself for once again feeling anxious and insecure among your peers. But what if your uneasiness wasn't your own, at least not entirely? What if it stemmed from some of your colleagues? If you knew you'd just tuned in to the tension in the room that existed before you came in, you'd be able to say to yourself, "Whatever I'm feeling has nothing to do with me. I'm wondering who's stressed out here?"

Science confirms this concept of subconsciously sensing other people's fears. Several studies have shown that the smell of people's fear can subconsciously trigger fear in others.[5] Let me give you another example of how protective sensitivity can backfire. You meet a friend for coffee. Being keenly aware, you quickly detect that he's miffed and stressed. You rationally know his negativity has nothing to do with you, because he goes on and on about his troubles at work. But still, your protective sensitivity interprets his emotions as a threat, which then causes your subconscious to quickly turn on its flight or freeze response. As you're feeling more anxious and tense, chances are that in return, your friend's subconscious inner protector senses the shift of your emotions as alarming. He may feel misunderstood, judged, or uncared for, making him switch into flight, fight, or freeze mode. As he becomes more defensive and changes his tone of voice, facial expression, or body language, your inner protector's urge to protect you doubles. Round and round this feedback loop goes. Eventually, both of your defense mechanisms can turn a relatively harmless conversation among friends into a stressful conflict.

You can see that using your self-protective radar system to sense, take on, and react to other people's emotions doesn't necessarily increase your safety. Instead, it may jeopardize it, like trying to avoid drowning by gulping down the water rather than calmly swimming to the shore. Yet because your sensitivity can make things worse, it doesn't mean that sensitivity is a useless flaw or weakness. On the contrary. Sensitivity is a gift and an incredible power. It just comes with the obligation to harness this ability and use it wisely. If you had Hulk-like physical strength, you would need to learn not to take other people's anger personally, because your defensive reaction could quickly annihilate them. Uncontrolled sensitivity can also cause a lot of harm—it's just you who suffers. Yet, in contrast to Hulk's muscle power, which creates a sense of safety through a wall of intimidation, sensitivity can help you pierce through others' protective walls of anger, judgment, and negativity and understand better what they feel underneath. The key to turning sensitivity into this extraordinary power is compassion. But how can this form of compassionate sensitivity protect you from the hurtful anger and judgment of your fellow human beings?

Most of us have been frightened of the dark at some point, especially when we were little. A coat hanging from its rack in the corner becomes a ghost staring menacingly at us. The settling floorboards signal that someone is creeping through the house. And the cat scratching at our door pushes us into a panic because we're convinced an unwanted visitor is about to snatch us. We get up, turn on the light, and "eureka!" there was nothing to be afraid of. Blending your sensitivity with compassion is like turning on the light in your mind. With compassionate sensitivity, you can pierce through people's often terrifying defense layers and recognize that behind linger fear, insecurity, vulnerability, and pain.

Knowing that those who scared or overwhelmed you are just trapped in their own suffering makes it easier to accept that their survival responses aren't a reflection on you or a sign of danger. Compassionate sensitivity is like a force field that keeps other people's energies on the outside. While your sensitivity provides you with the awareness and understanding of their emotions, you no longer feel overwhelmed or responsible for what they're going through. Such a force field doesn't make you a callous and self-centered person. You appreciate that we're all in the same boat and on the same journey. That we all, from the first to our last breath, try to shake off the baggage of the past, overcome the worries about the future, and resolve the questions about who we are and where we go from here. We all just want a little bit of peace, love, and happiness. The difference is that with the power of compassionate awareness, you'll navigate through this journey with much greater calmness and ease.

......

These five principles may still not have fully convinced your inner protector to let go of its invisibility pattern, and that's ok. Right now it is more important that you, the conscious adult, accept that you have more to gain by growing into Empowered Authenticity than staying in hiding. Your subconscious needs your conscious conviction and guidance to even consider changing course and taking on new perspectives and patterns.

As you may remember from before, turning off the invisibility pattern isn't enough. To grow beyond it, you also want to retrieve those precious aspects of yourself that this pattern tried so hard to hide from others—until they became forgotten and invisible even to yourself. This is where we will need to go a little bit deeper and once again work consciously with your subconscious mind. Are you up for that?

THE MISSING LINK

No matter the circumstances we grew up in, or how we were raised, most of us will spend a good deal of our adult lives trying to peel away and erase the early imprints, beliefs, and expectations that covered up large parts of who we truly are. Like Michelangelo, who created his masterpiece *David* slowly and meticulously, chiseling away the layers of marble that were not part of the statue he saw within the block of marble. Yet there's another, more straightforward option. We connect directly to the source of all the delicate and precious aspects of our truth—the innocent little self.

Let's assume that the innocent self is you before you switched on the invisibility pattern. Then certain events or relationships shook you up, making you wonder whether it is all right for you to freely express and explore your authentic self. To make sense of these unsettling developments and determine how to stay unharmed, your subconscious established a set of beliefs, such as "The world is a hostile place," "People can't be trusted," "I don't belong here," or "I'm not good enough." Sure, these beliefs weren't especially reassuring, and even added fuel to the flames of worry and insecurity, but given that your abilities to fend for yourself were minimal at that age, your subconscious installed these guidelines to keep you on guard.

As I mentioned earlier, beliefs are strong filters of the subconscious that can enhance whatever external information supports them and delete anything that doesn't fit their notion of yourself and the world. In other words, whatever you believe, you perceive. For example, based on the limiting beliefs that fuel your invisibility pattern, you may be keenly aware of how negative and judgmental people are, how risky it is to speak your mind or show vulnerability, or how nobody seems to care. These observations confirm the general idea that you need to hole up to protect yourself. With this "interpretation" of reality, it becomes almost impossible for you to notice and appreciate anything or anyone who may have helped you to feel safe, seen, and cared for.

One of the most challenging aspects of self-protective beliefs from your early years is that they don't come with an expiration date. So even though you've grown up and are no longer tiny and helpless, your subconscious is still operating under the same playbook it established decades ago. It's stuck in the past, which explains why as soon as the invisibility pattern kicks in and takes over, you turn into a scared child—incapable of dealing with whatever people or situations you're confronted with. I know I repeat myself, yet to heal and outgrow the invisibility pattern, you need to embark on a *search and rescue mission* to retrieve the part of you it tried to protect in the first place—the innocent self.

But how do you locate a part of your subconscious that has been kept invisible for so long? The best way to start this mission is to go back to before you switched into survival mode, when you still felt safe, loved, and accepted. Maybe you were very imaginative and built worlds of dragons, knights, and wizards right in your backyard. Or perhaps you were utterly fearless, full of energy and curiosity, always scaling the highest trees or jumping with delight from the five-meter diving board into the deep end of the pool. Perhaps you felt deeply connected to nature and could get lost in awe and wonderment as you spent hours watching a butterfly emerging from its cocoon, or an army of ants boldly carrying breadcrumbs ten times their size. Or you loved to put on little skits and performances to make people laugh and clap. Maybe you were a toddler who was just open and friendly to everyone, trusting in people's innate goodness. And with your sensitive nature, you always recognized when others were struggling and wanted to help them feel better. Enjoy contemplating those early years and remember the innocent child you used to be.

The following questions will help you to jog your memory:

- What is your earliest happy memory?
- What was the name of your favorite stuffed animal?
- Which room in the house you grew up in did you like the most—and why?
- Who were your best friends and what games did you play with them?
- What role did you like to play when you created imaginary worlds (e.g., the princess, the knight, the magician, the hero)?
- How did you relate to animals and nature?
- What was your favorite movie or book when you were very little?
- What are your best memories of holidays or family gatherings as a child?
- What were your beliefs about the world, life, and God?
- Did you believe in Santa Claus, the Easter Bunny, or other magical beings?
- Did you speak to an invisible friend? If so, what did you talk about?
- With which five attributes would you describe your little innocent self?

If you have trouble remembering who you were before your invisibility pattern kicked in, you may want to ask your parents, siblings, or childhood friends how they remember you as a child. You could also pull out the old photo albums or family vacation movies, or go to the attic and search for the earliest artwork you gave your parents for their birthdays. Finding evidence of who you were and how you engaged with the world at that age can remind you of who you are at your pure and innocent core, even though these characteristics may be quite different from the adult personality you and those around you have become accustomed to.

My wife, Danielle, used to break out laughing when I told her at the beginning of our relationship that the core of who I am is carefree and easy-going. She saw me more as a strong-willed achiever—charming and kind-hearted—but certainly a man with a plan and not some happy-go-lucky, laid-back dude. Yet eventually, as I got more in touch with the hidden aspects of myself, she learned to love and appreciate the spontaneity, curiosity, and playfulness of little *Pinepan* (which is what I called myself as a child because, due to a slight speech impediment, I wasn't able to pronounce my name properly).

The precious aspects of the innocent child are neither outdated nor irrelevant to your current life. You may have known for many years that something inside you is missing, because you don't feel quite as alive or connected to yourself as you would like. You may have always sensed that under your cover of aloofness and unapproachability lingers the yearning for closer and more intimate relationships. That even though you don't show or talk about your emotions, you're highly sensitive and vulnerable. Or that somewhere deep inside abides a source of artistry that longs to be revealed and expressed. Unearthing the gifts of your innocence and bringing them to the light of your current life will make you feel more complete, and it will also demonstrate to your inner protector that there's no longer any need to disguise who you truly are.

But what are you supposed to do if you can't recall a time when you could just be your innocent and pure little self, because the circumstances you were born into were so difficult and dysfunctional that you were forced to live in survival mode for as long as you can remember? Rest assured, there's an innocent child inside you that your invisibility pattern tried to conceal and protect from the world. It's there. The true nature you were born with. And the following process will help you to reconnect to this part of you.

● ● ● ● ● ●

DEEP EXERCISE

UNCOVER THE HIDDEN GIFTS OF YOUR INNOCENCE

Every child is an artist. The problem is how to remain an artist after he grows up.

—PABLO PICASSO

The following process will help you resolve and override the invisibility pattern and its need to protect you. With the help of your subconscious, you'll go back in time to meet the younger self that decided hiding out was the only way to stay safe. As the safe and compassionate grown-up, you can resolve the inner child's confusion and fears that activated the invisibility pattern in the first place and thus help this mini-you gently release its grip on the invisibility pattern and instead hold on to you.

Here is a summary of the following five steps:

Step 1: Embodying the Kind and Compassionate Adult.
Here, you get ready to show up for the innocent self as the calm and compassionate adult it can trust and feel safe with.

Step 2: Back from the Future. In this step, you meet your younger self, right after a scary or confusing event occurred that caused you to want to shrink, hide out, and become invisible.

Step 3: Let's Talk. Sitting next to the inner child, you listen to its fears, insecurities, and confusions, and then compassionately answer any questions it may have. You reassure this part of you, with patience and kindness, that it no longer has to hide out because you, the adult, will keep it safe.

Step 4: Show Me the Truth. As the little self takes you further into the past to a time before it lost its innocence, you get back in touch with the gifts and treasures the invisibility pattern has been protecting until now.

Step 5: Coming Home. In this final step, you bring the innocent self back into your heart, where it can safely explore, express, and share its untapped gifts and potential with you.

This healing process can also help you connect with and address the root cause of any other survival patterns. You just need to meet your younger self somewhere around the time when the particular pattern started.

For most of this journey, you will have your eyes closed. So you want to read through these instructions first and maybe take some notes. Then go through this process either in one sitting, or step by step, taking some breaks in between. Ultimately, there is nothing you can do wrong. Just being open and curious about finding your hidden gifts is enough for your subconscious to gradually reveal them.

Step 1: Embodying the Kind and Compassionate Adult

You've probably experienced this time-warp phenomenon. No matter how old, mature, and accomplished you are, no matter how many years ago you left home to build your own life, whenever you visit your folks, after only forty-eight hours, you revert to feeling and acting like a child or teenager. You may have the strongest intentions not to let your mom take care of you as if you were ten years old, not to allow your dad to make you feel inadequate when he questions your choices, and not to enter the who's-done-better contest with your siblings. But somehow, with expert precision, your family can still locate and push the buttons they installed in you many years ago.

As annoying as this form of regression may feel, it also makes a strong case for the existence of the inner child. Whenever your invisibility pattern is triggered, why do you feel precisely as you did when you were bullied in the schoolyard, made fun of by your siblings, or scolded by your parents? Because in those moments, a little scared self wants you to shrink back into hiding. After nearly twenty years of experience working with people who've been struggling with fear and anxiety, I've found that the pace and depth of a client's healing are directly correlated to how much time they spend fostering a compassionate and supportive relationship with their inner child.

In a moment, you'll meet the inner child that lost its innocence and went into hiding. You could say that this child is also the part of you that kept your invisibility pattern running. As you go back in time to where this pattern started, try to stay calm and compassionate no matter what memory emerges. Being angry and frustrated at the injustice you may have been subjected to can be as unhelpful to the inner child as getting entangled in their pain and anxiety. Instead, you want to show up for this part of your subconscious as the solid, caring adult it can trust and feel safe with.

To get started, find a quiet place to sit and take a few moments to tap into your inner source of love, kindness, and compassion. Think about someone you adore and care for. Remember how it feels when you're comforting a scared or sad child, holding a loved one in need of a hug, or giving a friend who feels lost and confused some heartfelt advice. You can also think about your favorite pet: maybe the dog that taught you about unconditional love, the cat that relished lying in your lap, or the horse that came running across the pasture when it saw you. Imagine also how the people or animals you love and care for may feel about you. How they are grateful for your support and feel at ease in your presence, trusting in your heartfelt support. As you contemplate these precious moments, notice how your mind becomes more calm and clear and your heart increasingly open and light. Now you're ready to meet your inner child.

Step 2: Back from the Future

Close your eyes, take a deep breath in, hold it for five seconds, and then gently exhale through your mouth. Inhale, hold, and exhale this way three more times. Then think about a time early in your life when you felt anxious, insecure, disappointed, or betrayed. Pick an event during which it felt as though you may have lost part of your innocence. It doesn't have to be the most difficult or traumatic memory of your childhood, but a situation that made you, maybe for the first time, want to shrink, hide out, and become invisible. You don't have to spend much time thinking about the details of this story, just enough to know where you can find your little self.

Then imagine you're in the house you grew up in, standing in front of your bedroom. Notice how everything looks, smells, and feels so familiar it's as if you'd never left. It's nighttime, and the difficult memory you recalled has just happened during that day. As you enter the room, you find your younger self sitting in bed, wide awake. What do you read in their facial expression and body posture? What do you believe they feel? And what do you feel as you watch this child? Are you touched by their struggles and eager to comfort and help this part of you? Or do you feel detached, neutral, or even judgmental and appalled by its vulnerability? If you sense the latter, go back to step one and reconnect to your source of kindness and compassion. You don't want to approach this sensitive aspect of your subconscious with anything but an open heart and mind. Otherwise, the inner protector may feel the need to protect itself even from you.

Step 3: Let's Talk

When you're ready to be the caring grown-up this part needs, gently approach the child and let it know that you've come from the far future to meet them. Pull a chair next to the bed, sit down, and look at your younger self with a friendly smile. Ask what happened that day and what events or people may have frightened or hurt them. Find out what emotions the child still holds on to. Is it anger at somebody's wrongdoing or frustration with themself? Does this part of you feel pain, sadness, disappointment, or fear that the world isn't safe? Or is there any guilt, shame, or a belief of not being good enough or not belonging anywhere? Give this child a voice and let it explain why it chose to hide out and become invisible as the only way to survive.

Then ask the child if there are any questions or areas of confusion that have made it difficult to find peace and resolution with what occurred. This part of you may ask, "Why me?" "Was it my fault?" "What have I done wrong?" or "What's wrong with me?" Or there may be confusion surrounding the people who hurt or scared your younger self. It might want to know their reasons for being so cruel, judgmental, or neglectful. Listen patiently and attentively to gain a deeper understanding of what this subconscious part is feeling—and thus what you've felt when you were in their shoes. Keep in mind your job is not to associate yourself with the child's hurt and fear, but to remain steady in your role as a source of love and compassion.

Next, answer the questions and resolve your younger self's bewilderment in the way you wish someone would have talked to you during that time. Provide this part of you with a different and more empowering perspective of the challenging incident it told you about. For example, you could say that whatever people did to them wasn't their fault or a reflection of their truth. The most common reason people cause others pain is because they don't know how to deal with their own wounds and fears. Those who may have appeared the most frightening and powerful are often, in reality, the most frightened and powerless. Tell the child that you're sorry that they felt so anxious, sad, and alone that hiding out seemed like the only option to stay unharmed. However, the past isn't the blueprint for the future, but more a library to learn from and grow. And although you sincerely appreciate how tenacious and committed this part of you has been in their protective efforts, the adult you will take over now, as you're more experienced and better equipped to ensure your safety.

Chances are the kid, your inner protector, doesn't yet buy that (a) you're genuinely the more capable guardian, and (b) you can be trusted. So you may want to share with the younger self the Five Principles to Enjoying Life in the Open:

Safety through invisibility is an illusion. Hiding the gifts and strengths of your authentic self only increases the likelihood of getting hurt, and prevents you from creating a purposeful and fulfilling life.

Whose life is it anyway? There's nothing worse at life's end than the regret of having relinquished your dreams and desires to accommodate the anxiety-driven need to be safe.

The meaning of life is more than just making it to the end. The purpose of life is to discover and share the vast and magnificent truth of who you are. Staying in invisibility mode is the surest way to miss out on fulfilling this purpose.

Reality is relative. Whatever we call reality is a subjective interpretation of the subconscious mind, and, therefore, entirely different for each person. This is why other people's judgment is more a reflection on them than you, and why what you think of yourself should matter more than the opinions of others.

The best protection is compassion. Since you no longer have to take anything personally, you can begin to change course. Instead of not wanting to be seen, you can see, sense, and understand with compassion that most people live behind a protective wall. With compassionate sensitivity, you can feel peaceful and secure while being more understanding of those who may have appeared threatening in the past.

It goes without saying that the more you believe in these five principles, the more convincing you'll appear to your younger self.

However, rather than expecting the child to fly into your arms with tears of relief and happiness running down its cheeks, you may have to visit them several times before they start to have faith in you and your message. But rest assured that at some point, whether during your first visit or after several conversations, you'll notice how this child feels increasingly comfortable and at ease with you, the adult. At that point, you can imagine holding their hands or giving them a big hug, reassuring them that you'll love, protect, and guide them from now on. Tell this part of you that they are no longer alone and always have a safe, warm, and welcoming home in your heart, where they can relax and be themselves.

Yet, for your inner protector to be willing to retire the invisibility pattern, you need to provide it with a new job description that isn't focused on being safe but on creating more joy and fulfillment in your life.

Step 4: Show Me the Truth

"I know you're much more than what you've allowed yourself to be in this world. Can you show me who you were when you still felt safe just to be your true self?" Ask your inner child something along these lines to help them remember their hidden qualities. Then let them lead you further back, to a time when you still had your innocence. This can be one of the memories you recalled while preparing for this journey, or you may find yourself in an event you hadn't thought about for a long time. What is your younger self doing in this situation? What do they think and feel about themself and the world they live in? What do they do when they act freely and without hesitancy or inhibition? Skip through several events and discover more of the unique traits of your personality your inner protector had been hiding. This may be from when you still knew how to have fun, be creative, and play with others with complete trust and openness. You may see yourself daydreaming, being completely engrossed in the magic of the now as you delight in an ice cream sundae, or feeling deeply connected to the forces of nature as you walk on a beach.

Go beyond just looking for specific gifts, such as friendliness, creativity, courage, and boundless optimism. As you observe the child playing, creating, and exploring, imagine you can peek into their heart and find at their core the light of their signature energy. While in the past your invisibility pattern has dimmed this beautiful and powerful light to avoid drawing unwanted attention, in the safety and delight of this moment, that light can shine brightly like an inner sun. Gaze into its glow and recognize the different elements of this signature energy. Do you detect sensitivity, kindness, and purity? Do you notice curiosity, openness, and joy? Or maybe you sense trust, courage, and love? Without overanalyzing, intuit what the true nature of your inner child is all about. Open your heart to embrace the indescribable innocence of who you were—and deep inside, still are.

Earlier I asked the question, how do you connect to your innocent self if you never had the chance to feel safe enough to explore who you are and do things you loved? What if your invisibility pattern had to protect you since your earliest childhood and there are no memories to remember your truth?

In this case, rewriting history with your subconscious mind becomes especially useful. Tell your younger self, "I know your childhood was difficult and that you didn't have the support and protection that would have allowed you to simply be yourself." Then ask, "If you would know that you're now safe and loved, what would you like to do?" You may have to wait for an answer and continue to gently encourage your inner child to start showing you its deepest unfulfilled desires. It's like giving them an empty canvas and a color palette. At first, they may be unsure about how to start, but once they realize there's no judgment or limitation to creative expression, they will show you their secret dreams.

Your younger self may build an imaginary world where everything is possible—flying, eating candy from trees, riding dinosaurs for fun. Or it may show you all the simple things it dreamed of having or being allowed to do if it had grown up in a kinder and more supportive environment. Going on sleepovers with friends, adopting a little puppy as a companion, camping in the mountains, performing funny skits to an applauding family. The possibilities are endless. Whether you're whisked away to an enchanted world or find yourself in a redesigned childhood, the unfulfilled wishes the child shares with you in the safety of your mind will reveal about the aspects of your innocence that have been kept invisible until now.

You may spend five minutes or an hour watching or playing with your younger self. As you gradually remember who you were or who you could have been before you lost your innocence, you're filling an internal void, one you may have always known existed but weren't sure what to do about. No accomplishment, relationship, or purchase could give you a sense of fulfillment because what you were missing couldn't be bought or gained from the outside. Reconnecting with your younger self—and the lost parts of your authentic self—could be likened to life-changing moments such as falling in love for the first time, holding your newborn child in your arms, moving into a new place that finally feels like home, or finding your passion. Until you had those experiences, you didn't know what you were missing, and you didn't know how much your heart and the love within it could grow and expand.

Don't worry if you don't feel any transformational expansions right away. It can take a little while before you're able to fully appreciate this younger self, and until this part of you that used to feel left to their own devices accepts you as someone safe and trustworthy. What will help is to give this part of you a new home.

Step 5: Coming Home

Imagine you're back in the bedroom where you initially met your little self. You probably look at this child now with a much greater appreciation and admiration than you did at the beginning of this journey. You may have an even stronger desire to take care of this vulnerable child. So gently look into their eyes and ask, "Do you now remember who you are? Do you know that the gifts you were hiding are precious and powerful? And do you realize that without you and your gifts, my life will never be as rich and fulfilling as it could be?"

Wait a few moments to let these questions sink in. Sometimes all you'll get from your younger self is a blank stare or an "I don't know." This is completely okay. It just means that this part of you still needs a bit more time and reassurance. It's more common though, that you'll get a "yes" or a small nod of your inner child's head as a sign that they agree with you.

Here comes the most important question for your younger self: "Would you like to come with me so I can take care of you and show you you're safe, wanted, and loved?" Again, patiently wait until this little you is ready to say "yes," then gently take them into your arms and float out of the past back above the present moment, into the warmth and comfort of your heart. There, together, you create a comfortable and cozy space as their new home. Softly reaffirm to the child: "You are safe now. You belong here. You no longer have to protect yourself—and you no longer have to be my protector."

From this moment, this inner child is in your care. I know being the loving guardian of your little self may sound like a daunting task considering your already overflowing plate. But don't worry, it doesn't need your attention 24/7. All it takes for this inner child to shift out of survival mode completely are two things: (1) guidance and reassurance from you when they're triggered and (2) a little time and space to gradually explore and share more of their true gifts and untapped potential with you.

......

WHAT DEFINES YOU?

"If you're not afraid of the voices inside you, you will not fear the critics outside you."

—Natalie Goldberg

Choosing authenticity over invisibility, freedom over safety, and purpose over comfort takes courage and the conviction that whoever you are and whatever you carry inside you matters to the world. Yet if you've been ridiculed and rejected like Lizzie Velasquez, a young woman from Texas, the option to hide out for the rest of your life may appear tempting. Unlike Lizzie however, you probably haven't been made fun of by millions of people.

Lizzie was born with a rare combination of genetic diseases: Marfan syndrome, which affects the connective tissue, and lipodystrophy, a disorder where the body is unable to produce fat, making it almost impossible for her to gain weight, no matter how much nutrition she puts into her body. At five feet two inches, the young woman weighs only sixty pounds. Lizzie, who is also blind in her right eye, has paper-thin skin that is easily injured and ages fast. Her childhood was marked by surgeries, diagnostic tests, and countless visits to hospitals and doctors. But Lizzie calls herself lucky because she grew up with a loving family who treated her just like her healthy siblings.

Until she started kindergarten, her family's love and support had felt completely normal to the point she couldn't see that she looked different from other kids. Her parents had always told her, "You're beautiful, smart, and can accomplish everything. There's nothing wrong with you. You're just a little bit smaller than the other kids." However, when Lizzie started school, she noticed how other kids pointed or pulled away from her, apparently scared of her appearance. Little Lizzie's sense of self got shattered, as she couldn't understand why her schoolmates treated her so badly when she hadn't done anything to them.

It wasn't until she entered high school that Lizzie started to regain her confidence. She decided to be brave and join activities, make friends, and learn to be more outgoing. Even though the first steps were scary, Lizzie knew her efforts would pay off. She joined the school newspaper, became a photographer for the yearbook, and even tried out for cheerleading. Finally, she felt that she could be herself around her peers.

Then, when she was seventeen, she made a devastating discovery. Putting off her homework, Lizzie innocently searched for something entertaining to watch on YouTube. When she came across a video called *The Ugliest Woman in the World,* she clicked the link without much thought. To her horror, she realized that someone had posted pictures of her on the web. The video already had more than four million views. Many people had posted hateful comments, calling her a monster, somebody who should have been aborted or should commit suicide, and worse. Feverishly, Lizzie scrolled through the comments, hoping to find one person who'd stood up for her. But nobody had the courage or decency to say, "Leave the kid alone. You don't know what she's going through."

You can imagine Lizzie's utter devastation. For days she shut herself off from the world, crying her eyes out, telling herself her life was over. But then, from somewhere deep inside, a realization bubbled up in her that changed everything.

In her TEDx talk, Lizzie asks the audience, "How do you define yourself?" She describes how she used to define herself by her appearance. She hated her tiny legs and arms and found her thin face disgusting. Every night she prayed that somehow the syndrome would disappear, or she could find a way to scrub it off. The day she stumbled across the YouTube video, all the self-rejection for looking so different from everybody else became unbearable. But after several days of despair and self-pity, something clicked inside. Lizzie realized her life was in her hands, and she could choose to make her life a good experience or a bad one. She could decide to let the people who called her a monster define who she is, or choose to be grateful for what she has and let those traits define her. In her talk, Lizzie describes how she no longer dwelled on the hateful YouTube comments but instead used the negative remarks as a ladder to reach her goals.

In the years since she discovered the atrocious video, she graduated from college and published three self-help books: *Be Beautiful, Be*

You; Choosing Happiness; and *Dare to Be Kind.* Lizzie also starred in a documentary film about her life and her own original series called *Unzipped.* Her uplifting YouTube videos have received more than fifty-four million views. Lizzie has become an inspiration for so many people who also believed they weren't worthy and acceptable enough to be seen by the world. In an interview, Lizzie shared that she wished she knew who posted *The Ugliest Woman in the World* so she could send flowers and a thank you card, because that video changed her life for the better.

Lizzie's story is a powerful example of how we can erase the harshest criticism and rejection once we choose to love and appreciate ourselves. But it also raises the question, how did Lizzie find the strength and courage to accept and believe in herself? She often credits her unbreakable spirit and optimism to her parents, who always loved and supported her unconditionally. Her parents' staunch belief that their daughter had no reason to hide or feel less than anybody else enabled her inner protector to accept her choice to become the best and most noticeable version of herself.

But what if you never heard such supportive and unconditionally loving messages from your mom and dad? What if they were too busy to realize you would have needed more encouragement? Or what if they were struggling with their own survival patterns, unable to find peace and acceptance for themselves? Where can your subconscious protector borrow faith and confidence to come out of hiding permanently—and become fully empowered?

FROM HIDING TO SHINING

In every real man a child is hidden that wants to play.
—FRIEDRICH NIETZSCHE

Let's recap for a moment. By now, you've discovered that the invisibility pattern protected the younger part of you who, at some point, lost trust in it being safe to be yourself. Since the world no longer appeared warm and welcoming, your subconscious decided to preserve some of the most precious and vulnerable aspects of your truth by hiding them, hoping that one day they could be brought back to light. However, since the invisibility pattern continued to run unchallenged for many years, you eventually lost sight of the hidden gifts your subconscious tried to protect. Being invisible was no longer just a necessity; it became a part of your identity.

When you journeyed into the past as the compassionate and caring adult, you helped your younger self address the trauma that started the invisibility pattern in the first place and reminded them of the hidden gifts and qualities that make them—and you—unique. Once you guided your inner child to their new home, your loving and caring heart, you released them from their exhausting mission to protect you through contraction and concealment. Now you've regained access to the aspects of your personality that had been kept in lockdown for many years.

Sounds marvelous, right? Well, the skeptic in you may have joined the party by now, wondering if it's really possible to erase a survival pattern that has served you for decades, and then on top of it, harness the untapped potential that you may not have known existed in the first place.

Here's an example of how recovering her innocence has changed one of my client's lives. Anna, a young writer in her thirties, knew she was sensitive. For her, any form of criticism felt like a complete rejection. She felt like an utter fraud upon hearing her editor suggest corrections. A friend not understanding her sense of humor seemed to her like betrayal and abandonment. A date not calling her back meant she was unlovable and would always be alone.

Her invisibility pattern made her either avoid social gatherings or keep conversations and interactions to a minimum.

She attributed her sensitivity and shyness to two major challenges in her childhood. First, her mother, who came from Eastern Europe, dressed her daughter in, as Anna described, "the most hideous and old-fashioned ways." Because Anna grew up in Los Angeles, colorful folk dresses and knee-high wool socks didn't elicit a warm and welcoming response from her cool and stylish classmates. The other root of Anna's sensitivity was that her mother wanted her to become a competitive gymnast. While the other kids were hanging out and bonding, Anna's free time was defined by jumps, flips, and painful falls. The stress of memorizing complicated routines and the pressure to win the weekly competitions—aka to make her mom and her coach happy—took a toll on her. Even years after she had quit gymnastics and finished school, Anna still felt under constant scrutiny from anyone around her.

When we traveled back to her early childhood, Anna tapped into a memory of when she was four years old, the time before she lost her innocence. She remembered being in the pool and climbing up the three-meter diving board without fear or hesitation. Once she reached the top, she jumped off the board with complete delight and excitement. Anna, who hadn't thought about this event in a long time, realized that some of her hidden treasures were courage and a zest for life. Tears streaming down her cheeks, she said, "I can't believe I've forgotten how fearless and fun I really am. This little girl reminds me that living my truth is far more important than avoiding other people's judgment."

During the following weeks, Anna made an effort to check in daily with the little girl she had brought back into her heart. She imagined sitting with her younger self on a couch, sipping hot chocolate and chatting about the day's schedule. When, out of habit, her inner protector brought up worries and concerns, Anna reassured this part of her that she could relax and let the adult take care of any issues that may arise. Then she visualized how she would approach formerly challenging situations, such as a meeting at work, a phone call to her mom, or going on a date with the courage and lightness she had recovered from her innocent self. She pictured the forcefield of compassion surrounding her while she would confidently interact in situations where she used to feel small and insecure.

Quickly her friends noticed that Anna was different. "Whatever you're doing, keep it up." "I like the new unapologetic you." "You look so young and energetic; what's your secret?" Yet even though such positive remarks were flattering, Anna made sure not to give them too much weight. She told me that she now understands that whether she's judged or praised, the opinions of others say very little about who she is.

For many people, including myself, reclaiming and integrating the hidden gifts of our innocent self has added a new and enriching facet to life. Some, like Anna, have restored their bravery and chutzpah. My client Christine, who as a child was often scolded for being spacey and inattentive, retrieved her ability to daydream and get lost in the bliss and beauty of a sunset, or the scent of the enormous pine trees surrounding her home. Reconnecting with the essence of her inner child also allowed her to break through a decades-long struggle with insomnia and finally enjoy deep and restful sleep again.

For me, being reunited with little Pinepan meant I regained a sense of trust in life and the universe. Don't get me wrong, the happy-go-lucky kid in my heart didn't make me careless, complacent, or irresponsible. My adult self wouldn't allow that to happen. However, where I once would either ruminate about the past or diligently plan ahead, Pinepan reopened my mind and heart to play again and appreciate the little joys in life more fully—and more frequently. I no longer feel the need to overthink and micromanage every move I make. Instead, I'm more able to discern between those things I can control and those I have to either let go of or let unfold the way they're meant to.

EMPOWERMENT ROUTINE

The goal of this daily routine is to foster a close and caring relationship with your inner child, to encourage it to let go of its invisibility patterns and share with you and the world the gifts of its truth.

Step 1: Connect

Ideally in the morning, find a quiet space to sit down and go within. Close your eyes and take a few breaths in and out. Then in your mind's eye meet the younger self in its safe and cozy place in your heart. Imagine sitting together on a soft couch or a warm blanket on the floor, chatting about the upcoming day. In the beginning, you may notice the child still needs reassurance about why it's safe to be no longer invisible. Don't feel discouraged. Instead, go patiently through the Five Principles to Enjoying Life in the Open or any other reasons that will remind your younger self that you have their back.

The following affirmations can also help to put its mind at ease:

- This is my life.
- I choose to be my authentic self.
- I choose to express and share my gifts and talents with the world.
- It's safe to be all I can be.
- I belong here.
- Who I am and what I contribute matters.
- I'm not responsible for other people's emotions and opinions.
- My shield of compassion deflects the negativity of others.
- I take responsibility for how I feel about myself.
- I'm fully committed to treating myself with kindness, support, encouragement, and appreciation.
- This is my life—and I choose to live every day without regrets.

Step 2: Choose

Remind this part of you that one of the most important purposes in life is to discover, embrace, and share with the world the best and most authentic version of yourself. As you choose to take more and more ownership of your life, you're eager to express the gifts and qualities this part of you has kept hidden in the past. Together, decide which of these precious aspects of your authentic self you want to focus on today. You may choose the courage to be noticeable, speak up and voice your opinion, share an idea, or just wear colorful socks. Or maybe you want to express more of your creativity by taking an art class, cooking a new dish, or writing a letter to your spouse. You and your younger self may also decide to make more room for fun today, such as going to the zoo, flying a kite in the park, or having lunch by the river instead of in front of the computer.

Visualize how you want to experience whatever activity you choose. Imagine how freeing and self-affirming it will feel to bring out aspects of yourself that you haven't fully accessed since childhood. After a couple of minutes of rehearsing these special moments of the day, give your inner child a hug and a kiss and open your eyes.

Living in the open is possibly still scary for the inner protector. Try to strike a balance between daring to be different and being mindful that your younger self needs some time to learn that life outside its comfort zone is safe and enjoyable.

Step 3: Express and Appreciate

The best intentions become the biggest disappointments when they lack commitment and follow-through. Make it your daily goal to take the newly recovered aspects of your personality for a spin, and to practice this form of self-actualization without worrying what other people may think about it. If you notice others' judgment or negativity in response to your explorations, use the shield of sensitive compassion to deflect their energy, while at the same time reminding yourself that their reactions and criticism are just reflections of their own fears, discomforts, and insecurities.

At the end of the day, spend a few moments celebrating with your little self that expressing more of your authenticity was safe and enjoyable. Share with this child how you and your contributions mattered, and how they brought you one step closer to reaching *empowered authenticity*. Another day fully lived—without regrets.

7

THE PROCRASTINATOR PATTERN

Waiting for Tomorrow

Tomorrow is often the busiest day of the week.
—SPANISH PROVERB

FROM RELIEF TO REMORSE

Procrastination is often associated with being lazy or disorganized. However, contrary to popular belief, the procrastination pattern isn't necessarily a sign of apathy or a lack of motivation. I used to (and still do, at times) procrastinate by becoming very busy. The more I tried to avoid my desk with its pile of unfinished tasks, the more I became interested in vacuuming, cleaning windows, or changing light bulbs. Being busy and productive served as a conscience-soothing excuse to postpone other more challenging matters. My wife, Danielle, calls this habit *doing all the right things for the wrong reasons.*

I don't know about you, but after a day of riding the procrastination train, I never slept well. Usually, I was plagued by nightmares, such as sitting in a math test I hadn't studied for, or realizing on

Christmas Eve that I hadn't bought any presents for my parents, or one of my favorites, walking around town without pants. Obviously, a part of my subconscious mind wasn't too pleased with me putting things off.

While you may not be tormented by nightmares of running around naked in public, I'm pretty sure some part of you hasn't been thrilled with your procrastination patterns either. Most people procrastinate not because they are lazy or indifferent, but because they struggle with overwhelm, lack of confidence, fear of potential failure, judgment, or other kinds of discomfort and pain. Our subconscious mind creates procrastination by using denial and distraction to keep us safe. While this survival pattern is a part of the avoider trifecta (victim, invisibility, and procrastinator), it isn't just limited to the avoiders among us. Procrastination may be the busiest and most ubiquitous of all self-protective habits.

Okay, you may believe you are too busy or driven to procrastinate. However, I'm sure that upon closer inspection, you'll find areas in your life that your procrastinator has under lockdown. Don't get me wrong, there's a time and place for everything; just because you may be currently focusing more on your career or raising kids than being in shape, developing your spirituality, or starting a hobby, doesn't mean that you are stuck in a procrastinator-driven survival mode. As the saying goes, "Everybody procrastinates, but not everybody is a procrastinator." So, how do you know whether procrastination keeps you in survival mode?

DOES PROCRASTINATION HOLD YOU BACK?

According to studies, approximately one in five people are chronic procrastinators.[1] Yet, considering the results of a meta-analysis by the University of Calgary, which showed that 80 to 95 percent of college students procrastinate, particularly when it comes to doing their coursework, the procrastination problem may be on a steep incline. [2] Compared to fifty years ago, most people today are dealing with the challenging combination of, on the one hand, facing enormous pressure and stress at work and home, and on the other hand, having access to infinite ways to distract themselves. With more than two hundred channels on TV, daily sports events, countless devices to surf the web, and all-day breakfast in fast-food restaurants, the temptation to choose mind-numbing instant gratification over discomfort-causing effort is, for many, too great.

So the chances are that you may also have a slight procrastination problem. Here are six signs that can tell you if your inner procrastinator has been too active:

1. You Avoid One or Several Parts of Your Life

A widespread way to procrastinate is to prioritize the urgent and the more convenient aspects of our lives and ignore the important and more challenging ones. Whether you're a self-proclaimed workaholic, always busy and stressed out, a devoted caregiver, proud of being selfless and giving, or someone who likes to be in control of your life, it may have never occurred to you that you could also be dealing with a serious case of chronic procrastination. Yet why is it that you can never find time to go to the gym; that you promise yourself to watch your diet, right before you take another bite of your jelly donut; that you tell your spouse for months you'll schedule a date-night; or that you continue to download self-help books even though you know that you most likely will never read them? How long have you let these facets of your life simmer on the back burner?

You may have come across the wheel of life before. It's a powerful tool that gives you a clear visual representation of whether your current life is well balanced or whether certain parts need more of your attention. This concept was first introduced by Paul J. Meyer, founder of the Success Motivation Institute. Starting from the center, color each section of the wheel according to how positive you feel about that particular aspect in your life. The more content you are, the more you color. Once you've finished, notice how *round* your wheel appears—and whether you have *successfully* procrastinated on attending to certain areas of your life.

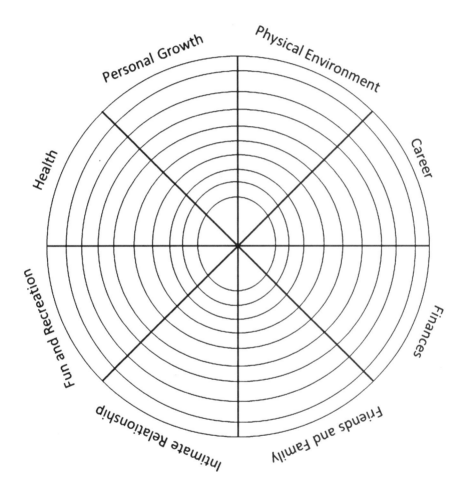

The Wheel of Life

For each of these eight areas of your life, the colored wheel shows how content you feel and where you could place more attention.

2. You're Easily Getting Distracted

Think about the last few times you had to deal with a problem, a deadline, or an unpleasant task. Did you suddenly notice a stain on the carpet that needed urgent cleaning? Got sucked into decluttering your inbox or found yourself aimlessly surfing the web? Or did you tell yourself that before you tackle the issue you need first to get a latte, eat a piece of chocolate, or take a power nap? As you search for instant gratification, how often do you end up postponing a timely and relevant activity until another time? You may have diagnosed yourself as dealing with a minor case of ADHD, yet most likely, you're dealing with a procrastinator pattern that makes you squander your time to avoid making a mistake, getting hurt, or feeling overwhelmed and uncomfortable.

3. It's Difficult for You to Make Decisions

Making a choice is scary for the procrastinator because of the risk of making the wrong one, and the notion that any decision is a reflection on you. Even the most straightforward choices, such as what to wear to work, what gift to buy for your mom, and what restaurant to go to for lunch, become almost life-and-death decisions. What if you regret your pick and feel remorse and guilt afterward? What if others don't approve of your choice and judge and embarrass you for it? The procrastinator prefers lingering in limbo, with the excuse of just having to gather more information, to dealing with the consequences of a possible fumble.

4. You Use Alcohol or Drugs to Escape Discomfort

Procrastination and substance abuse often go hand-in-hand. If you usually, right before you pour yourself a drink or light up a joint, think something along the lines of, "I am too overwhelmed, anxious, frustrated, confused . . . to deal with *this* now," you know that your procrastinator tries to rescue you from the unpleasantness of life by getting you into a more relaxed frame of mind. Downing a stiff one, pulling on a doobie, or popping a pill are ways to avoid the stress of whatever your procrastinator deems too hard to tackle. Until the effects of the drugs wear off that is, and you're facing an even taller mountain of unresolved issues.

5. You (and Others) No Longer Trust Your Word

How many times can somebody break their promise to you before you stop believing them? The answer for most people lies anywhere between one and five times. Now, if you're honest, how many times have you told yourself and others that tomorrow you'll take action, address the problem at hand, or start making a change? And how many times did you not follow through with your pledge? Or worse, to avoid fallout, how often have you resorted to lies and half-baked truths, making excuses for your failure to follow through on a commitment? You know you're knee-deep in the procrastinator pattern if the moment you boldly declare that "Tomorrow I'll get things done," your spouse or friends either snicker or roll their eyes to express their *Yeah, I'll believe it when I see it* doubts. Procrastination undermines trust and confidence and thus sabotages close relationships, including the one with yourself.

6. You're Dealing with Health Issues Due to Stress and Overwhelm

Studies found that procrastination is associated with higher levels of stress, anxiety, depression, insomnia, fatigue, and more illness.[3,4] Of course, stress and its associated health issues can be caused by many other factors besides procrastination. But if you notice that your physical symptoms regularly increase with the size of your "still-not-done-list," it's time to make a change.

Do any of these examples hit home? No need to make yourself feel bad; nobody is safe from procrastination. The gist is that whenever you hold off doing something because it could make you uncomfortable, even though you know how important it is to you or somebody else, you can bet that your inner procrastinator has pulled in the reins.

This of course prompts the question: What drives the inner procrastinator to prevent us from following through with our agenda, even if it means that we end up feeling anxious, stressed, ashamed, and even sick afterward?

HOW PROCRASTINATION GETS YOU OFF THE HOOK

I know this title sounds like you and I aren't responsible for dawdling around and postponing specific tasks and responsibilities indefinitely. It's all the fault of our subconscious, right? Actually, nobody is at fault because there is fundamentally nothing wrong with any of the survival patterns, including procrastination. Blaming our subconscious for getting in our way is like blaming the brakes in our car for slowing us down. Our subconscious just does its job to keep us alive and unharmed. However, since many of its protective patterns started early in our lives, it's our responsibility to review and revise our subconscious operation manual. Being aware of our patterns, as self-sabotaging as they may appear, is the first step to updating them. So, let's look more closely at why and how our inner procrastinator gets us to abandon or at least postpone our best intentions.

Avoidance of Discomfort and Boredom

Common Rationalizations

If it is too hard, it's probably not right for me. Life is too short to do things that aren't fun. This is so tedious, I'm just wasting my time.

With this form of procrastination, the typical sequence is straightforward. First, you have a sincere intention about how you'll spend some solid time and energy resolving an issue, cleaning up a corner of your life, or making some progress with one of your goals, all of which you've ignored for quite some time. These could be washing the dishes, paying the bills, getting a haircut, or calling your family doctor for your yearly checkup. You're gung ho, ready to dive in, and convinced that this time you'll make progress. But the closer you get to taking action, the less clear and enthusiastic you feel. It's like approaching the edge of the platform before your first bungee jump. Every inch you move forward, the resistance to taking the leap increases. And just as the opposition is almost unbearable, you hear a comforting voice inside saying, "Why don't I watch a little TV first?" Or, "I wonder how many likes my latest Instagram post received." Or, "Isn't it time to have lunch—it's already 11:30 am?"

While at first, you may defy the temptation to quit your plans, as soon as you give in and give up, you feel strangely relieved, maybe even elated, like a kid who got away with playing hooky. You may even convince yourself that the timing wasn't right in any case because you need a higher level of stress and pressure to do your best work. Like in high school or college, where you put off tasks until the very last minute, but you still got decent grades by pulling all-nighters.

Yet, as the sun goes down, so does the rewarding feeling of avoiding unpleasant chores. Soon a glaring sense of failure, doom, and shame takes over. After you've lectured yourself with insults and threats, just like a stern parent would do, you heave yourself back up, filled with new intentions and promises that tomorrow everything will be different.

At first glance, I have to admit, this part of your subconscious may appear more like a close relative of Jeff Bridges's "the Dude" in the movie *The Big Lebowski,* who spends his time bumming joints and listening to whale sounds on his tape recorder. But the truth is, your inner procrastinator isn't a lazy bum determined to shun all responsibilities. All it wants is to at first protect you from agonizing over dull and annoying tasks and then—as certain aspects of your life are getting more out of control—from facing the mess it helped you create. Like comfort food, procrastination doesn't offer solutions to improve your life, but it provides a compelling mix of pleasant distractions and instant gratification.

Sure, putting off washing the dishes, paying the bills, getting a haircut, or calling your family doctor for your yearly checkup could be interpreted as pure laziness or ignorance. However, when you listen more closely to what motivates the procrastinator, you may notice that washing the dishes and paying the bills may stand for getting the house and your life in better shape. And since neither are in excellent condition, focusing on a pile of dirty plates makes you feel simultaneously overwhelmed and like a failure. Better to watch another episode of *Master Chef* on Netflix, even though you hate cooking yourself. The resistance to paying a visit to the hairdresser may be associated with the discomfort of having to chat with the stylist or stare at yourself in the mirror for way too long. And going to the doctor may trigger the fear of getting some bad news or once again being lectured that you still haven't lost the extra pounds. The point is, don't just assume your procrastinator is hooked on self-indulgence and convenience; instead, try to decipher what exactly this part of you is concerned about as it slams on the brakes.

Avoidance of Failure

Common Rationalizations

I want to do this right; this is too important to me. Tomorrow I will be in a better headspace. I just need to get organized, make a list, and do some more research; then I'll be ready to start.

One of the strongest motivations for the inner procrastinator to kick into gear—and kick your plans to the curb—is the fear of not meeting expectations and letting others down. Your spouse asks you to surprise her for her birthday, and instead of being excited, your mind becomes utterly devoid of any brilliant ideas. You're afraid of making the wrong choice and disappointing her. Rather than asking a friend or taking some time to reflect on what your beloved may enjoy, you find yourself drawn to clean out the garage or trim the hedge along the sidewalk. Or your boss wants you to do some critical research for their next presentation in front of the board, but instead of feeling flattered and motivated by their trust in you, just thinking of this project gets your stomach tied up in knots. To distract yourself, your research focuses on your next vacation or the summer movie release schedule. When the stakes appear too high and the risk of failure too real, your procrastinator barges in like a firefighter, pulling you out of the flames of worry and insecurity into the safety of denial and diversion.

Rachel, a young college student, was told since she was little that she was uniquely gifted, and destined to make a big splash in the world. While in the beginning, she loved the attention and praise she received from her parents and grandparents, when she hit puberty, she struggled with the idea that she always had to be the best among her peers. At that time, the pressure didn't come so much from her family, who reassured her that all they wanted was for her to be happy. What weighed her down were her own unreasonable expectations that she shouldn't only be at the top of her class, but also win every math, speech-writing, and history competition she participated in.

When she was fifteen years old, to the surprise of her teachers and family, she started to procrastinate around studying and doing her homework and even skipped classes. Rachel told me she felt too exhausted and overwhelmed to focus. Whenever she tried to sit down to prepare for a test, she was overcome by almost paralyzing tiredness, so all she could do was either take a nap or distract herself by watching videos on YouTube. Unfortunately, this procrastination pattern continued in college. As we dug deeper into what could motivate her inner procrastinator to take over, she admitted that her exhaustion was worse when she believed she couldn't get an A on an upcoming exam or compose an outstanding essay. It almost seemed better to not show up at all than to be just average.

You may have experienced firsthand the bumpy *all or nothing* ride. And, like Rachel, you may have noticed that you procrastinate the most when your high expectations of yourself collide with your doubts you might not meet them. When your perfectionism is potentially setting you up for failure, your procrastinator steps in to save you from pain and embarrassment. At least that's the intention. When I asked Rachel why having a mediocre result would be worse than getting an F, she told me she felt more in control by choosing to give up rather than giving her best and not reaching her potential. This way, she could still tell herself that she could have achieved another excellent result if she had just tried. Obviously, the procrastinator has its own logic to justify its patterns.

Avoidance of Overwhelm

Common Rationalizations

I'm too busy at the moment, but I'll start as soon as I've finished x, y, and z.

Procrastination doesn't mean you are a lazybones. Some of the most hard-working people are the biggest procrastinators, especially when it comes to taking care of themselves.

When your plate is full, and the calendar has no white space left, your mind gets overloaded because everything appears equally important and pressing. This is when your procrastination pattern plays triage and pushes aside all the items on your list that may feel less relevant to an immediate objective and more difficult to handle. In my practice, I've found that pleasers often procrastinate when pursuing their dreams and desires to devote their entire energy to others. High achievers use procrastination to avoid becoming distracted by fun and relaxation, which might prevent them from reaching their lofty goals. And people who love to be in control postpone developing or deepening personal relationships to avoid the perceived discomfort of intimacy and vulnerability.

In this regard, busyness and overwhelm can be both—a trigger and a form of procrastination. Like in the examples above, you may be one of the busy bees who deliberately use the socially acceptable excuse of overwhelm and lack of time to hide the fact that you are chronically putting off something essential you don't want to deal with. Of course, your inner procrastinator doesn't consider that it will inevitably cause you an even greater amount of overwhelm once you're forced to face those aspects of your life you've neglected for far too long.

Avoidance of Change

> **Common Rationalizations**
>
> I am not sure if I am ready for this. What if this change will cause only problems? This may not be the right direction, but I just thought about another great idea.

Procrastination can kick in to save you when you're about to commit to a project or an ambitious goal that could make a difference in your life. Let's say your New Year's resolution was to lose twenty pounds in the first three months of the year. Almost immediately, the fear of change and getting out of your comfort zone activates your procrastination pattern. Come April, you've neither gone to the gym (despite your gold membership) nor stopped competing for customer-of-the-month at the drive-through of your local fast-food chain. Or you're determined to finally pay your overdue taxes but don't take any steps toward reaching this goal. As your subconscious recognizes your looming defeat in light of continued inaction, it steers you toward something new: another idea, project, or shiny object that will distract you from your initial goal.

When I met Bryan during his first appointment, he told me his goal was to become a life coach, helping people get unstuck and pull their lives together. However, in the next sentence, he admitted that a big part of his drive to support others was that he hadn't succeeded in overcoming his own immobility. "It isn't that I'm not motivated enough to reach my goals," he said. "I'm constantly reading self-help books, attending seminars, and watching hours of empowering videos on YouTube. The problem is, I'm good at starting something but terrible at staying committed and following through."

He told me that whenever he tried to make a business plan or practice the coaching tools he'd learned, he suddenly felt the urge to relax, crack a beer, or smoke a joint. A voice inside of his head would say something like, "Don't be too serious; life is short," or "If you study too much, you're no fun to be around," or "Your friends are in the pub having a good time. You should be too." At first glance this sounds like an addict's rationale. (And it's true that addictive behavior can be an extreme form of procrastination.) Yet as I just mentioned, to understand somebody's behavior, we need to understand what's driving it in the first place.

When Bryan was four years old, his dad left his younger brother and him and never looked back. Bryan's mother, who wasn't the most organized person herself, struggled to keep a job and raise her two boys on her own. She looked for relief in alcohol and countless short-lived relationships with men, who were usually anything but stable, upstanding citizens. At first, Bryan and his brother were eager to be good kids, please their mom, and do their best in school. Yet no matter how hard they tried, their mother had neither time nor interest in providing her boys with anything but the bare minimum, which didn't include decent food, clean clothes, or support with homework. In school, they were scolded by their teachers for their lack of preparation and ridiculed by their classmates for their outdated clothes, lack of hygiene, and overall unkempt appearance.

Once they became teenagers, the boys figured that trying to be good and fit in didn't appear to be a winning strategy. Since their mom was usually absent and left the brothers to fend for themselves, the brothers decided that skipping school and going fishing or roaming through their town streets was much more rewarding than sitting through boring lectures.

With tears running down his cheeks, Bryan told me, "I can't believe how neglected and alone my brother and I were throughout our childhood. The only people who wanted to hang out with us were other misfits from similarly dysfunctional homes. Through some of them, I discovered that alcohol makes me funny and popular." Bryan realized that his early procrastination pattern had kicked in when his efforts to succeed in school and fit in with his *normal* peers appeared to fail. His inner protector pulled him away from anything and anybody that could embarrass or reject him, and steered him toward getting drunk, a behavior that seemed to ease his pain and get him at least some recognition and a sense of belonging.

Since then, Bryan struggled with moving forward in life. After barely passing his GED, he couldn't convince himself to attend college. Staying at a job for longer than a year was impossible, because he bailed as soon as he felt any kind of criticism or pressure. His procrastinator also impacted our work. No matter how strongly he expressed his commitment to *this time* follow through with the homework I gave him after each session, low and behold, the next time we saw each other, he had to admit that he had stalled after just one or two days of good intentions.

Bryan explained to me that while he was consciously determined to get the most out of our sessions, a subconscious part didn't want him to change and succeed, because he was afraid he would lose the only attribute that had gained him approval and friends: the ability to be fun. Yet to be fun, he needed to drink. Alcohol loosened him up so he could be less serious. So Bryan dealt with competing commitments: he could be either tipsy and entertaining and thus have friends, or he could be sober, sit at home, and focus on his personal and professional growth and possibly end up being alone. For his inner procrastinator, the prospect of becoming an outcast again outweighed career and financial stability concerns.

It wasn't until the young man recognized that although his procrastinator wanted to keep him safe, he was on his way to becoming just as dysfunctional and ultimately hopeless as his mother, who'd abandoned him when he needed her the most. "It's crazy, all my life I felt neglected and abandoned by my mom, and now, I'm repeating the same pattern with myself." Yet, this time, Bryan chose to have compassion for himself rather than beating himself up for his addictive behavior. He entered into a rehab program, not with the usual shame or self-loathing, but with renewed determination that he could turn his life around because, for the first time since he'd started drinking, he didn't associate being sober with losing his personality and friends. Instead, he accepted that committing to his health and sobriety was his way of providing himself with the kindness and care he'd never experienced when he was a boy.

......

These are just a few excerpts from the vast playbook of the procrastinator. Its mission is mainly fueled by two fears: The fear of failure, which is tightly connected to the underlying limiting belief of you not being good or capable enough. And the fear of pain and discomfort, which is about the unwillingness to leave the familiar comfort zone. Who knows how well you'll do *out there,* and whether being different won't come with a greater risk of being judged and rejected.

This may not be the first time you want to tackle your issues with stalling and falling behind. You may have tried many times to improve and change, only to procrastinate right before or after the first step. Deflated, you gave up on the notion that you'd ever overcome this self-defeating habit. Yet keep in mind that until now, you may have approached procrastination as a weakness and flaw, without appreciating its protective mission. With the following four steps, you'll learn how to end this survival pattern by empowering your inner procrastinator instead of fighting it. Ultimately, as a part of your subconscious protection team, it always had your best interest in mind—even if its (non)actions overshadowed its good intentions.

8
....

SELF-RELIANCE

The Key to Owning Your Actions

*Honesty and reliability are the pillars of confidence and
  inner peace.*
If you can't count on your word, who can you trust?

"Stop being lazy." "Suck it up buttercup and get going." "You just need to manage your time better." These are a few classic phrases that could easily make it on the *10 Things You Shouldn't Say to a Procrastinator* list. No matter how negatively your procrastinator pattern affects your life, anger, blame, and shame are terrible long-term motivators for change and only reinforce the subconscious need to avoid. As you're ready to outgrow this limiting habit, remind yourself that, like all the other survival patterns, its intention isn't to harm but to protect you, albeit in a rather clumsy way. So try to approach the following four self-empowering steps to end procrastination from a place of kindness and compassion—but also clarity and commitment. After all, you've already decided with the invisibility pattern to no longer postpone joy, growth, and fulfillment for the illusion of being safe.

STEP 1: STOP, LISTEN, AND QUESTION

How do you know it's time to procrastinate? Since the subconscious mind drives procrastination, you may not be consciously aware of the moment you switch into this pattern. With the willpower of a sleep-walker, you find yourself checking your emails, calling a friend, getting a coffee, or mindlessly staring out of the window just when you're about to attend to a task. Yet rather than going on auto-pilot, notice that right before you make the subconscious decision to procrastinate, an inner voice pipes up with a negative or deflating comment about whatever you were about to do.

I've already listed some common procrastination-triggering thoughts in the How Procrastination Gets You off the Hook part of the previous chapter. Thoughts such as "If it isn't fun it's probably not right for me," "Let me relax for twenty minutes, and then I'll get going," or "This is too hard right now. I won't succeed with this task" can easily be interpreted as derailing messages from the subconscious headquarters, challenging your decision to do something productive.

But, you know by now that the subconscious mind isn't eager to control you. Instead, it prefers a conscious-subconscious collaboration, with the conscious mind in charge and the subconscious following its instructions. However, if there's a lack of clear conscious guidance and reliability, the subconscious continues to run proven familiar survival patterns, such as procrastination, to ensure your well-being.

I can hear you thinking, "How many times do I have to yell at myself after another bout of procrastination before my subconscious gets the memo? Or is my procrastinator just more stubborn than me?" Good questions. As I said before, shouting and self-loathing aren't the most effective communication styles to reach the subconscious. In fact, the angrier you are with yourself, the more you appear as a threat to your subconscious, which only enhances its commitment to be your bodyguard.

The good news is that your subconscious is always eager to learn, and no matter how hard you've been on yourself, it continues to look for your feedback and advice. So let's assume for a moment that the procrastination-triggering thoughts are not factual statements or commands, but only questions that your procrastinator would like you to answer:

- Is this the right thing to do, even if it isn't much fun?
- Would it be better to relax for twenty minutes before you get going?
- Isn't that too hard right now?
- Are you sure you will succeed with this task?

Do you notice how much more open and empowered you feel when you imagine your inner procrastinator asking you questions rather than making self-defeating remarks?

There's a neurological explanation, which has to do with how our brain responds differently to questions than to statements. According to Harvard University psychologist Daniel Gilbert, who has done extensive research on the science of lying, we react to a statement in two steps, no matter how wrong or outrageous it may appear. First, we accept the message as true, even for just a fraction of a second, before we go through the discernment process of believing or rejecting it.[1] Gilbert found that while acceptance occurs quickly and straightforwardly, the second verification step takes more effort and can easily get thwarted.

When we face a shortage of time, energy, or clear evidence, we're more likely to remain in automatic acceptance than proceed to discernment. Another factor that hampers our brain's ability to decipher a statement as true or false, is when we're bombarded with a constant stream of messages. As our mind becomes overwhelmed, it stops trying to comb through the massive amount of information to discern between truth and fiction. Eventually, it surrenders to accepting even the most implausible ideas.

While Gilbert's research focused on computing and analyzing external input, I believe that his findings are equally valid for our internal communication. As you have undoubtedly noticed, your negative self-talk is more often based on fiction and distorted views of reality than hard facts. Any of your procrastinator statements such as "If it isn't fun, it's probably not right for me," or "Let me relax for twenty minutes and then I'll get going," or "This is too hard right now" could be challenged and judged as untrue. However, since these negative thoughts usually create strong emotions such as doubt, frustration, worry, or insecurity, the discernment process is already impaired. Add in the often relentless repetition of self-defeating thoughts, and it's no wonder that the rational aspect of our brain, our conscious mind, abandons its truth-finding discernment process. Therefore, we often remain stuck in step one, accepting that the negative thought is correct even if it's a blatant lie from our subconscious mind.

Let me ask you, what's your mom's middle name? You probably stopped reading for a moment to think about the answer, right? Questions are powerful brain stimulators. According to Earl Miller, professor of neuroscience at MIT, it's difficult for our brain to process more than two mental tasks simultaneously, which is why questions can literally hijack our neurons.[2] So when you ask yourself a question, you have your brain's full attention.

Now here's where the magic happens. If you turn a negative thought into a question, you not only light up your neurons, but you also skip step one, acceptance, and go right to step two, discernment. In other words, you no longer accept a potential self-defeating statement as accurate, but immediately put yourself in the role of the authority who decides what you want to believe. From a subconscious perspective, the conscious adult takes charge and allows the subconscious to step back from its habitual need to protect you.

The technique of turning a negative thought into a question also works for all other survival patterns. It gives you the power to decide how you want to perceive yourself and your life, rather than remaining trapped in old, self-limiting distortions of reality. Again, notice the difference between hearing, "This is not safe." And, "Do you know if this is safe?" Or, "You are not good enough to succeed." Versus, "Are you sure you are good enough to succeed?"

Converting the procrastinator's negative remarks into questions is very effective, because instead of activating its pattern, this part of you is eagerly waiting for your response. But what are you supposed to answer?

STEP 2: WATCH OUT FOR THE FORK IN THE ROAD

I heard a speaker in a seminar say, "Successful people always consider the long-term consequences of their actions. People who struggle focus more on fast relief and instant gratification." Or in the words of Gloria Steinem: "Rich people plan for three generations. Poor people plan for Saturday night." While I'm not a big proponent of generalizations and simplifications, *short-term living* is one of the procrastinator's hallmarks. I highly regard the intelligence of the subconscious mind, and I don't believe it's ignorant and unaware of the negative consequences of making you procrastinate. However, what may have been missing is your conscious analysis of the two immediate choices you face right before you're about to procrastinate.

Take a moment and picture yourself standing at a fork in the road. The left, well-trodden path shows you the immediate and long-term consequences of your procrastination pattern. You may first sense the instant relief of letting yourself off the hook. But then, also pay attention to the inevitable procrastination hangover, which sets in later. Notice how guilt, frustration, and anxiety eventually culminate in an overwhelming sense of defeat and worthlessness. Visualize what will happen during the next forty-eight hours after letting the procrastinator again take the lead. This can be a pile of dirty laundry, a stack of unpaid bills, your body being overweight and under-exercised, or an image of you sitting late at night in front of your computer, alone and disconnected from anything that could be joyful and meaningful.

Then, assuming you continue to repeat the same pattern during the coming weeks and months, see yourself standing at the end of this left road, one year in the future. Are you aware of the external fallout of remaining in this pattern—the lack of change, growth, and success, and the possible loss of relationships, opportunities, and security? Also, understand the mental and emotional impact procrastination has on your future self. What do you think and feel about this version of yourself?

Now switch your focus to the right path, representing the choice to go ahead and carry out your plans. At the beginning of that path, you may see struggle and strife, trial, and tribulations, resistance and reluctance. But you'll also notice how following through and accomplishing even the smallest objectives on your journey increases your confidence. As my friend Gerhard likes to say when he's about to climb a steep mountain path on his bike, "All I think about is how amazing I feel once I'm up there." Envision the completion of what you had planned to do. You may see your closet filled with clean, neatly folded clothes, your desk free of bills and clutter, and yourself *flying* on the elliptical at the gym with a big smile. Imagine how one empowering decision to procrastinate procrastinating creates a profound ripple effect throughout your external and internal world. Can you see this engaged and committed version of yourself one year down the road? What do you think and feel about this future self?

As you consider both pathways, be completely open and honest with yourself. Don't underestimate the harm you do to yourself and your life by putting your tasks, responsibilities, and goals on hold. Nor do you want to overestimate how quickly and profoundly overcoming procrastination will improve you and the circumstances you're in. I'm not saying you shouldn't drool a little with excitement when you see your empowered future self on the right side. Yet, suppose you're visualizing yourself as a multi-millionaire, dating Jennifer Aniston or Brad Pitt (or both) and having just completed your third Ironman. In that case, your subconscious will pull the plug on your dreams and switch back into inertia because your expectations are surely delusional and set you up for painful disappointments.

The goal of this process isn't to accurately design your future, but to shift out of the nearsightedness of short-term thinking and remind yourself that you're not a puppet on strings held by a hyper-protective subconscious. You have the power to choose your life path by deciding whether it's in your best interest to procrastinate or be self-reliant. This conscious decision gives you a much greater sense of control and relaxes your subconscious because it prefers to serve you rather than lead you.

Behavioral scientists have discovered that asking people about what they'll choose to do in the future significantly influences their choices. Vicki Morwitz and colleagues found that simply questioning people if they were planning to buy a new car in the next few months increased the purchase rate by 35 percent.[3] In another study, asking citizens whether they would vote in an upcoming election increased the likelihood of casting their ballot by 25 percent.[4] This so-called *mere measuring effect* was further confirmed in studies exploring the frequency of exercise.[5,6] Researchers concluded that by making someone wonder about their future behavior, they automatically and instantaneously create a subconscious image of that behavior. The mere measurement effect is more pronounced when people imagine themselves taking action, rather than somebody else doing so.[7]

Bringing this all back to overcoming procrastination: you're significantly more likely to actualize your intentions by visualizing the right path, where you're paying the bills, using your gym membership, or studying for your test. Of course, you can argue that by envisioning the left path, you may also be more likely to engage in procrastinating behavior again. The two prime concerns of the subconscious mind—to avoid pain and discomfort and to seek out pleasure and joy—come in handy here. As you consider the procrastination path, recall clearly and viscerally how bad it feels to let yourself down and face a growing pile of problems because of it. This way, you stimulate the so-called away-from-pain motivation of your subconscious. Then ignite the toward-joy motivation by basking in the glow of feeling excited, proud, happy, and accomplished, as you are laying out the results of the right path.

A word of caution: don't assume just because you chose to step into the role of the architect and creator of your reality that your inner procrastinator will immediately drop its habits and surrender to your guidance. As we discussed, your subconscious may not trust you yet because so far, you may have appeared neither exceptionally reliable, nor firm in your resolve to break through procrastination. Steps three and four will help you to create a more powerful trust-based conscious-subconscious collaboration.

STEP 3: MAKE YOUR WORD COUNT AGAIN

If your procrastinator has stubbornly ignored your efforts to become more proactive and self-reliant, you're probably not utilizing one of your most incredible powers—your word. Words can create, teach, inspire, and connect. And they can do just the opposite—deceive, destroy, deflate, and alienate. Sticks and stones can break my bones, but words can never hurt me, sounds nice, but unfortunately it isn't really true, especially when it comes to your relationship with yourself. How often do you judge, criticize, and kick yourself verbally when you're already feeling down? The negative consequences of beating up on yourself are serious, as they often trigger anxiety, depression, lack of self-worth, and low energy. But a possibly even more severe way your words can hurt you is when you lie to yourself.

Let's talk about *lying* for a moment. Most of us have been guilty of fibbing, exaggerating, or withholding information from time to time. We usually make ourselves feel better by rationalizing that this was an exception or just a white lie and that we are generally honest. But hasn't the invention of social media made dishonesty a daily form of communication for many of us? Some call Facebook, Instagram, or TikTok the venues of our vanities, where we can showcase to thousands of our "friends," how extra-ordinary our lives and experiences are, when in reality, we feel ordinary and lonely. We usually don't post about the worries that our romantic partner may have become disinterested, that we're so depressed that we can't get out of bed, or that we're dealing with debt and are afraid of losing our home. Pretending on social media to be someone we are not, which is a form of lying, has become normal.

Here is another example of how lying became mainstream. Since the 2016 United States election, politicians and media have played with reality like kids with an Etch A Sketch. We have entered an era where alternative facts, fake news, and blatant lies are increasingly the norm, while truth has become a rare commodity. The fact that the University of Washington in Seattle is planning a course on The Art and Science of BS (which doesn't stand for Bachelor of Science), shows that we're heading toward a potential truth-telling crisis.

Of course, lying has been an issue since ancient times, which is why it's been included in most religious texts as a no-no. I'm sure that most people would agree that lying has harmful and destructive consequences for both the liar and the person being lied to. Yet this doesn't prevent us from being somewhat dishonest with ourselves, especially when we've been playing tug-of-war with our inner procrastinator.

Do you realize that your subconscious protector hasn't been willing to surrender its place at the helm because you constantly lie to yourself? No matter how boldly you may declare in the morning that today you'll tackle all the long-overdue issues that have been hanging over you like Damocles's sword, as the evening rolls around, all you have done is once again gone back on your word.

Regarding procrastinating, there are three significant problems with lying to ourselves. First, our brain gets used to lying. Neuroscientists found that the more we lie, the less we experience shame, guilt, and other negative feelings about it. And the more we get away with meddling with the truth, the bolder and more frequent our lies become.[8] So dishonesty shifts from being the exception to becoming the default.

Second, to cover up the consequences of procrastination, we are more likely to hide the truth from the people around us, especially those we love and care about. We tell lies about the changes and the progress we made, because we're afraid of being found out as not worthy, not good enough, or not loveable. Yet, after each lie, our fears increase because we're building our sense of security and worthiness not on reality, but deception. More likely than not, the lies and excuses for our procrastination eventually backfire, as others discover that we can't be trusted and relied upon.

But maybe the greatest risk of no longer being truthful is that we gradually stop believing what we think and say. Or, as the great Russian writer and philosopher Fyodor Dostoevsky wrote, it gets even worse: "Above all, don't lie to yourself. The man who lies to himself and listens to his own lie comes to a point that he cannot distinguish the truth within him, or around him, and so loses all respect for himself and for others. And having no respect, he ceases to love." As our word loses validity, we lose power and confidence. When we can't trust ourselves, our efforts to improve are no longer taken seriously by the part of our mind that's already afraid of change. After all, can you blame your subconscious that it would rather hunker down in a familiar comfort zone than follow an unreliable guide into the unknown?

Here are three practical ways to make your word count again, to build self-reliance and thus re-establish a foundation of trust between your conscious and your subconscious mind:

Take Ownership

What do people who let you down frequently have to do to regain your trust? Do they need to be completely honest? Return your calls? Follow through with their word? Show up on time? Probably all of the above. And it may take some time for you to regain confidence in their trustworthiness. To restore faith in your own dependability, you need to become aware of how you used to undermine your integrity:

- Did you often make promises to yourself and others, even though you knew you wouldn't keep them?
- Did you have too lofty goals and intentions that even for a non-procrastinator on a good day were impossible to achieve?
- Did you make excuses for your shortcomings, blaming others or the circumstance you were in rather than taking responsibility?
- And did you conceal the consequences of your procrastination habits through blatant lies?

Let's be clear, the procrastinator pattern doesn't want you to become a flake and perpetual liar. It's your conscious choice to lie to yourself, to cover up for the survival pattern of your subconscious mind, and to pretend to others and yourself that you are more dedicated and committed to reaching your goals than you genuinely are. Unfortunately, as you now know, your lack of credibility makes it rather impossible for you to convince your subconscious protector that it is time to let go of hiding behind procrastination.

The good news is that you don't have to become holier than the pope himself to get your subconscious to take you seriously again. I found that most of my clients' confidence levels shifted dramatically by just committing to change one or two of their usual dishonesty patterns.

For example:

- Instead of settling for denial and ignorance by pretending that you don't have a procrastination problem, notice how liberating and empowering it feels to choose honesty and integrity over appearance and approval.

- Instead of making excuses for your past failures, take responsibility and deal with the consequences of your old survival pattern. Acknowledge and ideally apologize to those you've let down and disappointed the most, including yourself. Admit that you have been struggling with procrastination and pledge to empower yourself to outgrow this pattern.

- Instead of making yourself look and feel good by over-promising something you already know you'll under-deliver, commit only to the goals and improvements you're confident you can accomplish, even if they may appear minuscule.

Aim for Progress and Not Perfection

In a world that worships billionaires, megastars, and superheroes, it may seem complicated to admit that the best you can do right now is make small, incremental changes. But to gain traction as you start shifting out of the survival patterns, you want to commit to small steps consistently. So don't tackle everything you've been procrastinating about all at once. Avoid overwhelm and set yourself up for success by addressing just one of your procrastination habits to start. Contradicting the widespread belief in the ingenuity of multitasking, research has shown that people who focused on only one goal at a time were more committed and more likely to succeed than those who tried to implement multiple changes simultaneously.[9]

Let's say the bills are stacking up, your inbox at work is overflowing, you're eating mostly junk food, haven't exercised in years, and due to habitual Netflix-binging, you've lost touch with almost all your friends. While you can tell it's time to reinvent yourself, as they say, Rome wasn't built in one day. Choose to focus on the problem area of your life, which once you change it, will give you simultaneously the greatest relief and biggest boost of confidence and motivation. This could be going through your bills or improving your diet. However, don't try to frantically tackle all your unpaid debts at once. This would only increase the likelihood that you'll feel defeated and end up hiding again under the thick blanket of denial. Instead, commit to gradually paying off the outstanding bills and attend to the new ones as they are coming in. Similarly, decide to eat one healthy meal a day, or cut back on eating junk food to just three instead of six times per week. The point is, make your change goals realistic, achievable, and measurable so that at the end of each day, you can pat yourself on the back for following through with your intentions. "Start out how you can hold out," was sage advice our friend Kay gave Danielle and me right before our wedding.

Power Up and Plan Ahead

So you're clear about the change you want to make, you've set a goal, and you're all geared up to get going. But then suddenly, all the good intentions deflate like a popped balloon. Why? One of the surest ways to poke holes in your good intentions is to fuel them with the wrong kind of energy. Let's face it, thoughts starting with "I have to . . . ," "I need to . . . ," or "I should . . . ," evoke a sense of severity, urgency, and pressure and can quickly appear more like stern commands or scoldings by your mom or dad than empowering choices. Researchers also found that we tend to associate with *should* goals and events that need more deliberation, appear more abstract, and reside somewhere further out in the future.[10]

So, whenever you try to *should* yourself into making a change, all your procrastinator hears is a lack of concreteness, absence of instant gratification, and the possibility of severe consequences for potential failure. Prefacing your intentions with "I want to . . . ," "I choose to . . . ," "I'm happy to . . . ," or "I can . . . ," is less threatening, more motivating for your subconscious, and generates overall a greater sense of choice, joy, and empowerment.

Another effective way to turn good intentions into great results is by creating a precise implementation plan on when, where, and how you'll act to achieve your goal. Studies show that having a plan significantly increases the likelihood of changing a behavior and achieving the desired outcome.[11] Without such a plan, people tend to forget about their intentions or fall for their inner procrastinator's excuses of not having enough time, energy, or reason to pursue them. Of course, a poorly crafted plan can easily become the greatest obstacle to itself, as it may be too ambitious and challenging to follow through with, and its reward too delayed. Such an example could be wanting to get in shape by going to the gym every day, limiting yourself to 1,000 calories per day, and not feeling satisfied until you've lost at least 50 pounds. Your inner procrastinator will smell inevitable defeat and pull the emergency brake on your efforts faster than you can say "gym membership."

A well-designed plan needs to match the following criteria:[12]

Divide bigger goals into smaller ones. Example: Getting into shape by . . .

1. Creating a workout routine for the next two months
2. Reducing sweets and foods rich in carbohydrates
3. Addressing mental and emotional issues regarding weight struggles

Be specific about the implementation details. Example: I will go to Freddy's Gym on Monday, Wednesday, and Friday at 7 am for 30 minutes.

Use prompts, such as a reminder alert on your phone or laying your gym clothes out on a chair next to your bed.

Share your plans. Declaring to those you care about that you're fully committed to sticking with your plan and reaching your goals creates accountability to others and increases the likelihood of follow-through.

Make every day count. Establishing a new routine can feel like a long haul without an endpoint in sight. So regard each day you intend to follow through with your schedule as a desirable goal in itself.

Reward your efforts and acknowledge your progress. Start a success journal, and at the end of each week, write down what you've accomplished, what obstacles you were able to overcome, what you've learned, and how much you've improved. Each month, give yourself a treat, such as a massage, a new pair of shoes, or simply a day off.

Once your subconscious realizes that your plan to become empowered and self-reliant is safe and pleasurable, it will naturally shift into its pleasing mode and help you find more opportunities and creative ways to reach your goals. This was the case with Harriet, who expressed the following to me in one of our sessions, "I asked my husband what he sees as the biggest change since working with you. His response was quick and easy. 'You're back in control of your life. It isn't controlling you.'" When I first met Harriet, she described herself as "a complete mess, without motivation, desire, or hope to change." After a series of unfortunate events (job loss, marriage issues, and health problems), Harriet had spent most of the past two years in bed, feeling too anxious and depressed even to prepare a meal or take a shower. The narrative of her procrastinator circled around her past failures, her lack of positive qualities, and the meaninglessness of life in general. Obviously, this part of her had determined that the only safe place on earth was under the sheets. Harriet scolded herself as being "lazy, useless, and fat," which only solidified her procrastinator's determination to keep the young woman securely tucked away.

Growing up with a narcissistic and neglectful mother and a drug-dealing father, Harriet's childhood was anything but stable and safe. Confused and devastated by the lack of love and support, she tried to end her life when she was twelve years old, which she admitted was probably more to get attention than to "get away." When, despite this suicide attempt, her home life remained unchanged, Harriet's survival instincts kicked in. She decided that the best way to avoid the endless fights between her parents, her mom's verbal attacks, and the gnawing hunger due to lack of regular meals, was to hide in her room and bury herself in school books. This two-pronged approach of being invisible *and* an achiever, aka a straight-A student, seemed to pay off. She left home when she was seventeen, ready to take on the world.

Yet when her college classes became more difficult and her boyfriend started to cheat on her, another survival pattern kicked in, and Harriet became a procrastinator. Due to the lack of motivation and effort, she dropped out of college, stopped taking care of herself, and disconnected from her social network.

During our first session, she told me: "I want to stop shoving piles of mail into paper bags and throwing them in the back room when guests are coming. I want to get out of bed in the morning and face life without needing to schedule something to ensure that I will shower that day. I want to care about eating before I become so hungry that I'm cranky. I want to have a voice mailbox that isn't full. I want to stop being afraid to answer the phone when I don't recognize the caller's number. I want to live again."

For Harriet, the turnaround started when she became a mother: "When I looked at my baby daughter and saw what an innocent, loving soul she was, I realized at that moment that at some point, I too was that loveable. What could happen in my daughter's life that would no longer make her deserving of my love? *Nothing.*

There was a glimmer of recognition in that moment that I, too, must still be loveable." This glimmer sparked the young mother's willingness to heal the wounds of her past and grow beyond her survival patterns.

With more compassion and kindness toward herself, Harriet decided that rather than trying to strong-arm herself into becoming a healthier and better-functioning individual, she would focus on only one small improvement goal at a time. Harriet said that looking back, the first goal, which was simply to have breakfast and take a shower every day, became the catalyst for a complete transformation. "Now, one year later, the outside of me looks much different. I've lost fifty pounds. I smile more and have a calmer and more relaxed demeanor. I can even wear gray tops now because I no longer sweat at every social interaction. But the bigger changes happened inside. I used to feel alone in my sorrow and pain and hadn't even dreamed that I could *not* be depressed or anxious. There's not a moment in my life where I feel alone anymore. I always have me. That's enough. And what I didn't dare to hope for became a reality: I love myself."

STEP 4: EMPOWER THE PROCRASTINATOR

Let's look through the eyes of your inner procrastinator and evaluate how the previous steps impacted your resolve to protect through avoidance.

In Step 1, you are finally listened to and not just swatted away. You get answers to your questions and compassionate reassurances about your concerns. This, in itself, lightens the heavy weight of responsibility and makes you feel more open to considering that the conscious adult could potentially be trusted.

In Step 2, at the fork in the road, you, the procrastinator, are shown the negative consequences of your short-term living approach and how life beyond procrastination could be safe and more enjoyable and fulfilling. Being the procrastinator, your entire concept of navigating safely through time and space is put into question, which can be simultaneously devastating and freeing. Yet just seeing the map may not be enough for you to change course.

This is why Step 3 becomes so important. By taking ownership of the past and the present and crafting a simple and achievable plan that leads you into a brighter future, the conscious adult has introduced itself as the reliable leader to whom you, the procrastinator, can pass the baton. So far, so good.

Yet, as with all the other survival patterns, once the procrastinator's job is made obsolete, the logical question is: *Now what?* Since there's neither a retirement community for subconscious protectors, nor is it possible to get rid of a part of your mind, your best option is to give the procrastinator a new job description. But what is the procrastinator good at? No, it isn't frittering away time, it's actually the opposite.

You've probably seen this scenario plenty of times with your kids or nieces and nephews. After a long and full day without much time to rest, rather than gladly heading to bed, the kids put up a fight, insisting that they want to stay up with the adults because they're not tired at all. Yet the children's tirades, tears, and temper tantrums just prove they're wired-tired and in desperate need of getting some shut-eye. A similar phenomenon, though less rambunctious, also happens with adults in the form of *bedtime procrastination*.[13] If you know you should hit the pillow and get some rest after a long and busy day, but you somehow find yourself spending the next several hours glued to the TV or getting lost in the endless maze of YouTube, you're probably dealing with bedtime procrastination.

According to Christopher Winter, author of *The Sleep Solution*, bedtime procrastination is especially prevalent in people who never seem to have time for themselves because they're too busy taking care of others. In a study published in *Frontiers in Psychology*, researchers from the Netherlands found that people have difficulty sticking to their intended bedtime after a particularly task-oriented and demanding day. Interestingly, the extent of bedtime procrastination correlated directly with how many desires the participants had resisted during the previous day, such as having a meal, taking a nap, reaching out to a friend, or watching something casual on the internet.[14]

You may wonder why the procrastinator would want to prevent you from getting your well-deserved slumber. What does this survival pattern try to protect you from? It appears that the subconscious considers over-busyness a potential threat because it may lead to a lack of balance and joy in life. The correlation between resisting pleasure and procrastinating bedtime suggests that by focusing on pleasurable activities, the procrastinator wants you to make up for the missed opportunities to have some lightness and fun. And this is exactly what the job of the empowered version of the procrastinator can be.

Don't get me wrong, I'm not an advocate of bedtime procrastination. Yet once the procrastinator no longer focuses on survival, it can support you in creating a more balanced lifestyle, with a healthy and enjoyable equilibrium between your ambitions and obligations and your pleasure and leisure. Overcoming procrastination doesn't mean you have to fall into overdoing and overachieving patterns. Focusing on the little things that make life sweeter and more enjoyable is a valuable talent for inviting more balance into your life. So the job of the empowered procrastinator can be to remind you of the importance of having fun, giving yourself a break, and rewarding yourself with simple treats.

The empowerment of the procrastinator and its balancing effect on your lifestyle is a perfect example of how you can transform different survival patterns to create more fulfillment, joy, and peace in your life. And this chapter shows once again that when it comes to your subconscious mind, there is always more potential to discover and harness.

PART III

Taking a Stand

From Pleasing Others to Loving
Your Authentic Self

9

THE CHAMELEON PATTERN

Fitting In at All Costs

Don't ask me who I am, just tell me who you want me to be.

As we all know, chameleons are fascinating creatures with a unique ability to change the color of their skin to blend in with their environment. Of course, there are other animals—such as the octopus, the squid, or the cuttlefish—that can make themselves *disappear* by rapidly mimicking their surroundings. Yet, it is the chameleon that is used as an analogy to describe the human pattern of adjusting our behavior, attitudes, and maybe even beliefs to please those we're with.

Imagine the following scenarios: You're sitting at the weekly business lunch. As usual, your boss holds court, boasting about their adventures during their latest exotic vacation. Suddenly you notice that everyone at your table is hanging on every word, alternating, in unison, between smiling, nodding, and laughing. But the worst is, you behave precisely the same, as if somebody had taken over your brain via remote control. After work, you meet with your friends for drinks, and even though you've complained to your spouse many times that you no longer enjoy the pernicious mix of gossiping, teasing, and throwing back shots, somehow you still fit right in. Come

Sunday, you're at your parents' for supper, as usual, dutifully eating your mom's pot roast and potatoes, even though you've been trying to stick to a vegan diet. Sounds familiar?

As much as we believe in free will and like to perceive ourselves as unique, independent-thinking individuals, deeply ingrained inside we all have the desire to belong and fit in, which is why we tend to conform to the norms and expectations of whatever group we interact with. This conformity can be as simple as adjusting how we dress, the topics we talk about, the movies we watch, the sports we play, and the music we listen to. Having something in common makes it easier to relate and interact. During conversations, we may subconsciously mimic others by adopting facial expressions, posture, physical tics (finger tapping, foot shaking), accent, and rhythm of speech to signal that we are harmless and facilitate understanding and cooperation. In fact, Neuro-linguistic Programming teaches methods such as *matching* and *mirroring* to create instant rapport between the practitioner and the client.[1]

The need to be a part of a cohort started when humans were still on the lower end of the food chain, exposed to wild animals and harsh weather conditions. From an evolutionary perspective, tribalism was an adaptive necessity; due to our rather inferior physical strength and resilience, we humans were ill-equipped to survive on our own. With tribalism came rituals of social bonding, rules that needed to be obeyed, and commitments that prevented members from putting their individual needs and wants before the safety of the clan. Those who didn't want to conform to the norms and agreements of the collective were either punished or ostracized from the group. Therefore, trying to be *like* everybody, in order to be *liked by* everybody, became an indispensable survival pattern.

As humans evolved and figured out how to conquer nature and the elements, the rigid tribal structures were gradually replaced by more loosely connected collectives, such as villages, cities, and nations, which allowed more freedom of self-expression and a greater diversity of lifestyles. What didn't change was our need to belong. According to a recent survey, approximately half of Americans feel lonely, indicating that despite our freedom to express our individuality and pursue our unique paths to happiness, humans are social creatures who innately crave to be a part of something.[2] The deeply rooted longing to belong and the associated fear of being rejected and abandoned drive the chameleon pattern to exchange individualism for commonality.

Provided that adapting our behavior to create a sense of connectedness with those we interact with is helpful, when does the chameleon pattern become a problem?

THE NATURAL NEED TO BELONG

When Terry retired from a stellar career in the health services department of her state, she started to suffer from anxiety, depression, and a sense of feeling completely lost. She couldn't understand how she had suddenly turned from being a confident, capable, courageous woman into, as she called it, "a pathetic and insecure loser version of myself." Self-compassion apparently wasn't Terry's forte.

When I asked about her childhood, her anxious irritation dissipated, as she told me about the sweet and sensitive girl she used to be. "See, the problem was," she said, "my father, who was funny and kind, was rarely at home. On the other hand, my mother was rather stoic and strict, and my sister and my brother were loud, self-absorbed, and demanding. There didn't seem to be a lot of room and patience for me to share my feelings and my sensitive side.

"For example, I decided to give my parents a special Christmas gift when I was five years old. On Christmas morning, I presented Mom and Dad with a little box I'd wrapped as artfully as I could. Once my parents opened their gift, they looked at me incredulously. 'I'm giving you the gift of God's love,' I happily announced. I felt so proud of my idea; I wanted them to know that I loved them and so did God. But instead of being touched by my sweet present, the whole family burst out laughing because the box was empty. I couldn't stand the shame and embarrassment and ran up to my room, crying and scolding myself for having such a stupid plan. At that moment, I decided that the best way to stay out of trouble was to keep my head down and my feelings to myself."

However, Terry's childhood only became more challenging for her. Her father, a successful executive of a multinational corporation, had been promoted to the go-to guy for the company's struggling outfits. From that time on, the only constant in her life was change. Every two years, Terry's dad uprooted his family as he was dispatched from the Midwestern United States to Costa Rica, Brazil, Belgium, Austria, and back to the US. As a sensitive kid, Terry suffered the most from constantly starting over again.

"The last day in the old school and the first day in the new school were always the hardest," she said. "I had barely time to dry my tears from saying good-bye to my friends when I had to deal with the anticipatory anxiety of whether the kids in the new school would accept me, let alone having to get used to a new culture, a different language, a difficult climate—you name it. But you know, at some point, all the pain, fear and worry were so exhausting that I decided to just focus on blending in and not getting too attached to anybody or any place." In other words Terry's chameleon pattern kicked in. Whether she lived in the Midwestern US, South America, or Europe, she could quickly figure out how she needed to dress, talk, and behave to be accepted by most people in her schools and neighborhoods. So, where is the problem? Isn't the ability to adapt and conform a desirable skill, especially in her situation?

In Terry's own words, the problem was that nobody—including herself—knew who she truly was. "With all the moving, adjusting, and focusing on how I was supposed to be, I never had the chance to ask myself what I was about and what I really wanted. As a result, people could easily manipulate me into believing that fulfilling their needs and expectations was more important than taking care of my own. And since acceptance and a sense of belonging were so crucial to me, I was happy catering to others." Not surprisingly, once Terry finished high school, she decided to become a nurse. Once she began her career, and it became apparent that she had a lot of talent for this line of work, she was quickly promoted into leadership positions, all the way up to becoming the head nurse in her department.

Terry loved her job and thoroughly enjoyed making a difference in her community. Her chameleon pattern seemed to fade away as a new ambitious, brave, and results-oriented side of her took over. She no longer tried to accommodate and conform to others because, for the first time in her life, she felt seen and appreciated for her unique contributions. Even when, years later, her husband became involved in a cultish religious organization and tried to sway her to join, she stood her ground and chose to divorce him rather than follow a group she didn't care for.

A couple of years after the divorce, the hospital Terry worked for "nudged" her into retirement to make room for a younger successor. At first, Terry felt excited to finally have time for travel, hobbies, and making new friends. However, shortly after her last day of work, she felt overcome by a heavy cloud of anxiety and depression. It hit her hard when she realized that her entire self-worth had hinged on her work and that without it, she still didn't know who she was. Almost overnight, her personality reverted to that of a scared and insecure child in dire need of finding a place she belonged to.

In her panic, Terry decided to move in with one of her brothers, who also had just retired. Terry figured that living with her brother and sister-in-law would provide her with the stability and security she craved. Unfortunately, her brother, who had always been controlling and judgmental, also struggled with his new role as a retiree. But unlike Terry, he expressed his difficulties by becoming even more demeaning and demanding toward his sister and his wife, which further triggered Terry's chameleon pattern.

Terry started to dress like her brother, speak with a similar tone, and share his interest in fishing and watching documentaries while walking on eggshells and staying keenly aware of any potential mood shifts in her sibling. However, in the end, the blend-in strategy seemed to backfire as Terry's brother became even more disrespectful, impatient, and abrasive, eventually forcing Terry to move out and find her own place. After a few months of living alone, Terry's depression and anxiety became so overwhelming that she finally reached out for help, which is how we met.

Terry's example shows the challenges and limitations of the chameleon pattern. Like the invisibility pattern, its mission is to ensure our safety by not drawing any negative attention. However, in contrast to the invisibility pattern, the pleasing chameleon doesn't avoid others but believes that our survival depends on their acceptance and support. This is why its motto is more along the lines of "Better fit in and live on, then stand out and be gone."

THE CHAMELEON IN YOU

Human chameleons don't enjoy the best reputation. Usually, we perceive them as spineless yeasayers whose opinions change like weathervanes in the wind. Therefore, it may be hard to accept that we all have inner chameleons. It may help to know that the inner chameleon isn't to be confused with an *opportunist,* whose motives are cunning, self-serving, and usually focused on gaining power and control. The intentions of the chameleon are more innocently centered around the basic needs to be safe and to belong. As in Terry's case, this pattern often originates during childhood as a self-protective response to a series of destabilizing circumstances, busy parents, bullying siblings, and frequent moves.

From a child's perspective, the chameleon's accommodating ways can appear as the most promising strategy to make it through our early years.

As I mentioned, the problem with living in the chameleon survival pattern is that you mainly identify with your surroundings, and therefore have difficulties developing a true sense of self. As you deny yourself the natural inclination to explore and express your authenticity, your insecurity, and thus your need to be accepted by others, only increases. Questions such as, "Who am I? What are my gifts?" and "What do I want?" are for chameleons as foreign as the concept that others could value and appreciate them for who they truly are.

Here are some classic signs that your inner chameleon is running at least a part of your life:

- You fluently change your persona to match the people you're with.
- You don't have strong opinions or preferences.
- Others easily sway you.
- You're good at reading people.
- If you think differently than others, you stay quiet, because you prefer to be liked than to be right.
- Even if you don't have a good time, you pretend to enjoy yourself out of fear of disappointing your company.
- When you're not sure how to be in a social situation, you look to the behavior of others for cues.
- After you interacted with others, you often ruminate on what you may have said or done wrong or what people may think about you.
- You feel empty, uncomfortable, and somewhat lost on your own.
- Even though it can be exhausting, being in a group of people makes you feel safe.

So, are you getting closer to acknowledging your inner chameleon? Even if you didn't have to deal with a difficult childhood, this survival pattern kicks in from time to time. In fact, given the increasingly paramount influence of the internet and social media on how we connect and interact socially, the chameleon pattern has been in high demand. And there are four reasons why.

HOW BLENDING IN BECAME MAINSTREAM

In our modern society, it isn't easy to establish a clear understanding of ourselves and the world. There seems to be an infinite number of influential voices and sources that tell us who and how we're supposed to be. Just a few decades ago, we mainly relied on our families, friends, teachers, religious leaders, and other authority figures in our communities to give us direction about how to grow up and navigate life. Now we're facing an overwhelming amount of opinions to sift through. Every day, we're bombarded by messages about what's acceptable, what's desirable, and what makes us losers. The ensuing confusion and growing uncertainty about what advice and trends to follow causes many a chronic state of stress and anxiety. When it comes to the chameleon, there are, in particular, four fears that can trigger this pattern to jump into gear: the fear of conflict and rejection, the fear of being average, the fear of missing out, and the fear of "the others." All four have the fear of *not belonging* in common, yet each of the fears elicits a slightly different response in the chameleon, depending on what group it wants to align with and belong to.

1. The Fear of Standing Out
I was nineteen years old when I started the fifteen months of mandatory military service in Germany. On my way to the air force base I was assigned to, my stomach was in knots, not knowing what I should expect. How would it feel to wear a uniform or

shoot a gun? Would bootcamp be tough and the drill sergeants merciless? And would I get along with my bunkmates? One thing I knew for sure from the beginning was that my name would be read out loud in front of many other recruits. Bad enough that, being six foot four, it was already challenging to blend in. But my unusual-even-for-German-standards first name, Friedemann, which means man of peace (rather unfitting for the occasion), would surely stand out like a ketchup stain on a white shirt. How I wished my parents would have named me Peter, Michael, or Hans.

Once I arrived at the base, my worries came true. Not only did I detect some snickering among the other recruits when the sergeant yelled my name across the parade ground, but he also called my name "completely ludicrous" and "impossible to remember." Without hesitation, the sergeant declared that from now on, I should be called *Julius,* which is my second name. You can imagine that after this introduction, my inner chameleon was on high alert, vigilantly studying the other young privates to figure out how to become one of them.

You're probably familiar with how your inner chameleon responds to this initial fear of drawing unwanted attention. First, it makes you scramble to determine the norms and expectations of the group or the authority figure it deems to be in charge. Then it makes you take on camouflage by adjusting your appearance and behavior, with the attempt to strike the delicate balance between not standing out and still getting some acknowledgment and approval from others. Unlike the invisibility pattern, the chameleon doesn't like you to become unnoticeable and disappear. Instead, it aims for the sweet spot of being perceived as pleasant and acceptable without getting too much attention. Like a paper towel holder in the kitchen, you know that it's there, but you neither love nor hate it.

Often the fear of standing out is limited to a specific context and set of people. During your school years, being seen as a loner wasn't an option. You needed to belong to a group, such as the popular kids, the athletes, the artists, or if all else failed, to the geeks or the goths. Later in life, you notice the chameleon pattern during get-togethers with the in-laws. Even though you dread the obligatory visit, the idea of rocking the relationship scares you more. So you show up, bite your tongue, and play nice. You laugh at the inappropriate jokes of your spouse's dad and nod in agreement with his extreme right-wing views, even though you've been a card-carrying Democrat your entire life. Or at book club meetings, you serve snacks and sweets you usually avoid, pretend that you've read the whole book, and drink far more wine than you intended to. And in your family, you're the only one who gets along with your annoying brother because you never question his opinions, giving him precisely what he needs, which is to ALWAYS be right. Even with your spouse, you may from time to time turn to the chameleon pattern by holding yourself back from doing something on your own, or going along with their preferences to avoid an argument. Yes, good relationships are made of a thousand compromises, but isn't it equally true that good relationships need honesty and authenticity to grow and thrive?

For many people, the fear of standing out isn't just limited to specific situations but has become the creed they live by. The so-called traditionalists firmly adhere to societal norms and values, such as family, religion, and hard work. They find safety and comfort in conforming because they value being loyal, law-abiding citizens rather than pursuing their unique dreams and purpose. Traditionalists believe in the importance of moving through life in an orderly fashion—finish school, start a career, get married, have kids, become involved in your community, retire, take care of the grandchildren—the end. While we may initially think of our parents and grandparents as the generations of traditionalists, I find that more and more young people are struggling with the notion of not being at the stage of their lives they're "supposed" to be. Some of my clients in their twenties and early thirties feel afraid of falling behind because they don't have a senior position at work, a mortgage, a family, or a retirement plan—and they don't like golden retrievers. Their inner chameleon is freaking out because it assumes that there's a blueprint for a *normal* life they must follow to be an acceptable member of society. The fear of standing out and the need to fit into the mold of the tribe make the chameleon blind and numb to the fact that we are all unique individuals and that we all have a particular set of qualities and talents, a specific purpose, and a path to follow that has never been walked before.

2. The Fear of Not Standing Out Enough

One of the great paradoxes in our modern society is that while we seem to have a strong urge to express and expose ourselves, we also have an increasing fear of being judged as not good enough. Or, as a friend once said, "We all want to stand out but are also terrified not to fit in." For many, the desire to be unique and the need to be accepted have become competing commitments. As peer pressure and social media–driven expectations have raised the stakes on what is cool, successful, and trending, they have also created new parameters for fitting in: "Keeping up with the Joneses" has been replaced with "Keeping up with the Kardashians."

Although the *fear of standing out* and *the fear of not standing out enough* both have *the fear of not belonging* in common, the former causes you to contract and blend in, while the latter drives you to do, have, and be more so you're not left behind. The chameleon pattern triggered by the first fear may replay critical remarks and stern statements your parents issued to keep you in line. The chameleon triggered by the second fear turns more to social media influencers for guidance about how to gain attention. You may spend most of your money on the newest gadgets, fashionable clothes, and the hippest clubs and restaurants. You may speak the slang of those you admire, stay up-to-date on the latest trends, and make sure your social media profile portrays somebody with an exciting lifestyle.

The chameleon of the standing-out-to-fit-in paradigm can turn into an inner critic who relentlessly compares you with others, pointing out what you have too little of and where you are too much, until one of the most self-destructive emotions emerges: shame. More than any other feeling, shame can make you feel small, inadequate, and completely worthless. The toxic combination of shame and fear increases the urge to do, have, or be extraordinary—no matter the cost.

A study by the All India Institute in New Delhi found that between October 2011 and November 2017, 259 people died while attempting to take selfies.[3] Almost three-quarters of those who died were men under the age of thirty. The researchers pointed out that most deaths occurred due to high-risk behavior, such as standing on a slippery cliff, playing with fire, or using firearms. Other dangerous trends to stand out are social media challenges that encourage daring and risky behavior, such as lighting parts of your body on fire, choking yourself to blackout, eating a spoonful of cinnamon, or rubbing an eraser on your skin until it causes abrasions. These contests have caused countless injuries and even fatalities worldwide, mainly among teenagers and young adults. At first, it may seem hard to understand that online *dares* encouraging participants to harm themselves would get any takers. But no matter how dangerous such games may appear, what counts more for most contestants is that these internet platforms allow them to escape their dull reality and their difficulties in relating to and connecting with others. Again, yearning for a sense of belonging overtakes common sense.

3. The Fear of Missing Out

Fear of missing out, or FOMO, is another phenomenon that has become more pervasive with the rise of social media. Yet personally, I experienced the fear of missing out long before Mark Zuckerberg was out of diapers. When I was thirteen years old, a couple of years before girls showed interest in me, a group of neighborhood boys started a bi-monthly dinner and games get-together. For me that sounded fun, and something much better to do on a Saturday night than sitting with my parents on the couch, eating Toast Hawaii with ketchup and watching either a silly show (Germans' sad attempt to be funny) or a badly dubbed Hollywood classic. Like most boys at that age, the arrival of testosterone in my system took me on emotional roller-coaster rides and often left me confused and insecure. Sensing my insecurity and desire to be included in their circle, these boys came up with a rather cruel game. They told me I would be invited to their dinner parties only if I collected enough points during the two weeks in between. Whether doing chores for them, helping them with homework, or playing tricks on smaller kids, each task gave me a random number of points. But as hard as it was to gain points, it was just as easy for these boys to take them away from me, usually for no apparent reason. I know kids can be mean, but my desperation for acceptance made me a willing participant in their scheme.

The fear of missing out made me humiliate myself and lose sight of reality. I started to believe that there was nothing more important than belonging to this group and became more stressed about gathering enough points. Thank God it took me less than a year (and a new friend) to figure out that these kids really wanted me at their parties because I was fun to be around, and thanks to my mom, I was a rather good cook. Once I told them I no longer had time for their silly games, their invitations kept coming anyway.

Fear of missing out is the combination of needing to stay continually connected with others and their activities, and constantly worrying that they might have exciting experiences without you. While most people experienced FOMO long before the name was invented, the prevalence of this fear has grown exponentially since the invention of social media. There are about three billion social media users worldwide, or more than 40 percent of the world's population.[4] In the US, almost 80 percent have a social media profile.[5] Since Facebook, Instagram, and its cousins make it possible to have "friends" worldwide, for many, social media has become the predominant form of socializing. The advantage of this extensive connectivity is that we can quickly get in touch with an unlimited number of people, stay updated on their lives, and get an overall sense of not being alone in the world. Several studies showed that social media users are often driven by loneliness to spend several hours daily scanning, chatting, and posting. Social isolation may be one of the reasons why, as some research suggests, people who suffer from depression and social anxiety feel drawn to social media interactions as their primary leisure time activity.[6]

Yet the downside of a social-media-focused social life is that we become inundated with an overwhelming amount of information, opinions, and options—more than we can digest or take advantage of. Researchers demonstrated that while some participants gained a certain amount of satisfaction from interacting with their virtual friends and monitoring their activities, others reported that social media use made them even more anxious and depressed.[7] One study found that among college students, 75 percent of participants struggled with some degree of FOMO. Those who suffered the most were also more likely to visit social platforms first thing in the morning and right before going to bed. Conversely, researchers discovered that limiting access to social media resulted in a decrease in loneliness and depression.[8]

A client of mine described it this way: "The pain of missing out and feeling abandoned is unbearable. At first, it feels like panic. I can't think rationally and feel that my whole life has just fallen apart. Then I spiral into self-loathing, telling myself that nobody loves me and that I'll always be alone. I even have thoughts such as *I'll never belong anywhere*, and *the world would be a better place without me*. I know I'm overly dramatic, but it feels so real. Then some instinct kicks in, and I start frantically looking for a way to connect with somebody or just post something interesting on Instagram. As soon as I get a response or a like I feel somewhat relieved, but also more determined than ever to never be left out again."

FOMO is a significant call to action for the chameleon because it brings up the fear of not being good enough and the fear of abandonment in equal force. In particular, social media-triggered FOMO becomes a massive challenge because there are just too many options available, too many places to be, and too many roles to play. You constantly scan for fun events you don't want to miss out on. You worry when you don't know what your friends are up to. And you end up feeling shattered when you find out they're having a blast without you. The chameleon urges you to post about your "fun" times and never allows you to disconnect from the scene, even if you're ill or on vacation. To avoid the pain of missing out, you spend more time trying to keep up and stay in touch with others rather than focusing on what you can enjoy and experience in the present moment.

4. The Fear of "The Others"

Guido Menzio, an Italian-born economist at the University of Pennsylvania, calmly scribbled notes about a math problem he was working on while waiting for his plane to depart. The woman seated next to him, watching him write some strange formulas she didn't understand, felt increasingly uncomfortable with the man. Whether it was just his obscure notes or his dark hair and beard, minutes before take-off, she alerted the cabin crew that she might be sitting next to a possible terrorist. A few moments later, the captain approached the unsuspecting economist and asked him to get off the plane to meet with FBI agents that were waiting for him at the gate.

Cases like this are more and more common. Fueled by the fear of terrorism, people eye their fellow travelers with great suspicion, especially if they appear Middle Eastern. Although the notion of "better safe than sorry" is understandable, it also bears the risk of us becoming increasingly prejudiced and paranoid.

We are living in a strange dichotomy. On the one hand, we seem to be growing closer together. Modern technology allows us to connect and interact instantly with almost anyone around the world. The media feeds us live updates about any global developments. Traveling to the most exotic places has become more accessible and affordable. And within our communities, there appears to be a greater diversity of cultural influences, and more freedom to pursue and express our unique lifestyles. On the other hand, political movements that base their ideology on fear and anger against those who don't share their same values and beliefs are rapidly picking up steam.

Growing up in Germany, we were taught early and thoroughly about the horrific atrocities the generations before had committed during the Third Reich. I remember how guilty and ashamed I felt being German when I learned about the Holocaust and the many unimaginable acts of cruelty Jews, Romas, gays, lesbians, and others endured. Yet, when I visited Mauthausen, a concentration camp in Austria, everything I'd heard, read about in books, and seen in films became much more real. I'll never forget the eerie laboratories where doctors conducted horrendous medical experiments, the gas chambers disguised as group shower facilities, and the crematory ovens, which shockingly still emitted a stench of smoke and ashes. The crimes against humanity Germans committed must always be remembered to honor the millions who suffered and died, and to remind us that history will repeat itself if we're not careful.

I often wondered how a little Austrian man could have seduced an entire nation to make him their *Fuehrer*. Why did most Germans believe in this sociopathological ego-maniac as their savior, and why did they accept his lies and doctrines as the truth? How could ordinary people denounce their neighbors and close their eyes to their government's brutality and inhumanity? My parents, who were teenagers during World War II, told me that when Hitler arrived on the political scene, Germans were desperate for a change. Still reeling from the aftermath of World War I and the Treaty of Versailles, there was hope that someone like Hitler would make Germany great again.

A little more than seventy years after the fall of Nazi Germany, we face a global resurgence of populism and nationalistic tendencies. Most Western nations observe a growing popularity of politicians who use divisiveness and "us versus them" messages to fuel the frustration and worry of those who already feel disenfranchised by the establishment. And similar to the rise of Hitler, religious and political movements worldwide are preying on people's worries, fears, and anger as they are looking for someone to make their lives safer and better again. To obey *God's word,* abortions, transgendered individuals, and homosexuality are labeled as evil sins. To preserve jobs for US citizens, illegal immigrants are locked in cages like animals. To protect the nation, refugees who desperately flee their war-torn and poverty-stricken regions are eyed warily as terrorists.

The segregation of a group of people to preserve the tribe is a fundamental protective mechanism that has been abused throughout history. And now, with perceived threats and conspiracy theories broadcasted 24/7 via biased news outlets and social media, racism, xenophobia, and homophobia are on the rise. The humanitarian philosophy of "live and let live" is replaced with the self-protective "us versus them" dogma.

The chameleon pattern makes us respond to this kind of fear-mongering and demonization of others, with the need to huddle more closely with those we feel connected to and protected by. In the extreme, this can lead us to blindly follow the perceived leader of the tribe while justifying our fear- and anger-fueled actions with broad generalizations, close-mindedness, and dismissing contradictory ideas. The atrocious attack on the US Capitol on January 6, 2021, is just one of the more recent examples of this dangerous trend. We must be aware that prejudice is one of our mind's survival patterns to make us feel safe. We fear that which we don't understand, and avoid or attack that which we're afraid of. Preconceived notions about those who think, believe, and live differently from us are self-protective patterns.

I am pretty sure that most people see themselves as accepting and open-minded and would feel insulted being called prejudiced. Yet new populistic movements have created a divide among families and friends. Fundamental values of decency, honesty, and compassion no longer seem to unite nations but are denounced by some as wimpy, unpatriotic, liberal, and "woke."

Now, you may consider yourself tolerant, progressive, humanitarian, or a devout follower of your religious beliefs and, therefore, unaffected by the fear of others. Yet have you noticed that you feel a sense of righteousness and superiority whenever you watch a political program that supports your views or discuss the injustice in the world with like-minded friends? Instead of being curious about those on the other side of the political spectrum or having empathy for their fears, anger, and confusion, you find solace in the fact that you and your friends share all the same outrage and disgust for those "deplorables" who are *obviously* ignorant and completely misled by populists.

Whether in the schoolyard when we were little, or more recently in the office at work, many of us have taken part in or at least witnessed bullying. We may have silently stood by with a strange mixture of pity for targets and relief that we weren't in their shoes, yet unwilling to stand up for them. When the chameleon pattern is triggered, our need to belong and be safe can quickly suppress our decency and humanity. Yet don't chastise the chameleon as wrong or evil. Instead, please take this as another reminder that we shouldn't ignore any of our protective patterns because they have all the potential to bring out the worst and the best in us. It all depends on whether they make us focus on surviving or thriving.

10

SELF-REFLECTION

The Key to Owning Your Truth

*How can we be at peace with ourselves
when we suppress our truth just to appease others?*

One of the primary reasons you've probably picked up this book is that you're tired of how living in survival mode makes you feel anxious and powerless. By now, you've already seen how each survival pattern has its own way of making you give some of your power to the people or circumstances that appear threatening to you:

- In **victim** mode, you lose the power to grow from the past by holding on to anger and resentment toward those who've hurt you.
- In **invisibility** mode, you diminish the power of self-expression by suppressing your inborn desire to be seen and heard.
- In **procrastinator** mode, you relinquish the power to impact your life by deeming your goals, tasks, and responsibilities too challenging and uncomfortable to accomplish.

Now, in **chameleon** mode, you hand over the power of individualization to anyone who may provide you with a sense of safety and belonging. As you assimilate and adjust to their thoughts, beliefs, and behaviors, you gradually abandon your natural inclination to discover and express your true self.

If life is a journey, tagging along behind others certainly won't help you find, let alone stay on, your path to creating the most meaningful and fulfilling existence. Just as conforming yourself to the desires of others won't help you find out who you are. The problem with the inner chameleon is that it isn't curious about who you are, because it assumes that whoever that might be isn't enough to get approval from others. Therefore, this part of your subconscious stalls your self-awareness efforts and instead uses its heightened sensitivity to scan your environment for clues on how to be and act. Sure, this strategy may sometimes work to avoid hurtful rejection and loneliness. Yet, as with the invisibility pattern, the painful regret of denying yourself your birthright to discover and express your unique self will eventually be much greater.

What if you could get in touch with the real you, your essence, the core aspect of your true self? And what if you could show your chameleon that sharing and living from this authentic truth is far safer and more rewarding than merely surviving in the obscurity of conformity?

HOW YOU DISCOVER YOUR AUTHENTIC TRUTH

No matter whether your chameleon survival mode has been dominating your life or only made an appearance once in a while, like most, you probably haven't spent much time reflecting on your authentic truth. And so, you may wonder, "I have been like this all my life, is there more to me? How can I start looking for something if I have no clue what it is? And what if I find my authentic truth, but I don't like it?" First, like all of us, you are so much more than you have believed you are. And you probably already had some experiences where you were in touch with your authentic self, which is also directly connected to your innate goodness. So no matter what you discover about your truth, more than likely, these findings will enhance your life in significant ways.

So let's assume that you agree that it's desirable to know, trust, and be your authentic self. Yet, you may ask, "Exactly what parts of me constitute the true self that I should know, trust, and be?" The quest for your truth isn't like searching for the holy grail, hoping to stumble across something you don't even know exists. Trying to connect to your truth is more like facing a 5,000-piece jigsaw puzzle you just poured from its box onto the table. It all starts with gradually filling in the blanks and putting the pieces in place. Think about *love* as an example. While it's difficult to describe its essence accurately and fully grasp its countless layers, you know how love feels to you and how you express it. So, if you were to try to define what love is, you would start by recounting your experiences with this most powerful emotion. Similarly, the best way to start searching for your authentic truth is to take a closer look at how you've shared yourself with the world so far.

When it comes to gaining a sense of our truth by looking back on how we showed up in life until now, we can either have the mindset of an explorer or an exterminator. Unfortunately, most of us are using the latter by meticulously highlighting our faults and shortcomings rather than acknowledging our strengths and gifts. Our parents, peers, preachers, or teachers may have instilled in us that we shouldn't feel too good about ourselves because (a) this would only lead to complacency and arrogance, and (b) there is always plenty of room for improvement. Thus, we are used to focusing more on our flaws and failures than on our gifts and strengths, which creates a somewhat distorted and negative self-image.

How can we develop a sense of self if we're only aware of what's missing? Just as we can't define a dog by the lack of its ability to purr, we can't define ourselves by only paying attention to what we're not. As you've experienced reconnecting to the treasures of your innocent self, we're all so much more than we allow ourselves to believe—and more than the feedback of others made us believe. When we shine the light of awareness on our innate treasures and qualities, we gain a much more accurate and fair perspective on who we are—and our purpose for being here. So let's go deeper and further into discovering the truth of your magnificent authenticity.

GETTING IN TOUCH WITH YOUR GOOD BITS

Let's start this journey to connect to your authentic truth by taking an inventory of your life. As you contemplate some of the highs and lows you've experienced, you'll better understand the traits, gifts, and qualities that defined you. Going back to the jigsaw analogy, the more of these inner qualities you can piece together, the easier it will be for you to gain a sense of that overarching self, the authentic you that is the source of all of your gifts.

Approach this reflection on yourself with an open mind and a kind heart. And try not to brush aside accomplishments or obstacles, telling yourself they weren't unique or challenging enough. The goal is for you to gain awareness, acceptance, and appreciation for how you've shown up in your life without judgment or comparison.

With that goal in mind, answer the following questions:

- What are six of your accomplishments in life? (An accomplishment is any goal you reached, any success you experienced, or any positive change you made, no matter how small or big. It can range from learning to ride a bike to memorizing the multiplication table, leaving your home to start your own life, getting married, et cetera.)
- What are six challenges and obstacles you've overcome? (Maybe you struggled with kids who bullied you in school or

your parents separating. Maybe you were ill or had an accident and had to go through a long recovery process. Maybe you quit smoking or dealt with a painful breakup. Challenges and obstacles are any situations that ask you to dig deep and find the resources and motivation to keep going.)

- What are six happy memories in your life?
- Your truth is less defined by your actions and more by the inner strengths that fueled them. From the list of personal qualities below, choose for each accomplishment, obstacle, and happy memory two personal qualities that helped you get there. Be inquisitive and find different gifts and strengths for each memory (This list of personal qualities is certainly not complete, so feel free to add traits you think also describe you.)
- From the list below, which are the five qualities you express the most in your day-to-day life?
- Which personal qualities do you value but haven't been able to express? And how would your life be different if you could share these qualities? (For example, you have been too busy to travel and be adventurous or to explore your creativity. Or you love learning and would like to go back to school but have been bogged down by financial constraints.)
- If you got stranded on a deserted island, which of the personal qualities would you rely on?
- Which qualities do you admire the most in others?
- Ask two people who love and care about you which of your qualities they value most.

PERSONAL QUALITIES

Adventurous / accepting / altruistic / ambitious / attractive / autonomous / authentic / balanced / bold / calm / charismatic / committed / compassionate / confident /

consistent / cooperative / courageous / creative / curious / dependable / determined / devoted / diligent / disciplined / diverse / eager to learn / easy-going / efficient / empathetic / enthusiastic / expressive / fair / faithful / free / friendly / forgiving / funny / generous / giving / good / gracious / grateful / happy / hard working / harmonious / helpful / honest / humble / humorous / imaginative / independent / innocent / inquisitive / insightful / intelligent / intuitive / joyous / jovial / kind / knowledgable / learning / listening / lively / loving / loyal / motivated / open-minded / optimistic / organized / outgoing / patient / passionate / peaceful / persuasive / playful / polite / purpose-driven / reliable / resilient / resourceful / respectful / responsible / service-focused / serious / sincere / selfless / sensitive / sociable / spiritual / strong / thoughtful / trusting / trustworthy / warm / wise

While answering these nine questions isn't enough to describe all of who you are, it allows your chameleon self to realize that you're so much more than a reflective pool for others. Are you getting a glimpse of your authentic self? Let's take your body as an analogy. Each body part has an essential and unique role, but taken alone, none of them is sufficient to define the entirety. Only when all parts are integrated into an overriding wholeness and governed by cellular wisdom does your body become fully functioning. Just as your limbs and organs don't explain your whole body, your true self isn't only a collection of the personality qualities you expressed or gravitated to the most. What defines your uniqueness is the essence, or truth, which is the source and nexus of all your traits and qualities. It's impossible to capture this essence in words, but you can certainly sense it. Sounds too esoteric? Maybe. But let's imagine that connecting to such a source within would transform your understanding of yourself—and consequently change your life. Wouldn't it then be worth it to send the skeptical part of your mind on a little coffee break so that you can fully immerse yourself in discovering your essence?

WHAT IS YOUR ESSENCE?

Before we go on the journey to connect and realign with your essence, I would like to address some questions and doubts you may still ponder.

Let's assume for a moment that there's a part of your consciousness that existed before you were conceived and will continue to exist beyond the expiration date of your physical body. This notion isn't new to you if you have any form of spiritual belief. And if you're agnostic or atheist, you probably still agree that even newborn babies have particular traits that distinguish them from others. And if not, take the notion of your essence metaphorically as a reminder for your inner chameleon that you're a unique individual with more to offer than just trying to be like everybody else.

Admittedly, although I grew up Lutheran and believed in the existence of a soul, my science-trained mind initially frowned upon the notion of an essence. But the fact is that ever since I got in touch with my essence during a time when I felt lost and confused, I'm at peace and at home with myself in ways I've never experienced before. Since then, I've seen similar transformational changes in many of my clients, who despite their initial skepticism, wept when they connected to that most authentic aspect of themselves for the first time. Therefore, I trust that we all carry an essence, a source of undeniable truth underneath our stories, beliefs, and patterns. While as children, we still remember this truth, eventually, this awareness fades away as we're trying to cope with the pressure and expectations of our parents, teachers, and peers.

But no matter how much we may have lost touch with our essence, it remains steady and available at the core of our being. It's the source from where we can draw the most powerful aspects of ourselves, such as unconditional love, compassion, selflessness, and forgiveness, even for those who have hurt us the most. It's the light that gives us hope, strength, and direction as we pass through the deeper and darker valleys of our lives. And it's that inner wisdom that knows who we are, what we desire, and why we're here. In nature, a tiny seed contains all the information and potential to grow into a tree, a lion, or a human being. Similarly, our essence holds all the information and potential we need to evolve into the fullest expression of our truth.

Many people equate the search for their truth with finding a purpose for their existence, which they hope could be a career, an activity, or a new role in life, that will bring them the peace and happiness they have been longing for. However, to know *your* purpose, you need first to know yourself, which is why this form of truth searching has it backward. And here's why: Truth-based purpose is about making our unique contributions to the world. These contributions aren't necessarily about pursuing illustrious careers; just because we're doing meaningful work, doesn't mean we're living our truth. In my case, being a physician wasn't in alignment with my essence since I felt mostly drained and unfulfilled during that time.

Furthermore, we can make authentically purposeful contributions with seemingly very little impact on the world and without any acknowledgment from others. We may find our purpose in feeding stray cats in our neighborhood, helping refugees to get settled, growing a small garden in the middle of a city that serves as a sanctuary for insects and birds, or creating art that only a few can appreciate. We may not feel that we're living our purpose until later in life when we find our calling as a loving grandparent or a dedicated caretaker for our ailing spouse. The point is, our essence isn't defined by what we do, but by who we are. Therefore, we can live in alignment with our truth, irrespective of what we do.

Often it's easier for us to see the truth or the essence in others than in ourselves. For example, what do you love about your parents, siblings, partner, or children? Are there specific characteristics you admire, adorable quirks that make you smile, or unique ways they make you feel loved, safe, valued, or cared for? And are you aware of their essence, even though you may not be able to describe it?

This quotation, often attributed to Albert Einstein (but the source is unknown), captures the notion of our essence beautifully: "We are slowed down sound and light waves, a walking bundle of frequencies tuned into the cosmos. We are souls dressed up in sacred biochemical garments and our bodies are the instruments through which our souls play their music."

When Danielle and I met, we quickly realized that what we felt for each other was more than just chemistry and infatuation. We felt a deep connection with each other because we could sense and appreciate each other's essence. Yet, even twenty years later, we still can't clearly define the other person's essence. However, connecting to it helped us never lose sight of why we fell in love with each other in the first place, no matter how much we've changed and grown.

The question "Who am I?" is as old as humankind. Yet most who've claimed to have found a clear answer probably just stopped digging deeper. Our mind is simply too limited to be able to comprehend the unlimited nature of our truth. As Eckhart Tolle said, "The ultimate truth of who you are is not I am this, or I am that, but I am."[1] The quest for our truth is a life-long journey because there's always more to explore and unearth. While I have gained a better understanding of many aspects of my truth throughout the years, I still can't describe to you what it's all about. For example, since Danielle and I moved to France, I discovered *Farmer Fred,* a part of me that loves riding tractors and horses, mowing fields, building fences, and sporting a five o'clock shadow. As long as we stay open, curious, and courageous enough to stretch our comfort zone, we'll be continuously surprised by what our essence reveals about us.

Searching for your truth doesn't mean you have to struggle with self-doubt and question everything you know about yourself. The opposite is true. On your quest for your essence, you'll reach a point where you feel at peace with yourself, as if you've found your way back home. You'll be comfortable in your skin, accepting of your gifts and shortcomings, and grounded in a deeper understanding and appreciation for what makes you a unique and essential part of the vast web of life.

I had the pleasure of interviewing Dr. Carla Manly, the author of *Joy from Fear* and *Aging Joyfully*. During our conversation, she shared that she believes that we're all born with pure joy, which shines brightly inside our hearts like a candle in a tea-light holder. As we experience disappointments, pain, fears, trauma, and sadness throughout our life, the candle holder accumulates the emotional baggage and limiting beliefs like layers of soot that gradually obstruct our view of the inner light of joy. In other words, when we feel dark and heavy, overwhelmed and bogged down by life's challenges, we need to remember that we haven't lost our innate joy; we've just lost *sight* of it.

I find this metaphor also perfectly fitting for our essence because most people, including myself, perceive that inner truth as a brilliant light at the center of our being. The roles we play, the identities we hold onto and the self-protective patterns we rely on are all layers that are supposed to hide our vulnerabilities and perceived limitations. Yet underneath, the light of our essence never stops radiating in its original strength, patiently waiting for us to rediscover who we truly are.

With the following deep exercise, you will be able to remove those protective layers that have obscured the awareness of your authenticity so that you can freely reconnect with your essence. Again, whether you take this journey literally or metaphorically, this process teaches your subconscious to release the survival-driven beliefs and patterns that govern your life so you can realign with your truth. You may want to repeat this process multiple times to gain more knowledge and insights about who you are.

• • • • • •

DEEP EXERCISE

REALIGN WITH YOUR ESSENCE

◊ Find a quiet space where you won't get disturbed for the next ten to fifteen minutes. Then set your intention to reconnect with the essence of who you are by peeling off all the false identities and beliefs about yourself you've accrued throughout the years. Now lean back, close your eyes, and take a few deep breaths in and out.

◊ Imagine entering a beautiful room that appears safe, cozy, and somehow familiar to you. You see a chaise longue in the middle of this warmly illuminated space, which invites you to rest and let go. As you're lying on its soft surface, stretching out comfortably, you immediately feel more peaceful and at ease than you have in a long time. All the tension and weight you've carried with you is lifting out of you, allowing you to finally relax.

◊ As you drift deeper and deeper into a blissful state of relaxation, a beam of light starts shining from above onto your body. At first, the light envelops you like a soft blanket, making you feel held and embraced like an innocent child. Then you notice how the rays of light further soften and relax your body—from the surface of your skin to the core of your being. You become lighter and lighter, weightless, like a feather, until the light gently scoops you up into the air. Higher and higher you float, until you reach that particular place, beyond time and space, from where you can look down and see your entire life's path—from now back into the past.

◊ From this bird's eye view, you can see yourself below, resting in the present moment, your physical body calmly waiting for you to eventually return from this journey. As you start following the path back into the past, you watch your life rewinding and yourself becoming younger and younger, more and more innocent and pure. Retracing the steps helps you to remember when and why you adopted certain survival patterns, and who you were before you did. You notice that by going back in time, the roles you've played, the beliefs you've taken on, and the identities you've relied on are gradually removed, like layers of old clothing covering your body.

◊ The more of these obstructive layers you release, the more you become aware of a light radiating from the core of your younger selves. At some point you reach your twenties, your teens, back to when you were ten years old, nine, eight, seven, six years . . . until you can see yourself as a tiny baby in your crib. Notice the light of this baby's essence radiating from its core through every pore of its being. You've already seen this brilliant light with all its purity and unlimited potential when you reconnected with your innocent self.

◊ Now float above your birth and watch how you courageously left the safety and comfort of your mother's womb. Can you appreciate that even as a tiny being, your innate desire to expand and express your truth, follow your path, and fulfill your mission was much stronger than the fear of the unknown? Then continue to float even further back when you were still a baby in your mother's womb. From month nine back to eight, seven, six . . . to when you were nothing but a fertilized egg, a single cell, beginning to settle in your mom's uterus.

◊ Take a deep breath, and go one step further back to arrive at the place before your conception and before you embodied. Float back to the origin of your consciousness, your limitless, infinite essence. You can imagine this source of your truth as a bright beam of light, a brilliant sun or a shimmering sea of liquid luminescence. Slowly descend from your vantage point and become aware of what you see, hear, smell, taste, and feel as you gently approach the light of your essence, enter it—and become one with it.

◊ Being immersed in your essence gives you a sense of wholeness, peace, and freedom, like finally returning home and realizing how much you have missed being there. And while you feel more closely connected to yourself than ever, you simultaneously feel one with the entire universe. A drop in a sea of light—you are the drop, and at the same time, you are also the entire ocean. Embrace the pure essence of who you are without trying to judge or define it. You may recognize qualities you already know about yourself, such as compassion, creativity, humor, love, and joy. However, ultimately, words can't do justice to its boundless nature. There is nothing for you to comprehend rationally. So just enjoy being reconnected with the most authentic aspect of your being.

◊ As the traveler from the present time, you may have brought with you some of your emotional baggage, self-defeating patterns, confusions, and limiting beliefs about yourself and the world. Here at the source of your truth, you can cleanse yourself from these residual layers, like washing away old sweat and grime in a clear, refreshing body of water. You can free yourself from anything that makes you feel worried, insecure, or not good enough. You can let go of the patterns of assimilating and deferring to others or the need to make yourself small and invisible.

◊ Reconnecting with your essence also realigns you with your life's mission, like a compass needle pointing north. You now understand that you came into this life with a far more significant purpose than just survival. This higher purpose, which we all have in common, is to discover and share with the world your authentic truth with its multitude of gifts, treasures, and talents. Your mission may be to become a source of goodness, love, kindness, and compassion, so those who feel lost and lonely realize they also belong and matter. Or shine the light of your essence as a beacon of hope and inspiration so that others will feel encouraged to live up to their potential. There is no need to overthink the specifics of your purpose. Trust that the more time you spend in alignment with your essence, the more clarity you will gain.

As you're now deeply connected with the source of your truth, you can ask any questions about yourself and your life. Your essence has all the information and wisdom you need to pursue a path toward a life of purpose and joy. For example, you might wonder:

- Is any aspect of my essence still hidden, needing more attention and space to be explored and expressed?
- Am I on the right path, or are there course corrections I need to make?
- What steps do I need to take to live beyond survival mode?
- What can I do to become the fullest expression of my truth?
- What is my unique mission for this life?
- How can I accept, appreciate, and love myself more?

Your answers may come to you straight away as words, insights, images, or just feelings and sensations. It's also possible that you may have illuminating dreams or find yourself in the next few days thinking, feeling, and acting with greater self-assuredness, from a place of *knowing who you are,* without being able to explain what that *knowing* means. But no matter how, you will get your answers.

◊ Continue to realign and recalibrate for a few more minutes within your essence and bask in the rewarding realization that you have found your way back home to yourself. Can you appreciate that who you are is enough—and whatever you choose to share with the world from this consciousness will make the difference you are meant to make?

◊ To complete this process, clear your past from your survival patterns by illuminating the entire path you were on with the light of your essence. Visualize how this light infuses all your younger selves, liberating them from self-sabotaging habits, so that each can stand tall and secure, filled with the brightness of their essence. As you follow your newly illuminated past back to the present moment, you feel a huge weight is lifted. You're coming back to the now with a clean slate, ready for a new beginning, poised to let your essence guide you on how to be the authentic and empowered creator of a joyful and fulfilling life.

◊ Gently float above now and smoothly enter your body and the light of your essence at your core. Take five long and deep breaths, and sense your light expanding until it fills all your cells and your electro-magnetic field six feet around you. Then, when you're ready, open your eyes, feeling renewed, refreshed, and remembered.

······

You may already notice a remarkable difference in how you feel about yourself after the first go-around of this process. Or it may take several visits to your source to feel more aligned with your truth. Yet, not to rain on your parade, you will most likely find out that the uplifting and self-empowering energy you gain from this journey doesn't always stay with you throughout the day. From feeling high on self-reflection, you can suddenly tumble into the familiar pit of self-doubt and insecurity. Does this mean that this process didn't work or that you're a hopeless case? Of course not. While it's desirable to stay in constant connection to our authentic truth, for most of us it takes time and commitment to get there. Yet rather than viewing resurfacing survival patterns as a devastating sign of defeat, remind yourself that *contrast* is one of the most effective and motivating learning tools.

Isn't it true that we appreciate our health much more after we've recovered from an illness? That honesty feels more essential after a betrayal? That we only realize how much some people mean to us when they are gone? In *Travels with Charley: In Search of America,* John Steinbeck wrote, "What good is the warmth of summer, without the cold of winter to give it sweetness." Once you have tasted the calm and centered sense of self-awareness that comes with being in alignment with your truth, dabbling once again with the fear of rejection or not fitting in will feel like returning to an old imprisonment after delighting in complete freedom. So don't label the return of your survival patterns as a failure. Appreciate how the contrast of how these habits make you feel gives you greater clarity and eagerness to approach your life in alignment with your authentic truth.

The *realign with your essence* process isn't enough to live through and from your truth. Going back to your source is like finding your true north again so you can continue your journey through life with an inner point of reference, sure-footed and undistracted by other people's judgment and opinions. Knowing your path is only the first step. Walking it is the thousands that come after. Like any traveler, to stay on your path you need to consult your compass frequently. At least now you can be sure that no matter how far you've strayed off, through the connection with your essence you will always find your way back.

PSYCHOLOGICAL FLEXIBILITY: THE BRIDGE TO AUTHENTIC LIVING

Remember Terry, who started to struggle with the chameleon pattern after she retired? Once she reconnected with her essence her confidence and self-worth dramatically improved—and were right away put to the test when a few days after our session, her upstairs neighbor had another one of his rowdy Wednesday night parties. In the past, she was too afraid to complain about the loud music, the laughing, the yelling, and the stench of marijuana descending on her bedroom. But not this time. When at 2 am the festivities were still in full swing, she marched up the stairs to give her neighbor a piece of her mind. He was a big guy in his early forties, who she usually wouldn't want to mess with. But something inside told her that she had to stand up for herself. When her neighbor opened the door and gave her a puzzled look, Terry politely but firmly explained that he needed to turn down the music and put out the joints. "I told him that this was a non-smoking building and that he had no right to pollute the air we were all breathing. Plus, most neighbors had to go to work tomorrow but couldn't sleep because of the ruckus he and his friends were making. At first, he swore at me and told me to get lost. But I wasn't backing down. I told him if he wouldn't shut the party down, I would call the police with a noise complaint. And I would also file a complaint with the landlord the next day. Before I left, I asked him if he understood what I was saying, and he just nodded. I don't know whether it was what I said or how I said it, but fifteen minutes later, all was quiet and the air smelled fresh again. I was so proud of myself and slept for nine hours straight."

Terry's transformation from a bashful girl to a badass lady is a powerful testimony to our infinite possibilities to change and grow. Now that you have a deeper appreciation for your authentic truth, you may also surprise yourself when you suddenly approach situations that used to make you feel small or anxious with a completely different attitude.

One of the constants in life is change. While change is inevitable, how we respond to change is optional. Some people believe that being authentic means that we always need to be the same, no matter the circumstances. Yet, just like a diamond, our truth has many facets and ways to shine. Depending on who or what we are dealing with, it is up to us to consciously choose our most resourceful and authentic response.

Let's use the analogy of your body again. If your body were your authentic self, your limbs, organs, and systems would be its expressions. While moving, reaching, digesting, and sensing are all essential, they are not equally beneficial for all conditions. Your legs are useful to hike a mountain but not to digest food. Each part of your body contributes uniquely to help you navigate life. Your responsibility is to stay aware of your body's needs, use it to its best abilities, and be committed to making it stronger, healthier, and more flexible. You live with authenticity when you are aware of and guided by the values of your truth; when you are open to sharing your gifts and talents and remain curious to discover more of who you are—irrespectively of the external pressure to conform.

In contrast to other species, we humans have a vast ability to consciously choose alternative ways to respond to any given situation and reach our goals. But how can we adapt to our circumstances and remain authentic and true to ourselves? Through *psychological flexibility*. According to studies, mental and emotional flexibility is the foundation of creating a healthy and fulfilling life.[2] The lack of psychological flexibility has been a predictor of higher anxiety, depression, worry, and poor work performance.[3] Some define psychological flexibility as, "the ability to respond to stimuli in a manner that is functional given a particular context and that is congruent with personal values."[4] Others describe psychological flexibility as, "contacting the present moment as a conscious human being, fully and without needless defense—as it is and not as what it says it is—and persisting with or changing a behavior in the service of chosen values."[5] In other words, psychological flexibility is our ability to fluently adjust our thoughts, emotions, and behaviors to the people and situations we face. Sounds familiar, right? This description pretty much summarizes the chameleon pattern. But this isn't surprising because the chameleon's superpower is flexibility.

Yet while psychological flexibility is associated with less stress and greater joy, vitality, and meaning in life,[6] the chameleon pattern is fueled by fear, insecurity, and the need for acceptance. And while psychological flexibility promotes a higher degree of freedom for how to live each moment, the chameleon is trapped in an endless game of whack-a-mole, trying to adjust to *everybody's* expectations. So what is the difference between the two kinds of flexibility? With psychological flexibility, we choose to respond to any given situation in alignment with our values. In contrast, with the chameleon pattern we shift our values depending on who we want to be aligned with. Not because we have no values; but because we don't value ourselves.

Values are fundamental beliefs about what is good, right, desirable, and worthwhile. They are the foundation on which we build our lives, as they guide our perspectives and motivate our actions. When we live in accordance with our values, we experience more peace, happiness, and fulfillment. When we don't, we usually struggle with anxiety, insecurity, and self-sabotaging behavior.

You may wonder what it means to align your thoughts, feelings, and actions with your values. And how do you know your values in the first place? Your values and personal qualities often overlap, so you have already gained important insights about your values by answering the nine questions in the Getting in Touch With Your Good Bits section of this chapter. What you value in yourself and others, are usually traits that describe best how you prefer to engage with the world. Each of the different roles you play in your life has a unique set of values. For example, when it comes to your career, your values may be ambition, reliability, and connection. This could mean that you like to learn and advance in your career, focus on performing consistently well, and prefer to work in a team rather than alone. In your primary relationship, your values may be devotion, harmony, and playfulness, traits you would offer to your partner but also hope to receive in return.

Now that you have gained a greater understanding of and appreciation for your authentic truth, you can turn the chameleon's self-defense flexibility into psychological flexibility through a tool I call "Dynamic Awareness." This way you no longer unconsciously react to the people you are with, but instead consciously choose how you want to respond, again in alignment with your values.

A NEW OWNER'S MANUAL

There is a vitality, a life force, an energy, a quickening that is translated through you into action, and because there is only one of you in all of time, this expression is unique. And if you block it, it will never exist through any other medium and it will be lost. The world will not have it. It is not your business to determine how good it is nor how valuable nor how it compares with other expressions. It is your business to keep it yours clearly and directly, to keep the channel open. You do not even have to believe in yourself or your work. You have to keep yourself open and aware to the urges that motivate you. Keep the channel open.

—MARTHA GRAHAM

Dynamic Awareness allows you to use the principles of psychological flexibility to redefine your responses to the situations and relationships where you used to feel the most powerless and insecure. In regard to aligning with your values, let's assume that since you are reading this book, the primary value you want to focus on is to think, feel, and act from a place of self-empowered authenticity. In the future, you may want to choose values that are most fitting for each situation and facet of your life.

Psychological flexibility relies on three core elements: openness, positivity, and self-control. With openness, we are more curious and interested in new interpretations of situations that consistently trigger negative feelings.[7] And we are more receptive to defining alternative ways to approach these situations.[8] Positivity through joy, contentment, and love has shown to increase creativity, thoughtfulness, and the ability to access a wider array of mental and emotional resources.[9] Self-control or self-regulation is our ability to consciously modify our impulses and subconscious tendencies. Whether we resist our urges, delay gratification, control our habitual behaviors, or manage thoughts and emotions, self-control is a key element of self-empowerment.[10] With self-control, we can finally rise above living on autopilot with its numbing, reactionary self-defense patterns, and become the conscious creators of our reality.

Dynamic Awareness uses openness, positivity, and self-control to foster psychological flexibility. You can use this effective tool with all survival patterns, as it helps create a new blueprint for going through your day-to-day life and interacting with the world without losing your power or yourself. You'll replace the familiar guiding forces in your life, such as needing to belong, to be liked, or to be invisible, with the staunch belief that you are the source of your safety, that you are enough, that the gifts you offer to the world matter, and that your mission is to discover your truth and your purpose in this life. Let's get started.

DYNAMIC AWARENESS

Step 1: Center

Find a quiet space to sit down and reflect. Have a journal, phone, or laptop ready to take notes. Then close your eyes and take a few relaxing breaths. Think about one or two of your qualities you appreciate the most, such as being compassionate and generous. Remember how you feel when you embody these traits. Then picture these feelings as energy, like beams of light emanating from within. Trace these beams back to their source—the essence of your being at your core. Connect to this light, tune into its energy and notice how comforting and soothing it feels to align with your authentic truth. Imagine that your inner light expands and becomes brighter with every breath until it fills up your entire body, overflowing into the space around you.

Then affirm quietly or out loud: "I choose to be me. I live in alignment with my truth. My safety, worthiness, and belonging come from within."

Step 2: Reflect

Think of a person or a recurring situation in your life that triggers you to react subconsciously with avoidance or pleasing patterns. Then ask yourself: "What did I think and believe about myself, the other person, and the circumstances I was in, so I ended up feeling not good enough, anxious, and powerless?"

Let's use the three chameleon examples I mentioned at the beginning of chapter 9.

You're sitting at the weekly business lunch; you and everybody else are feigning keen interest in your boss's adventure stories. So your perception that triggers the chameleon pattern could be: "I need to pretend that I care about their monologues, otherwise I'll never get a promotion."

After work you meet with your friends for drinks, and even though you've complained to your spouse many times that you no longer enjoy the pernicious mix of gossiping, teasing, and throwing back shots, somehow you still fit right in. Your interpretation of this situation could sound like this: "If my friends knew that I have other interests and would like to spend my time differently, they would make fun of me—and then stop hanging out with me. I would end up alone."

Come Sunday, you're at your parents' for supper, as usual, dutifully eating your mom's pot roast and potatoes, even though you've been trying to stick to a vegan diet. So your limiting beliefs could be: "I am so different from my family. They don't know who I am—and they don't care to know."

As I mentioned before, the Dynamic Awareness process works with all survival patterns. So if you don't feel that the chameleon pattern interferes very often with your everyday activities, choose situations that trigger other disempowering patterns that usually leave you feeling drained and defeated.

Step 3: Rewrite

Now, openness, positivity, and self-control come in. Ask yourself: "How would my authentic self think, feel, and act differently in these situations?" and, "Which of my array of qualities would be best suited to engage with these people so that I stay empowered and connected to myself?"

So how would your authentic self respond to a self-aggrandizing boss? Keep in mind that being authentic doesn't mean you need to wear your heart on your sleeve and do as you please without consideration for another person. Your frustrated ego may want to tell your boss to shut his pie hole and let other people finally talk. As authentic and empowering as it may feel to express your anger, it probably wouldn't be self-responsible unless you don't care about getting fired. Emotions can give you valuable information on how you interpret your reality, but they are not necessarily reflections of your authentic truth. Sure, you can't necessarily control people or circumstances. But you can control yourself and choose not to react to your emotions, but to determine the most authentic and resourceful way to respond to the situations you deal with. Again, drawing on your values is the best guidance system for responding with authenticity once you have been triggered.

Let's say two of your most valued qualities are compassion and courage. With compassion, you could perceive your boss as, let's say, profoundly insecure. You could imagine that their only audience is their employees since neither family nor friends are interested in their stories. And with courage, you could ask them questions and then share a story of your own life, or bring your colleagues into the conversations with something like, "Judy, didn't you also go to Africa a few years ago?"

Your authentic response could also be just internal. For example, you may choose to keep your cool and with calm empathy watch the one-man-show, without getting upset at your boss for monopolizing the conversation or having to make him feel better by nodding like a bobblehead.

After work, instead of chugging tequila with your friends and making fun of those that aren't there to defend themselves, if your values are honesty and friendship, you can be honest with them and share that you no longer want to gossip and get drunk. You turn the tables and take charge of the energy and the conversation, rather than being on another one of your friends' wild rides. They may tease you and call you a party pooper at first. Yet, eventually, your authentic response may inspire them to take better care of their health and talk about more meaningful topics, which will also deepen your friendship.

For Sunday dinner with your parents, values such as love and respect may help you have a chat with your mom and tell her that you no longer eat any food derived from animals. You may suggest cooking a vegan meal, or give her some ideas on what she could prepare for you. And for the rest of your family, you remind yourself that those who judge others for their differences are usually the ones that are afraid to be authentic. You can have compassion for them, but you no longer appease their insecurities by denying yourself.

Take your time to choose new points of view and try out different self-empowering responses. There is no right or wrong, so pick the one that feels right, and most importantly, is in alignment with the overarching principle of being true to yourself.

Step 4: Rehearse

Until now, your newly defined responses from Step 3 are simply positive intentions. For them to become replacements for your self-limiting patterns, you need to translate them into the language of your subconscious mind—images, feelings, and sensations. Create an internal movie with bright, vivid colors and at least life-sized images, and visualize yourself authentically approaching the situations you used to struggle with. You can also look through the eyes of the future self and imagine what you will see, hear, and feel as you respond in these self-empowered ways. By rehearsing your future according to your updated owner's manual, you establish new neurological pathways and give your mind two scenarios: an old and limiting and a new and empowering one. Knowing you have different options for viewing and responding to people and situations puts you out of the passenger seat and into the driver's seat.

Step 5: Reinforce

Our mind, particularly our subconscious, thrives on positive feedback. Every dog trainer understands that consistent positive reinforcement in the form of a treat or praise is the best way to teach Fido a new skill. It works with us too. Since choosing how you want to authentically engage in your life is a new skill, it's essential to pat yourself on the back. Create a success log using a notebook, your smartphone, or your computer, and list every night how through Dynamic Awareness, you shifted your reality into a more self-affirming experience. Be generous with yourself and acknowledge even the smallest successes. Soon you will find that you have all the inner resources to authentically engage in challenging activities while pursuing a rich, meaningful life.

Use this process to gain mental, emotional, and behavioral flexibility, and establish trust in your essence with all its gifts and values. I know—it takes courage and strength to openly and honestly show who you are. But as you become more comfortable being vulnerable and sharing your truth, qualities, desires, and needs, you'll solidify your foundation of self-acceptance. And once you accept yourself, you're free.

11

THE HELPER PATTERN

Over-Extended and Underappreciated

I need you to need me. That's the only way I matter.

According to a friend, there are two types of people: those who, when somebody says, "I'm thirsty," jump up to get them a cold drink, and those who remain sitting and ask, "Did you eat something salty?" I certainly fall into the first category. I would serve a beverage to a friend whether they were thirsty or not. Do you also have a strong inclination to make sure that everybody has their needs met? Your sibling calls and complains that his computer is broken. You know that he looks up to you, and you immediately volunteer to buy him a new laptop, although you don't really have money for it. Your boss asks for volunteers to work on the weekend to meet an important deadline, and your hand shoots up before she can even finish her sentence. Or you're the only one who hosts family gatherings, while everybody else *may* bring a bottle of wine. Why are you the one who always caters to others? The helper pattern has many different expressions: pleaser, gift-giver, care-taker, peace-maker, responsibility taker, and savior to the martyr. This pattern is common in nurses, therapists, teachers, devoted mothers, and adult children looking after their ailing parents. It may be so deeply ingrained in your sub-conscious identity that you show up in all your relationships and encounters as the helper.

When Jim entered his forties, battered from another painful relationship where he devoted all his time and energy to fixing his girlfriend's problems, he decided it was time to focus on himself. His goal for working with me was to become more confident, especially in the romance department. Jim quickly realized that his helper pat-tern was rooted in the old belief that he was only lovable, worthy, and safe if he was taking care of others. Having been raised by a single mother who suffered from severe depression and suicidal ideations, he had to quickly become *the responsible adult* in the house. "If I hadn't diligently looked after my mom and my younger brother," he told me, "I don't know what would've happened with us." The bur-den of responsibility and the fear of becoming homeless or an orphan in foster care shaped Jim into a helper and savior. Throughout his childhood, Jim diligently kept an eye on his mom's mood swings. He tried to cheer her up when she went downhill, distract her when she had self-harming thoughts, and overall made her life easier by taking on most of the household chores. Naturally, Jim was always drawn to women who needed to be rescued rather than seeking out partners who could also take care of him. No exception, Jim's girlfriends were either needy or emotionally unstable, and they ended up leaving him once he was so drained that he had nothing left to give.

A few sessions into our work, he vowed to dedicate himself to finding security and validation from within rather than looking for confirmation from his relationships.

As life would have it, his mom called him just when he started to appreciate and care for himself more. She was in one of her emo-tional tailspins, with a mixture of depression, anxiety, and adamant negativity. Within moments Jim's empathy caused him to align with her struggles, feel her pain, and perceive the world through her dark and hopeless outlook. "I completely lost touch with myself. My mind started racing and all I could think of was how to save my mom." As usual, his suggestions to help her find a therapist or a new psychiatrist, schedule the first appointment for her, pay for the sessions, or at the very least, buy a meditation app to calm her mind were all met with the same answer: "No, this won't work. It's too late for me to make a change." Although Jim was all too familiar with his mother's resistance to getting help, it once again left him feeling powerless, anxious, and completely removed from his healing and growth. In a desperate email he sent to me, he said: "I wish I just didn't care so much."

ARE YOU BORN OR MADE TO BE A HELPER?

Just as Jim experienced, the helper pattern starts commonly during our childhood. It's often activated when one or both parents don't seem reliable or available to take care of us appropriately, whether because they were just too busy, were dealing with an addiction, or had a mental or physical illness. As I mentioned, parental neglect triggers subconscious survival patterns, which for some meant fending for themselves, and for others, taking their younger siblings under their wings while making Mom and Dad proud—or at least not upset. The little helpers want to rescue the family by stepping in as parent surrogates because they are sensitive and naturally operate from a place of kindness, love, and compassion. If the helper pattern was your response to the fears and uncertainties of your early years, you were probably a child who wanted to ensure that nobody struggled or was in pain. You cried quickly when you saw a person or animal suffer or when somebody talked to you in a harsh tone of voice. On the other hand, making people happy and seeing them smile gave you a sense of self-worth.

It's likely that instead of your family fostering your gentle nature, you were told you were too sensitive and emotional and needed to stop overreacting and toughen up a bit. Initially, you may have felt confused about why others weren't as considerate and caring as you, but their criticism of your nature eventually led you to believe that something was wrong with you. So you started hiding your thoughts and feelings and stopped asking for support. Assuming that you were different and somewhat flawed undermined your confidence and further increased your need for validation from others. Since pleasing others is what you're innately good at, you focused on earning your keep—and maybe a little bit of love—through being helpful and never demanding.

Since you became an adult, your subconscious has continued to rely on the helper pattern because it can accomplish more than most survival patterns. Being a helper and making yourself irreplaceable secures your relationships, provides validation, and keeps you safe from being judged and criticized since you're only known for your good deeds, rather than your needs.

Do any of these questions about your childhood resonate with you?

- Did you only get love and acceptance when you were good and helpful?
- Did you feel responsible for keeping the peace at home?
- Were you in charge of keeping the house clean, making sure that food was in the refrigerator, and that your siblings were fed, dressed, and helped with their homework?
- Did you often think about how to make a struggling parent feel better?
- Despite all your efforts to make others happy, did you frequently feel insecure and not good enough?
- Did you keep your problems to yourself because you didn't want to bother anybody?
- And when you dared to share frustration, sadness, or anxiety, were you reprimanded, disciplined, or punished by withholding affection?

Maybe not all these questions reflect your early experiences. But let's be clear, helpers aren't born that way—they're made. And you probably agree that your need to be helpful isn't rooted in you being catered to and showered with love and attention. The combination of instability, neglect, and conditional acceptance with reward and punishment are potent ways for a child to believe that it only has a right to exist when attending to everybody else's needs.

Still, you may wonder, "What's wrong with being helpful and considerate? Isn't this how we're all supposed to be?" Yes, of course kindness and caring are virtues we should strive for. But the helper pattern isn't just about being kind and supportive toward others; it is primarily about keeping us safe from rejection and abandonment. And as with all survival patterns, this one eventually also leads to disempowerment and disconnection from ourselves. So how do you know whether you're just a "good and giving person" or if you're operating in self-defense?

As a recovering helper, I understand how challenging it can be to suppress the urge to take care of other people's needs. The role of the peace-maker was assigned to me even before my birth. Soon after my older sister was born, my parents started struggling in their marriage. Using somewhat twisted logic, they thought maybe a second child, hopefully a boy, could fix their troubles. Lucky for them I showed up, and to leave no doubt about my job description, they gave me the unusual name Friedemann—man of peace. Thus, right from the crib I was given the responsibility for everybody in my family to get along. Obviously, I couldn't control my parents' or my sister's fluctuating moods, so arguments and fights still happened quite frequently. But as early as I can remember, as soon as tempers flared, my mom told me that I should step in and mediate between the three of them, like a diplomat in the Middle East trying to avoid another conflict.

Of course, the pressure of having to save my parents' marriage over and over again added a tremendous burden to my already anxious mind. I would break out in a cold sweat at the mere idea of them splitting up and having to live with my, at times, scary father (since my sister would certainly choose my mom). Yet a part of me also proudly relished when, after a six-hour mad drive through the Black Forest with my furious dad, my efforts to cool his temper succeeded, and he even apologized to my mom for treating her poorly. Even though the truce never lasted longer than a few weeks, the idea that I had facilitated the peace in our family boosted my self-worth. Once I left for college, I worried their marriage would quickly unravel without my appeasing influence. Surprise, surprise, the opposite happened. My mom and dad seemed to get along much better without their kids, which was a slight blow to my ego. In the end, my parents stayed together until they both passed, just three months apart.

The problem with being the designated helper and peace-maker was that this survival pattern became my identity and extended into other relationships. You already know how desperately I wanted to please the teenage cook-off clique. Lacking confidence regarding the opposite sex, I showered my first girlfriend with attention and gifts. I baked her cakes, recorded soppy mix-tapes, wrote her poetry, and dedicated all my free time to pleasing her. Unfortunately, the more I showed her my adoration, the more aloof she became.

Two years into the desperate battle to gain her approval, I crafted a marionette for her—in the shape of myself. I am not sure what I was thinking, but Freud would have gotten a kick out of this. All my friends burst out laughing, because they knew too well that she was holding the strings in the relationship while I was dancing to her tune. Their reaction and my girlfriend's steady coldness eventually broke my young heart. But as the saying goes, when the heart breaks, something breaks open.

What broke open for me was the realization that I deserved better than how she treated me. Once I decided to stop playing the pleaser game she suddenly became much more interested in me. However, her efforts were too little too late, and the relation-ship ended. I've since learned that I can't make somebody like me by giving them things they didn't even ask for. And that I can't win over another person's heart by pleasing them into submission. That didn't mean I stopped trying. I tried, not only with roman-tic relationships, but also with friends and colleagues. I broke this pattern when I realized that the problem wasn't a failure to please others enough, but rather, a failure to appreciate myself enough.

Maybe you've also felt this frustration of doing so much and never feeling that you and your efforts are truly valued. But like me, you weren't sure whether you were just kind and considerate or living in an insecurity-driven pleasing mode. Here's how you can tell if what motivates you is the joy to serve or the need to please:

- Anxiety is a good hint that you're operating from the helper survival pattern. You're anxious because you never want to upset anybody by saying or doing something wrong, and you're afraid of disappointing others by not meeting their expecta-tions, or Heaven forbid, by saying "no" to their requests.
- You feel guilty and ashamed when people are displeased with you or disapprove of your actions. Lack of self-worth makes you overgive without noticing when you have done enough, because you see others' needs as more pressing than yours.
- The pain and suffering of those you care about deeply affects you. You get caught up in their struggles and feel responsible for finding solutions. Since you can't create a healthy separa-tion from their problems, you tend to obsess about what to do and overextend yourself to provide some relief.
- You consider boundaries, let alone self-care, selfish, and tell yourself that giving is better than receiving. As far as you can tell, Mother Teresa didn't have spa days and Mahatma Gandhi

didn't go on vacation. So why should you deserve a break from helping others so that you can recharge?

- As the peace-maker, conflict makes you uncomfortable and needs to be avoided at all costs. So you quickly agree with others, even if you don't share the same points of view, or at least keep your opinions to yourself. You pride yourself on spotting any tension between your family members or friends early, and like a firefighter, put out the emotional flames before they flare out of control. Of course, you ignore how the responsibility of being constantly on the lookout for disagreements, juggling people's emotions, and managing their stress weighs on you.

- One of the most evident differences between the helper pattern and just being helpful, is what you expect from others. If the helper pattern is your modus operandi, your caring comes with an emotional price tag—approval and appreciation. I'm not talking about a simple "thank you." You need to be rewarded with praise to know that you matter. You want to be regarded as indispensable to feel a sense of belonging. And ideally, you want to be loved because you've always questioned your lovability. Somebody who is just helpful doesn't have a subconscious quid pro quo agenda.

- Your self-worth is defined by what you do for others and not by who you are. You identify yourself so much with your helper role that you feel useless and utterly uncomfortable on your own. Just as the people you care for don't ask you how you're doing or whether they can do something for you, you become less and less aware of your needs.

- Sacrificing your desires and yourself for others becomes your badge of honor, and your dugout. You vehemently decline anybody's support because you want to be seen as strong and capable. Plus, you tell yourself that in any case, you'll do a better job than they would. But deep inside, you're afraid of showing your needs and vulnerabilities because you don't trust that people care enough about you.

- You only stop being the always-stocked, free vending machine of good deeds when you get sick due to complete exhaustion. When your temperature hits 105 degrees Fahrenheit and you can barely make it out of bed, you give yourself permission to rest for a little while. However, rather than being kind and compassionate with yourself, you feel ashamed for being weak and letting down those who depend on you.

- Finally, you know that your helper survival pattern has run you ragged when you gradually feel mounting anger and resentment for all those who've taken you for granted. Yet you find yourself between a rock and a hard place, because even though you feel drained and unwilling to continue to overgive, you also don't feel secure enough to create healthy boundaries or ask for support. This is when you're heading toward becoming a martyr who, instead of taking responsibility, blames the selfishness of others for the pain and suffering the helper pattern caused you.

Let me be clear, I'm not trying to discredit all that you've done for others for so many years. Your heart is in the right place. The fact is that you chose the helper survival mode because you have a caring nature. Of the six survival patterns I describe in this book, the helper is the most benevolent and altruistic. While the three avoider patterns perceive others as potential threats we need to stay away from, the helper pattern allows us to find safety and solace by generously giving to others. And if the three pleaser patterns would meet for a dinner party, the chameleon would focus on fitting in with the most interesting and influential guests, the lover would be all over the "chosen one," and the helper would serve drinks, sweat at the stove in the kitchen while listening to sob stories of the depressed wallflower who is hiding there, and then spend hours cleaning up after everyone.

Nevertheless, assuming you can relate to one or several of the preceding descriptions, you probably agree that in the long run the exchange rate of receiving a fleeting sense of safety and worthiness for dutifully serving others is not in your favor. It's time for you to shift out of this survival pattern before you become even more depleted and unsure of yourself. How? First, we need to address all the typical excuses, aka limiting beliefs, your mind has been using to keep you stuck in the role of the helper.

RESOLVING THE FIVE MOST COMMON HELPER PITFALLS

Honestly, I wasn't one of those curious little boys who routinely took apart radios, toasters, or their sister's Barbies to figure out how they worked. Keeping the peace at home was already challenging enough. Instead of small appliances or dolls, I had to constantly unpuzzle the minds of my family members. Looking back, I'm grateful for the inquisitiveness I developed during that time because it has served me well, helping my clients navigate through the mazes of their subconscious minds.

One of the things I discovered with my clients is that we can't shake off self-limiting patterns unless we identify the mental traps that keep us stuck. For example, you want to lose weight, but deep inside, you're worried that being thinner will draw unwanted attention. Thus your subconscious continues to put ice cream and cookies in your shopping cart. You want to stop procrastinating but are subconsciously afraid that if you genuinely applied yourself and still failed, it would be evident that you're not good enough. You want a lasting romantic relationship, yet you're sure that nobody can be trusted. So as soon as your partner forgets to call you or shows up one hour late for your date, you call it quits. Just like you can't get out of debt without changing your unconscious spending habits, you can't overcome limiting patterns without addressing the belief pitfalls that make you hold on to them.

While you may have known for some time that pleasing others during your early years was more a necessity than a calling, you might wonder why you're still overgiving and overdoing. I already mentioned that the notion that you need to earn your keep and work hard to gain approval from those you care about is rooted in the belief that you're not worthy, safe, or loveable. Yet, after all the processes you've gone through so far in this book and all the empowerment keys you've obtained, you already know that your source of safety, worthiness, and love resides within you.

But there are five additional deep-seated, albeit outdated, beliefs that have kept your helper pattern firmly anchored in your daily life.

1. Giving Is Better than Receiving

Whether you were raised religious or just listened to your grandma, you're probably familiar with the adage, "It is more blessed to give than to receive." Even science has delivered strong evidence that volunteering and financially supporting others promotes health and happiness.[1]

Yet research also showed that "burnout," a syndrome of exhaustion, disillusionment, and withdrawal, is exceptionally high in professional and informal caregivers.[2] Nature, in its infinite wisdom, teaches us that the health of any ecosystem depends on the balance of giving and receiving. The symbiotic relationship between an anemone and a clownfish is an example of two organisms in such a balance. The clownfish provides the anemone with nutrition in the form of waste, while the anemone provides the clownfish with protection and shelter. Our dogs and cats offer companionship; in return, we give them food and tummy rubs. We human beings even have mutually beneficial relationships with bacteria. In our digestive tract, the microorganisms are essential to regulate our digestion, and in turn, the foods we eat also feed them. Just as we can't survive by only exhaling, or releasing water and waste from our system without taking oxygen and nourishment back in, receiving is an essential part of life. To quote Maya Angelou, "When we give cheerfully and accept gratefully, everyone is blessed."[3] After all, if there were only givers and no receivers, who would we give to?

2. I Like Taking Care of Others; It Makes Me Happy

That's one of the most common excuses I hear from helpers. My usual response is, *Really?* If there's only happiness driving your helper pattern, you may skip this chapter. Yet, if you're honest with yourself, you probably know that what makes you happy isn't only the act of giving, but also the acknowledgment and approval you might receive. But more often than not, your services and support have been taken for granted because you've played the helper role for so long and so well that others assume that this is who you are. How do you feel when you've once again bent over backward, saved somebody's day, or single-handedly managed their move to another house, only to hear them complaining about how hard they worked? Sad, frustrated, ashamed, disappointed? But still, your worries about disappointing others, and your hope that soon they'll value you for the good person you truly are, keep your helper mode going.

The sad truth is, like electricity at home or sunshine in Southern California, your services may only get noticed when they're absent. The fact that you may see caretaking as your primary source of happiness isn't just a reflection of your lack of self-worth and your need to be liked and appreciated. It probably also has to do with how little time you've spent figuring out other ways to feel happy and fulfilled, and how often you've told yourself that self-care is selfish, the next mental trap.

As a helper, peace-maker, or pleaser, you're spending your time and energy on supporting others, hoping to receive from them enough approval to feel a little bit more secure and worthy. The problem is that you usually don't evaluate how much of your resources you can give before running on empty—like a cook who feeds everybody they know but neither eats any of the food they prepare nor checks to see what remains stocked in their pantry. As a pleaser, you end up draining yourself until the only things you have left to share are your disillusionments and frustrations.

3. Self-Care Is Selfish

Do you feel unsure about what to do when you have some time and space to yourself? Does guilt creep up on you when you do something just for yourself? For the helpers, self-care is overrated, frivolous self-indulgence. Unlike cars that need maintenance or any other living being that needs rest, you may rarely give yourself permission to relax and rejuvenate when you're in helper mode. I've been there myself. Especially during my residency, the weight of responsibility for the health and well-being of others kicked my helper pattern into overdrive. At that time, I convinced myself that my needs were irrelevant compared to my patients' challenges. Lousy food, pots of coffee, too much wine at night, and zero physical exercise was the standard self-care plan for my colleagues and me. I wore the dark circles under my eyes with pride, as they were undeniable testimonies to my self-sacrificing dedication. And whenever somebody told me I looked like I hadn't slept in weeks, my helper consciousness somersaulted. If anxiety and panic attacks hadn't forced me to pull the brakes and reconsider my choices, I probably would have at some point become a two-hundred-fifty-pound cardiologist with two heart attacks under his belt.

After what I've observed with my clients and myself, I would argue that the need-to-be-needed is far more selfish than self-care. First of all, we all know about putting on the oxygen mask first when the airplane takes a nose-dive, and that we can't give from an empty cup. I'm pretty sure that the lack of R&R didn't make me a more gifted physician. But we keep on giving, even though we have less to offer, hoping we'll eventually be somehow rewarded.

The helper pattern can become selfish in three ways. First, when we push our help on others without them asking for support. Of course, it feels great to help an old lady cross the street, unless she had no intention of going to the other side. And it's tempting to cook a lavish meal for a dinner party, but nobody expected lobster and prime rib. Being always giving and supportive to people who didn't necessarily ask for our assistance or appreciate our excessive gestures is self-serving because we use them to make us feel good. And if those individuals don't shower us with gratitude and adoration for our exceptional generosity, we judge them with resentment as self-centered and inconsiderate. The helper pattern can require others to be our confidence boosters or punching bags without even asking them for consent.

Giving can also become selfish when we ignore that it has adverse effects on the receivers. Classic examples are the enabling spouse of an alcoholic who continues to buy liquor to keep the peace. Or the smothering mother who cleans, cooks, and does the laundry for her grown-up child who in return becomes increasingly unmotivated to become a self-reliant adult. I used to travel once a year for a few days to Germany to visit friends. During this time, my wife took over many of my daily responsibilities, including caring for our zoo, which consisted of six cats, four horses, a pony, and a mule. Every time I came back, she was so proud of herself, as she gained much confidence from managing our *farm*. Unfortunately, my helper pattern quickly took back the reins (and everything else from her hands) without considering how disheartening this must have felt for her. Think about how your helpfulness may stifle and even disempower those around you. And if it does, wouldn't it be a greater gift to share the responsibilities and get them involved, rather than diminishing them to the role of the passive receiver?

The third way the helper pattern can make you selfish is when you're hiding behind its mask. Many caretakers and pleasers I know focus on other people's needs and problems so as not to have to face their own. They protect themselves by keeping others at arm's length and never showing their vulnerabilities. You may be much more at ease asking questions and showing interest in your friends' lives than sharing what's going on in your own. During get-togethers, perhaps you're busy running around and making sure everybody is happy, because sitting still and having deeper conversations makes you uncomfortable. And your family only knows you as the organizer, the pinch hitter, the reliable brother or sister, who is always available to anybody in need.

Yet, as you avoid exposing your vulnerability, you're also eliminating the possibility of more intimate and balanced relationships. At first glance, this behavior may not appear selfish since you're the one who's shooting yourself in the foot. But what about those who would love to have you as a close friend or family member? The people who feel powerless watching you strive and at times struggle without ever asking for help? Or those who wrestle with feeling rejected by your wall of niceness and good deeds? When we control our relationships by refusing to show who we truly are, we selfishly value our safety more than the opportunity to share with others the greatest gift we have—allowing them entry into our hearts.

4. Pain Is Bad and Needs to Be Attended To

The helper pattern goes hand in hand with extreme awareness and sensitivity toward other people's needs and pains. Think about it. As a child, how often were you attuned to your mother's sadness, your father's irritation, and your sibling's insecurity without anybody talking about their feelings? The less the people around you expressed their emotions, the more you had to rely on reading their body language, facial expressions, and behaviors to stay up-to-date on what was happening with them. As the helper or peace-maker, you needed to know which fires to attend to first. I always considered sensitivity to be a gift *and* a liability. Sensitive awareness can help us navigate elegantly through the most challenging relationships. It allows us to understand others' points of view, and, even more importantly, lets us pierce through their protective masks and tune into their vulnerabilities. Once I intuitively understood that my father's rage came from his deep-seated insecurity, I no longer saw him as scary but just as scared, and my *duty* to tame his temper became somewhat easier.

While keeping tabs on the emotional state of those around us is a testimony to the helper's caring nature, feeling others' feelings (which many helpers do) can be pretty overwhelming. Do any of these situations seem familiar? You're watching on a TV show the protagonist having a cavity drilled, and right away you feel pain in your gums. You can't stand the thought of innocent children or animals suffering. And it breaks your heart when one of your loved ones cries with pain or sadness because you *feel* their hurt or sorrow. All you want to do is take their discomfort away. Helpers are known for an almost obsessive need to resolve problems and alleviate the suffering of others. You could say that the helper's sensitivity makes them too emotionally available and too empathetic.

At some point, I had to accept the harsh truth that no matter how hard I tried, taking on other people's pain didn't make them feel better. I don't know how often I patiently listened to my parents and sister complain, like a dry sponge absorbing their frustration, anxiety, and depression. Usually, such "counseling sessions" ended with them feeling *understood*—and therefore validated in their suffering—and me feeling drained and confused about why I couldn't convince them of a different perspective.

The problem with deeply feeling helpers and empaths is their skewed view on pain. In the book *The Art of Happiness,* the Dalai Lama talks about Dr. Brand, a world-renowned hand surgeon who spent many years working with leprosy patients in India.[4] Leprosy is a contagious disease that affects the skin, nerves, eyes, and nasal cavities, causing discoloration and lumps on the skin and, in severe cases, disfigurement and deformities. Dr. Brand discovered, to his surprise, that deformities and destructive effects of leprosy were not caused directly by the disease, but by the loss of pain sensation in the extremities. Countless times, he witnessed leprosy patients walk with sores on their feet or even exposed bones, stick their hands into fire, or remain asleep when rats chewed on their fingers during the night. Without the ability to feel pain, these patients had no protection from injuries and were thus utterly oblivious to how their daily lives ravaged their limbs. Through these experiences, Dr. Brand learned to appreciate pain as a clear and sophisticated message from the body about a subject of potentially vital importance. He believed that embracing the protective purpose of pain can help deal with it better when it arises.

What's valid for physical pain is also true for our emotions. Let's take anxiety as an example. The apparent protective purpose of this feeling is to alert us of potential danger. But, as I laid out in my book *The Fear and Anxiety Solution,* anxiety also calls our attention to the deeper mental and emotional wounds that caused it. Tending to these wounds, such as unresolved traumas, self-sabotaging patterns, or limiting beliefs, can lead to greater wholeness, inner peace, and self-empowerment. I can imagine that you may have picked up this book because anxiety, insecurity, or other emotional pain has nudged you to action. Pain is a wake-up call. Unfortunately, in the Western World, we tend to silence this messenger with medication, drugs, or alcohol rather than listen to what it has to say. Yet when we find the courage and strength to face its underlying truth, pain can become the catalyst for healing and growth. For many of my clients, their healing journey started when their emotional pain outweighed their fear of change. The point is that without any form of pain, we would probably shrivel in our comfort zones, utterly unmotivated to evolve.

When I started my coaching practice, my wife said, "If you're willing to take away somebody's pain, you are also willing to take away their chance of happiness." These words struck the core. As a designated helper and physician, I was convinced that easing people's suffering was a noble cause. Of course it is, yet not how I was used to. Twenty years later, I'm so grateful that Danielle pointed out my empathetic knee-jerk reflex of trying to take on my client's issues, which would have done nothing for their self-improvement, but for me, most likely would have led to a quick burnout.

You may ask yourself what I did about my empathy. Let's look at the next trap.

5. I Can't Help It—I'm Too Empathetic

Helper or not, most of us can intuit how other individuals are feeling. If we watch somebody bite into a piece of fruit, our saliva flows. A person screaming in agony after smashing his fingers in the door makes us wince. Images of refugees crying in despair as they hold the lifeless bodies of their children, who drowned trying to reach a safer country, break our hearts. The ability to empathize with one another is essential for functioning relationships, and the lack of empathy is often associated with sociopathological and narcissistic behavior.

Neuro-scientists found that empathy is hardwired into our brain thanks to *mirror neurons,* a specific class of brain cells related to social and emotional processing. The mirror neuron areas of our brain start to mature and shape our sense of empathy around age four.[5] Mirror neurons allow us to unconsciously sense another person's physical and emotional experiences and reproduce them in our brain.[6] According to Daniel Goleman, author of *Emotional Intelligence,* mirror neurons act as neural Wi-Fi. They attune our feelings to somebody else's internal and external state to understand better what is going on with them.[7]

As crucial as empathy may be for healthy social interactions, picking up emotions and energies from others can also be very stressful. Functional MRIs showed that in highly sensitive people (HSPs), mirror neuron activity levels were consistently increased, which may explain why sensitive people often avoid crowds, closeness, and intimacy.[8] But you don't have to be highly sensitive to experience empathy as overwhelming. In a study where participants were asked to watch short films of people in pain, those who entered into the experiment already feeling low or emotionally charged, reacted with significantly higher distress to what they saw than those who felt neutral at the start.[9] Similar to highly sensitive people, this form of empathetic distress was usually followed by guilt and the desire to withdraw from the situation.[10] In other words, our ability to handle empathy significantly declines when we are already struggling with our own emotional challenges and lack of energy.

We all agree that being stressed out doesn't bring out the most caring side of us. Usually, stress hormones signal to our mind and body that it is time to save our fanny, rather than look out for others. Yet empathetic distress creates an inner conflict as one side wants to avoid the source of stress, while another side wants to lean in and fix the other person's problems. Since the individual in need most likely also has functioning mirror neurons, watching and experiencing our stress response only adds to their discomfort.

A classic example is a small child tripping and falling. It immediately looks at its parents to gauge their reactions. When the parents appear freaked out and jump up to rush to the rescue, the child picks up their stress and concludes that the fall must have been surely something to cry about. However, when the parents talk in a calm and supportive voice and maybe even smile, the situation appears less scary and severe for the little one.

So how are you supposed to deal with your empathy? Shut it off, ignore it, or fight it? Since you can't just turn off your mirror neurons, none of these options would work. But what if you could notice other people's suffering from a healthy distance? With an open heart and mind, but still feeling calm and grounded within? What if you could turn to compassion rather than empathy?

The difference between empathy and compassion is that with empathy you don't only notice somebody's emotions and energies, you internalize them. On the other hand, with compassion, you're aware of another's internal experiences without losing the connection with yourself. Here's an analogy. Let's say you spot somebody drowning. Empathy makes you jump into the water and go down with them. With compassion, you stay on the shore and look for a life-preserver or a rope to throw them. Or, on an emotional level, when you see somebody stuck in the dark cave of their anxiety and depression, your empathy may ask you to join them. But your compassion encourages you to hold up the light of hope and positivity for them. In other words, empathy is the subconscious awareness of what others feel. Compassion is awareness plus consciously and proactively choosing how to respond from a place of love and kindness. And in contrast to empathy distress, compassion releases the trifecta of mood-enhancing neurotransmitters: serotonin, called the happiness hormone, dopamine, the feel-good hormone, and oxytocin, the love hormone.[11] So it's a win-win for all.

Here are a few questions that, next time your attention is drawn to somebody's struggles, will make it easier for you to shift from empathy to compassion:

- Does it help this person when I take on their pain, or does it make them feel even worse?
- What is a more positive and empowering perspective on what they're going through?
- Is this person helpless?
- Do I believe they have the inner resources to heal and grow from their struggles?
- Is there anything I can do to help them—or do I know of anybody who can?

- How can I compassionately support them without preventing them from becoming empowered and self-reliant?
- How can I remain responsible to and compassionate with myself?

By contemplating these questions, you will shift from empathetically reacting to quietly reflecting on the most compassionate way to respond.

But what if you take the compassion approach yet somehow can't come up with a way to help? Rest assured, you already bring more ease to the person you care about by simply staying calm and understanding. This is one of the reasons why people love to talk to their therapists. In a study, female participants were asked to undergo a functional MRI while receiving mild to moderate electroshocks (I'm not sure who volunteers for such an experiment). Naturally, all the women were somewhat anxious as they were lying on the MRI table, bracing for the unpleasant sensation. While they were waiting, somebody came and held their hands. If this person was a stranger, their stress level would already go down. Yet, if it was their husband, the anxiety almost wholly disappeared.[12] This example shows that instead of solving another's problems or taking away their pain, just showing up with calmness and compassion can be enough to give them the emotional and physical strength to face their challenges with greater ease.

......

Remember Jim, who believed he needed to be the savior for women in his life? During our work together, he learned much about himself and what he needed to feel happier and more self-assured. However, the most significant impact was the development of his compassionate presence—for others and himself—that allowed him to remain sensitive and caring without getting lost and overwhelmed by the struggles of those he loved. One day Jim decided that the best way to support his mom was to compassionately forgive and disentangle from her and thus release her from the imprisonment of his negative expectations. So rather than holding on to seeing her as hopelessly depressed and anxious, he started to visualize her waking up to her own strength, courage, and essence. "Every time my old helper pattern kicks in," he said, "I remind myself that I choose to do less caring and more of allowing her to be on her journey." A few months later, he shared with me that while his mother continued to have her emotional ups and downs, their relationship was filled with much more lightness, positivity, and sometimes even laughter.

To quote the football player Ralph Marston: "When your reasons to move forward outweigh your excuses for staying put, you will move forward." So with the limiting beliefs out of the way, the next step to switching out of the helper mode is self-commitment.

12

SELF-COMMITMENT

The Key to Owning Your Energy

You are the steward of your energy, the carer for your needs.
You have the right to exist and are worthy of your dreams.

OK, I can imagine you thinking now: "Great, I've gained more awareness about my helper pattern's onset and downsides and how I can avoid getting caught in its common pitfalls. But how do I shift out of this pattern without becoming callous and uncaring?" This chapter will give you the answer—and the fifth key to empowerment: self-commitment.

Mary, who was in her early sixties when we met, is a stark example of the potentially devastating ramifications of the helper pattern. Her childhood was defined by her overbearing and narcissistic mom, who abused Mary physically and emotionally. "I always felt that everything was my fault," Mary said during our first session. "Mom often said that I was too intense and too stressful and that I was the reason she would soon die, which scared me. When I accidentally hurt myself and started crying, instead of comforting me, she slapped me across the face, yelling, 'You disgust me!' But the worst was that she was a terrible cook and forced me to eat her awful food, even though I had to try so hard not to throw up every time." Luckily, Mary's father was the opposite; a kind and sensitive man who unconditionally loved his little girl. But he also was a target of his wife's cruel behavior, and unfortunately didn't have the strength to push back and protect his daughter and himself. When Mary was fourteen years old, her dad unexpectedly died. "This was the worst day of my life. I think he just couldn't take the constant stress and fighting anymore. But I couldn't grieve because I knew that now I was all alone in the world and the only way to survive was to do whatever my mom wanted, and to quietly swallow whatever she served me, literally."

The years that followed living with her mother shaped Mary into a guilt-ridden, insecure, and constantly anxious young woman. So it bordered on a miracle that when she turned eighteen, she somehow found the strength to attend college on the opposite side of the country. Yet as they say, wherever you go, there you are. Mary's pleaser patterns continued to define her life. In her romantic relationships, she attracted either needy or abusive men, who were always unfaithful. While her friends appreciated Mary's giving and supportive nature, they never bothered to ask her how she was doing. And her employers regularly took advantage of her boundless energy and unquestioning willingness to bend over backwards no matter how difficult the task. All the while, Mary felt guilty that she had *abandoned* her mom and continued to call her several times per week, obediently enduring the toxic onslaught of shaming, blaming, and complaining.

In her mid-fifties, fate suddenly seemed to smile on Mary. She met and later married a kind, decent, and loving man who brought two wonderful adult children into her life. She also decided to start her own business, which flourished and prospered right from the start. But instead of feeling happy and proud of herself, Mary struggled with one recurring thought: "Something bad will happen and take this all away from me. I just don't deserve to have so much luck. " So she wasn't too surprised when she developed a health issue in the form of increasing difficulties swallowing solid food, which sometimes even got stuck in her esophagus, causing her to panic that she might suffocate.

A gastrointestinal specialist eventually diagnosed her with CREST syndrome, an auto-immune disease that, besides other symptoms, is defined by scarring and narrowing of the esophageal tube. At first, the doctors tried to keep her esophagus open by stretching it a few times per year with an inserted balloon dilator. After a few years, the relieving effects of the treatment lasted just a few days before solid food again became painfully trapped in the mid-chest area. Meals became a major anxiety-triggering topic for Mary. One day, after she'd lost thirty pounds because all she could eat were smoothies and soups, her doctor gave her, as she called it, *a death sentence.* The physician explained that she wouldn't get any better and had to get used to living with a feeding tube.

As Mary left the clinic, she felt completely overwhelmed and paralyzed by the news. How would she tell her husband he would have to live with a disabled person? What would her friends think when she couldn't join them anymore for dinner? Would she even have any friends left? And what about her mom? How much would she blame Mary for getting ill? But amid these racing thoughts, which unsurprisingly were all about other people, an unfamiliar inner voice told her, "This is unacceptable. I will not live like this. I will find a way to heal myself." The power and sincerity of this voice silenced all the other worried messages. It was as if, for the first time in her life, she had permission to stand up for herself. Suddenly Mary knew what she had to do: heal the deeper reasons why her body attacked itself, which is literally what happens with auto-immune diseases. This was when she reached out to me.

Mary discovered during our sessions that her inability to swallow was linked to a conflict between two subconscious parts. One part of her believed she wasn't worthy enough to nourish and care for herself. This part, the inner pleaser, was steeped in shame and guilt for not doing enough for her mother and everybody else that needed her support. The other part of her felt angry with the pleaser and all those who had used and abused her. This more rebellious aspect of her subconscious refused to swallow the bitter pills life had served her. As an act of ultimate disobedience, this part preferred Mary to waste away rather than continue to *slave away*.

You may wonder why this conflict raged inside Mary at a time when her external circumstances were better than ever. As long as the helper pattern was triggered by anxiety due to dysfunctional relationships and demanding employment, her inner rebel was muzzled and pushed aside. However, once she was in a healthy marriage, enjoyed the freedom of running her own business, and was out of her mother's reach, the resistance to the helper pattern was unleashed. Ultimately, the inner battle of her auto-immune disease was caused by a fundamental question: Do I live in service to and at the mercy of others, or am I worthy of taking care of myself and being in charge of my life?

Whether you've been a pleaser or an avoider, or identified yourself mainly through your achievements, possessions, or relationships, the keys to empowerment you have obtained from the previous chapters will have given you greater clarity on your innate value. For Mary to understand and embrace that she was so much more than what she or others believed, she needed to peel away the subconscious layers of hurtful projections, rejections, and limiting beliefs of being flawed and unworthy even to exist. After several months of working together, Mary started appreciating her authentic qualities and innate goodness. Yet, the helper pattern made it still difficult to put herself first—until she discovered the power of self-commitment.

As you already know, each self-empowerment key uses the strength of the survival pattern it replaces. Self-responsibility uses the victim pattern's ability to keep track of the past so that you can learn and grow from it. Self-compassion counts on the invisibility pattern's sensitivity to reconnect with the gifts of your innocent self. Self-reliance takes advantage of the procrastinator's ability to see and ultimately value both task and pleasure. And self-reflection employs the chameleon's keen awareness to align with your essence. The strength of the helper pattern is the unwavering commitment to please everybody besides yourself.

So what will it take to shift the focus away from other people's needs and wants onto your own? Realizing that you have intrinsic value and deserve to care for yourself is crucial. But unless you show dedication to your happiness and well-being daily, your awareness of your worthiness will be as hollow as the love declarations of a serial cheater or the promises of a parent who never shows up for their kid's ball games or recitals.

Commitment is the safety net a child needs to grow and thrive; it's the foundation of mature love and the fuel that propels you to reach goals outside your comfort zone. Think about it; all the significant decisions in your life need your commitment to come to fruition. So once again, it's time to make an important decision: Are you viewing the empowerment keys you've obtained as desirable but non-practical concepts, like one of those gadgets you had to have but quickly ended up in the giveaway box in the garage? Or will you take advantage of these keys and implement them with self-commitment so that they can make a tangible difference in your life? Remember, being the most empowered version of yourself will benefit not only you, but also those around you. You will no longer give from lack and insecurity, hoping to receive some back-patting in return. Instead, you'll authentically share and serve with joy and purpose from the fullness of your heart.

Admittedly, self-commitment may appear a bit abstract and possibly even overwhelming. Where and how do you start? I'd suggest starting by committing to the most valuable gift you have to offer: your energy. Whether you're trying to defuse a conflict between your siblings, clean up after your kids, or burn the midnight oil to make your boss happy, what you expend is your energy. But just like the winner of a multi-million-dollar lottery ticket, you may have been overly generous and inattentive with your energy without considering that you might eventually run out of it. Self-commitment allows you to break free of the helper survival pattern by becoming a better steward of your energy and making your health and well-being a priority and natural necessity. Only when you learn to honor your needs and include yourself in your propensity to support and nurture, will you establish a balanced and harmonious relationship with yourself and the world around you.

Committing to managing our energy responsibly is similar to handling other resources, such as money and time. First, we need to feel worthy of having these resources, then we need to stop mindlessly draining what we have, and then we need to be open to generating and receiving more. So here are the four steps to becoming a responsible steward of your energy.

FOUR DAILY SELF-COMMITMENT ROUTINES

Step 1: Refill Your Self-Worth Account

It's challenging to change a pattern without addressing what drives it in the first place. Breaking habits such as chewing our nails, bouncing our legs when we're nervous, or eating lunch at our desk is almost impossible if we don't learn to manage the underlying stress. Similarly, as long as we depend on others to give us a sense of worthiness, we continue to fall back into pleaser patterns.

You've probably noticed that no matter how much validation you receive, it doesn't fundamentally change how you relate to yourself. Like a sugary treat doesn't provide much nutritional value, an approving smile or a "thank you" never has a lasting effect on your self-worth. Consequently, if you think about your self-worth as a bank account, you probably find it more often depleted than overflowing.

So to start replenishing your account, write into a self-worth journal every day two reasons why you could feel good about yourself. I know, this sounds easier said than done. Most people find it much more natural to criticize than appreciate themselves. Yet each day, you have most likely more than fifty reasons to compliment yourself; you just aren't in the habit of acknowledging them. Even though you show up every day, giving your best to all the different aspects of your life, you don't value who you are and what you have done.

Notice the many day-to-day contributions you make that you usually take for granted. Let's say you never forget to feed your cats, go to work even if you want to play hooky, always make your bed and never leave dirty dishes in the sink, check in with your neighbor because she seems lonely, and help bugs that are lying on their backs get on their feet. Also become aware of how you show up in the world. For example, you may be the friendliest driver on the road, cautious, considerate, and always waving to other cars to go in front of you, even if those behind you honk their horns. Or you love to laugh, and at times, sing in the shower. You're open to learning from your mistakes and becoming a better version of yourself. Freshly baked cookies make you think gratefully of your grandma, and whenever you see a falling star, you make a wish for those less fortunate than you. Keeping such a journal may make it easier to pay attention to how you express and share the unique gifts and qualities you've already explored in the chameleon pattern chapter.

If writing isn't your cup of tea, you may try the *inner cheerleader* approach. For several years now, I've employed a part of my mind whose job it is to provide me with positive commentary. The idea came after watching the 2006 fantasy comedy *Aquamarine,* which told the story of a mermaid who wore two talking starfish as her earrings. In the movie, these starfish constantly whispered encouraging messages into the mermaid's ears, like, "You are so beautiful, smart, and funny. Everybody loves you. You are just fabulous." Right away, my wife said, "It's like having a cheerleader on speed-dial. You know what you need to get me for my birthday." Needless to say, I couldn't fulfill her wish, but I started to use the principle of consistent encouragement as my new inner background music.

You know how when you're watching a movie, depending on the film score, you either relax into the chair, get ready to burst into laughter, or like me, close your eyes because the music becomes unnerving and you expect something horrendous to jump out from behind a door or nearby bushes? Our self-talk also creates a form of background score, which can be either uplifting or deflating. My inner cheerleader keeps pointing out everything I've done *well,* whether it's getting out of bed to brush my teeth, cleaning horse manure from our paddock, or refraining from checking my phone late at night. Yes, these are just ordinary things I could easily dismiss as unimportant. But as we all know, in any relationship, the small things matter the most. You don't have to end world hunger or win the Nobel Peace Prize to gain the right to appreciate yourself. There's no size minimum to feeling good about yourself.

Refilling your self-worth account is part of the equation. The other part of boosting your self-esteem is preventing yourself from eroding it. As I've discussed in previous chapters, stop yourself from depleting your confidence by judging and criticizing yourself, comparing yourself to others, and giving more weight to their opinion than your own. I suggest looking in the mirror with a smile rather than a horrified grimace. Be kind and compassionate when you mess up or don't fulfill your expectations. And always remember that perception is projection, which means that all of us can only see the world through the distorting filters of our minds. So whatever people are judging you for says more about them than it does about you. And whatever you are criticizing yourself for, you have the power to replace those distorting self-defeating filters with more encouraging and supportive beliefs. In the end, the only opinion that matters is that of the one person you spend every moment with until the end of your life.

If you still doubt that you can fill your self-worth account, rest assured that consistent self-commitment will help you get there. As the great psychologist Rollo May said, "The relationship between commitment and doubt is by no means an antagonistic one. Commitment is healthiest when it's not without doubt but in spite of doubt."[1] In other words, just by committing to acknowledge yourself, you already boost your self-worth—and thus become less dependent on the approval of others.

Step 2: Check Your Energy Balance

Have you ever avoided stepping on a scale because you worried you over-indulged in french fries, ice cream, and chocolate chip cookies? Or tried to ignore your bank statements after splurging during your vacation? Maybe neither of these truth-tellers scares you. But when was the last time you checked on the state of your energy? If you could measure right now the charge level of your internal battery on a scale from 1–10, with 10 being full, how high would it be?

No matter which survival patterns have dominated your life, it's more than likely that your energy level hovers around the low end because these patterns, due to their depleting nature, aren't designed to be active for a long time. Short-term, hiding behind victimhood, denying ourselves to be seen or heard, putting off the tasks at hand, or over-giving and over-pleasing can give you a sense of security or belonging. Eventually though, you realize that no matter how many people or situations you've avoided, and how many you've catered to or impressed, your struggles only worsen. Why? Because since you believe that your safety and well-being depend on external factors, you continue giving out more energy than you receive back. Let's see if we can put some numbers to this imbalance.

Imagine an old-fashioned scale, with two weighing pans suspended on either end of a bar at equal distance. Let's say the left pan measures all the energy you give out, and the right one all the energy you either get back or give back to yourself. On the left side, list your major, tangible activities during an average day. For example, you may write these items: waking up the kids, making breakfast, getting everybody ready for school, rushing through traffic to avoid being late for work, attending to my job, going grocery shopping on the way home, cooking dinner, helping kids with homework, or cleaning up before going to bed.

Now add to the list on the left specific times you're either in avoidance or pleasing mode. This could be managing a conflict between the kids, cheering up your partner since they are usually grumpy in the morning, apologizing to a road-rager who's giving you the bird, making sure to ask intelligent questions during the team meeting to impress your peers, worrying about calling back your sister because she'll make you feel guilty if you don't, agonizing about what to buy for dinner that everybody will eat without complaints, or obsessing about what super-cool gift you could buy your friends for their wedding.

Then give each item on your list of energy output a number between 1 and 10, depending on how much energy you expended.

Let's move to the right side. There you note all the activities—and non-activities—that gave you energy and nourished you, physically, mentally, emotionally, or spiritually. This could be a brief meditation before you get out of bed, followed by a hot shower and a green smoothie. Maybe during lunch, you listen to an uplifting podcast or sit on your favorite bench in the park. In the evening, you read a few pages in a captivating book or watch a funny show. And sometimes, you may even take a bubble bath, hoping that nobody will disturb you—for at least ten minutes. Then again, assign each item on your list a number between 1–10, indicating how much energy you've added to the scale. Now tally up both sides and see whether you have more energy going out or more coming back to you.

It's safe to assume that your left side is much heavier than your right side. To be fair, considering how many people struggle with stress, overwhelm, and exhaustion, probably most of our society suffers from energy depletion. At the same time, most don't know how to bring the energy scale back into balance. So we tell ourselves that there's nothing we can do to improve the situation, that we just don't have time to take care of ourselves, or that we have to get through this rough patch, and then we'll change. Then we rely on food, caffeine, and energy drinks to get us through the day, not realizing that we're pushing our body to draw on its vital reserves. If you floor a car that's already running on fumes, eventually you'll find yourself stuck on the side of the road.

Now let's start bringing your energy back into balance by removing some weight from your left side and adding more on the right side.

Step 3: Consolidate Your Energy with Unbreakable Boundaries

Earlier in the chapter, you dismantled the most common excuses for the energy-draining helper pattern. But to effectively prevent yourself from overdoing and overgiving, you need to learn how to set boundaries. Most pleasers and helpers find it more challenging to set boundaries than to endure the pain of getting drained, disrespected, or walked all over. The deep desire to get approval and the constant fear of rejection can thwart any efforts to speak out, push back, and stand up for yourself. But you're not alone.

The #MeToo movement sadly revealed how many men (and some women) abuse their power to exploit and maltreat their co-workers in the workplace. Yet sexual harassment, ranging from unwanted attention to abuse and assault, is only the tip of the iceberg. The uncertainties of the economy and unrealistic expectations of the shareholders have created a high-pressure work culture with very little room for gratitude, loyalty, and even humanity. Employees feel increasingly worried and anxious about being replaceable and are more willing to "shut up and put up" rather than stand up for themselves. They perceive setting boundaries as a luxury they can't afford. Not only in the workplace but in our society in general, there is a worrisome trend of disrespecting fellow citizens. Cyberbullying, road rage, domestic violence, and a resurgence of xenophobia and homophobia are just a few examples of where boundaries get aggressively broken daily.

Although boundaries are often ignored and breached, they're still the most effective way to protect ourselves from being taken advantage of and to preserve our dignity. Establishing boundaries is a powerful statement of self-commitment, as it shows that we honor and respect ourselves, even if it means we may lose approval from others. And as you'll see for yourself, just as a lack of boundaries invites a lack of respect, the opposite is true as well. The following four boundaries will make it easier for you to no longer unconsciously squander your energy on short-lived external validation.

Internal Boundary: Awareness

Recognizing that you need a boundary is the first and maybe most important boundary. This means paying attention to your feelings, respecting your needs, and taking responsibility for your safety and energy. Generally, you know somebody overstepped your boundaries when you feel confused, uncomfortable, frustrated, hurt, anxious, or ashamed. Yet in the past, you've used some or all of the pleaser excuses to talk yourself out of even noticing when you've given in to giving too much to others. And no matter how many times others kept on guilt-tripping you to provide them with the last bit of your energy, you continued to suppress your hurt and disappointment by telling yourself that you always overreact because you're just too sensitive.

As a sign of self-commitment, honor so-called negative feelings as messages from your subconscious indicating that it's time to pay attention to yourself. Don't ignore or argue with your emotions, but trust that they have a valid meaning for you. But let's look more closely at ways your boundaries get pushed aside.

The most direct boundary break is when people disregard your limits, after which you usually feel anxious and small. Apart from physical and verbal abuse, there are many less aggressive ways in which others, consciously or unconsciously, step across your boundaries. For example, some people assume that you're always available for them and ignore your need for privacy. Others don't accept your "no" for an answer, and continue to relentlessly bombard you with their problems, even though you've indicated that you're not comfortable listening to them. Or you may have encountered those who expect you to fulfill their needs, and if you don't, punish you with rejection and blame.

Another more subtle boundary breach occurs when people don't accept you and your choices. Let's say you start feeling good about your progress as you work on yourself. But your family shows you unequivocally that they prefer the "old" you. Or your excitement about a new interest gets squashed by your colleague's eye roll. And when you get together with your friends, they usually get a kick out of making fun of you, no matter how red-faced embarrassed you become. These underhanded ways in which those you want to feel close to and accepted by overstep your boundaries hurt the most and leave you feeling insecure and ashamed of yourself.

In my experience, the most common but also most elusive breakdown of our boundaries is the one committed by ourselves. Perhaps you find yourself still preoccupied with work on Saturday morning, rehashing a difficult conversation with a frustrated client from a few days earlier. Maybe you tend to take on your partner's anxious moods and quickly feel stressed and worried in their presence. Or at three o'clock on a Saturday morning, you fret about why, for Heaven's sake, you've agreed to help your buddy move, even though you would rather chill with your family. You break your inner boundary when you continue to give your mental and emotional energy to situations or people you can't change. The helper's insecurity and empathy often result in such an internal boundary breakdown. You ignore all your good intentions to focus on yourself and instead fall back into the old pattern of worrying about what you need to do to please others.

When you realize that your boundaries get frequently disregarded, your initial reaction may be to either attack or avoid those who crossed them—including yourself. However, are confrontation or retreat really the best ways to strengthen your boundaries? Let's take your health as an analogy; to avoid getting a cold, it isn't enough to eliminate bugs with disinfectants or stop leaving the house. You also need to strengthen your immune system. So how can you strengthen your boundaries?

External Boundary: Assertiveness

The best way to truly educate others about what you accept and what you don't is by giving yourself a voice that can't be ignored. My wife, a great role model for healthy boundaries, likes to say, "*No* is a complete sentence." As a helper, "no" wasn't necessarily a part of your daily vocabulary. So it can be helpful to practice saying "no" in easy and emotionally uncharged situations. Like at the take-out counter when you're asked whether you want extra napkins, with your friend who invites you to watch a movie, or with telemarketers who ask you if you can give them five minutes of your time.

There are, of course, wordier and more eloquent ways to stand up for yourself. Here are a few examples of what you can say if "no" feels too harsh or still too intimidating to you.

- Explain your needs and priorities: "I can't, because I need to focus on myself / my projects right now."
- Share your view: "I understand what you need, but I am working on making my needs a priority, so it doesn't feel right for me to help you with this."
- Express understanding for the other person's demand: "I know how stressed you are about this, but I really can't take care of this for you."
- Buy some time and then decline later: "Let me think about it. I need to see whether I will have the time and energy."
- Share your feelings: "You probably didn't intend this, but when you continued to ask me to do xyz, it really made me uncomfortable."
- Make a suggestion: "Unfortunately, I can't be the one who does this for you, but you may want to call X. He may have some availability."
- Ask for what you need: "It is really important to me that you respect my decision not to take this on."
- Call out pushy behavior: "I don't think you are hearing me. I

meant it when I said that I can't / don't want to do (or talk about) xyz."

- Negotiate. A boundary doesn't have to be as rigid and unmovable as the Great Wall of China: "I am not able to help you with everything now, but I can give you a couple of hours tomorrow."
- And when all fails: "I'm done. For my own sanity, this conversation is over."

It can be scary to speak up on your behalf and potentially be judged and rejected for doing so. However, staying small and powerless while others are taking advantage of you—knowingly or unknowingly—is even scarier.

Internal Boundary: Disconnection

Have you ever accidentally put your hand on a hot stove? While you may have touched the hot plate just for half a second, the pain afterward probably lasted for hours. Getting your inner boundaries breached can have the same effect. A troubling interaction of five minutes can occupy you for weeks as you continue to agonize on why you've been treated so badly, or what you've done wrong and what you should have done differently. However, unlike when you suffer a physical burn, you can choose whether you want the hurt to continue.

It bears repeating that even though we can't control the people or circumstances we're dealing with, we can always choose how to respond to them. Rather than spinning your mind around somebody's inappropriate behavior, remind yourself that you keep on giving your energy away every moment you are still thinking about them. To create an internal boundary that stops a person's negativity from triggering your doubt and insecurity, imagine watching the situation that bothered you as though it were a movie, ideally black and white, on a tiny little screen. As you observe the event from a safe and neutral distance, ask yourself these questions:

- Is the other person's behavior a reflection of who I am?
- How is this person's behavior a reflection of who they are?
- Why do I deserve to be treated with greater respect?
- Why is this person's behavior no longer acceptable for me?
- How can I set stronger boundaries next time?

Once you've answered these questions with self-commitment and self-compassion, you can turn the tiny screen off and shift your focus onto something more peaceful and positive.

Besides rehashing the past, what if-ing the future is another common way our inner boundaries crumble. You may worry about the endlessly growing to-do list that has become the measuring stick for your worthiness. Or you agonize about how to not upset your boss by announcing that you want to take a week off for vacation. Or you wonder whether you can even go on holiday while your mom has a cold. One of my favorite ways to stop my inner helper from turning on the mental hamster wheel is to hold a conversation with this part of my mind. In the victim and the invisibility pattern chapters, I discussed how to not lose our power by making assumptions or taking other people's opinions personally. To stop our subconscious from pushing against our inner boundaries, it needs to receive from us what it seeks to get from others—safety and validation.

Therefore, I'm telling my inner helper that it's safe to stop focusing on others because I have his back. I remind him of everything I appreciate about myself and why I know I am a good and valuable human being. I emphasize that I deserve to disconnect and pay attention to my needs and desires. And to further bolster my inner boundaries, I summarize the insights I shared with you when I discussed common pitfalls:

- Giving back to myself is essential for my self-worth and well-being.
- I am the source of my safety and happiness.
- Self-care is my commitment to myself and those I care about.

- If I tried to resolve all the problems of the people I care about, I would deny them their opportunity to become self-reliant and empowered.
- I believe that we all have inner resources to heal and grow.
- I choose to support others to the best of my abilities from a place of balance and compassion.

Internal Boundary: Shield of Compassion

Speaking of compassion, as we all know, even the most rational arguments and best intentions only have a limited effect on our subconscious, because this part of our mind responds better to feelings and visualization than words and logic. Now and again, you may empathetically sponge up so much of other people's needs, hurt, and expectations that you simply feel too overwhelmed to talk yourself into setting an inner boundary. This is when creating an energetic boundary in the form of a shield of compassion becomes very helpful. As I described in the invisibility pattern chapter, compassion for others can be a force field that prevents you from absorbing their emotions and energies. The shield of compassion affirms that while you care about and believe in others, you also acknowledge that ultimately it is their responsibility to attend to their needs and wants.

Here's a quick way to create a force field of compassion: As you did in the previous chapters, start with connecting to this emotion, thinking about anybody you feel compassion for. Then visualize compassion as a facet of the light of your essence at your core. Inhale and exhale and feel rays of compassion emanate from your heart. Let this brilliant energy soon illuminate your chest, your upper body, and then your entire physical being. Notice how you become more relaxed and centered as you picture the rays of compassion infusing every muscle, cell, and fiber. At some point, you can visualize the light spreading beyond the confines of your body, gradually forming a protective bubble, an energetic force field around you. Imagine how the shield of compassion keeps other people's emotions and energies at least six feet away from you. You are still aware of what they experience, but you don't lose focus on yourself. With this compassionate boundary, you gently restrict your helper pattern's urge to rush to the rescue. Instead, you can calmly reflect on the situation and choose how to approach it in a balanced and self-committed way.

Now that you have firmed up your inner boundaries, it is time to implement them.

External Boundary: Interrupting the Pattern

To quote the famous Brazilian writer Paulo Coelho, "If you think adventure is dangerous, try routine: it is lethal."[2] Living in survival patterns is your subconscious way of turning life from an adventure into a repetitive routine. Neuro-linguistic Programming offers an effective method called Pattern Interrupt to break out of this self-protective monotony. You use this tool to replace old mental, emotional, or behavioral habits with a new strategy. Let's say you want to stop chewing your nails whenever you get nervous. With pattern interrupt, you first analyze what triggers this unwanted behavior and what the habit looks like exactly. Then you pinpoint the moment when the behavior becomes an unconscious response. For example, if you bite your nails, that moment might be when you've moved your hand about four inches from your face. At that point, you have lost conscious control, and the behavior becomes automatic. The final step is to choose what replacement habit you would like to install, which for nail biting could be looking at your fingers or combing through your hair. Don't expect an old pattern to be erased and replaced after catching yourself one time. You may need to practice twenty or forty times to form a new habit. And most importantly, you still want to focus on reducing what activated gnawing on your claws in the first place—stress.

When it comes to replacing some of the old energy-draining helper survival patterns, you know by now what triggers them: your need for safety, belonging, and validation. And because you know more about establishing your boundaries, you already have alternative empowering responses at your disposal. Identifying when these patterns leave your conscious control and switch to autopilot may be trickier for you. Unlike nail-biting, there isn't necessarily a visual cue to indicate that your caretaking has gone off the rails. But to know when to say "no," you want to be keenly aware of the moment you're approaching the point of no return.

Let's draw on your past experiences with this behavior and write down the five most common situations when your inner helper ran the show. These could occur at work, at home, with friends, or with family. Then for each of these situations, ask yourself what specifically triggered your helper response. Was it something you thought or what another person said, their tone of voice, body posture, gesture, or facial expression? For instance, every time your daughter comes into your room right as you're crawling into bed, you end up spending at least an hour listening to her complaints about her "mean" girlfriends, even though you're completely exhausted. Whenever your boss looks for volunteers to work overtime, your hand shoots up as if you were trying to be a contestant on The Price Is Right, even though you already feel that you barely have time for yourself. Or when your partner tells you that you haven't been very attentive lately, you frantically search for ways to make them happy, although you already feel overwhelmed with everything else going on in your life.

Isn't it true that as soon as the phone rings, your immediate response is to pick it up? Or when your alarm goes off, you start to get out of bed? Our subconscious makes us automatically respond to certain stimuli. For your inner helper, such a stimulus could be your daughter's exasperated tone of voice, your boss's stress-induced intensity, and your partner's look of disappointment. Just as Pavlov's dogs salivated the moment they heard the ringing of a bell, this part of your subconscious springs into caretaking action at any indication that somebody might "need" you. This sudden urge to please is the sensation you want to be consciously aware of, because this is your choice point, the moment when you can decide whether you prefer to give your energy and time to others or yourself. The goal is for you in the future to be aware of what you're about to do before you do it.

When you go through your list of helper pattern examples, try to recall how you feel as this pattern gets fired up. This can be an emotion, such as empathy, anxiety, or even excitement. The choice point can also show up as a sensation in your body, like a rush, tension, or heat. Now, assuming that you're already maxed out and your energy scale is leaning heavily to the left, what would you need to say to yourself to stop your pleaser?

How about telling yourself that your daughter needs to learn self-efficacy and self-soothing to navigate relationship issues with greater confidence? At work, you could reflect on the fact that you're already doing the best you can, and it isn't necessary to overdeliver 100 percent of the time. What you do and who you are is enough. And with your partner, you may want to remind yourself how much you love them and are committed to making them happy. But still, since your scale is leaning dramatically to the left, it's equally important to commit to yourself so that you can engage in your relationship replenished and re-energized. Once you've stopped the automatic pattern in its tracks, you can calmly respond to the other person with compassionate but firm external boundaries and then, if necessary, attend to the concerns of your helper with inner boundaries.

Pattern interrupt is a powerful way to demonstrate to your subconscious that you're the trustworthy leader committed to being the source of your safety and worthiness. As with all methods though, there's just one in-built caveat: it works best when you use it regularly. Take some time to mentally rehearse each of the five scenarios you jotted down, noting how interrupting self-defeating patterns and applying your boundaries would make you feel more empowered and in charge of your life.

Between filling up your self-worth account, being aware of your energy balance, and consolidating how much energy you expend, you already have three self-commitment steps to becoming the steward of your energy. The last step is attending to your energy scale's right side.

Step 4. Replenish Your Energy

As goes the saying about the cobbler's children being barefoot, helpers usually don't help themselves. For you, the lack of self-care may not only be because of the lack of time but also because of the lack of ideas about how to recharge your batteries. At the beginning of our relationship, Danielle noticed that whenever I completed all my to-do's and was running out of people, animals, and plants to attend to, rather than looking for ways to relax and regenerate, I paced the house like a restless tiger locked in a cage. "It seems like you don't know how to relax and take care of yourself," she pointed out. And she was right. Before I met her, my idea of a self-care evening consisted of a Hamburger Helper dinner, two bottles of light beer, and three episodes of the TV show *M*A*S*H*. Yet pointing out my cluelessness about supporting myself wasn't enough. Through Danielle patiently offering me suggestions and modeling impeccable self-nurturing, I eventually learned to appreciate and practice the art of self-care. So trust me, if I could do it, you certainly can too.

If your idea of self-care comprises sleeping and eating, you may just as well add breathing. All three are fundamental to survival. To truly make a difference in your energy balance, you need to change your daily routines, schedule self-care appointments, and look for ways to rejuvenate outside your comfort zone. So let's divide replenishing your energy into three tiers: essential, enjoyable, and expansive.

Essential

These are the basic, daily changes to counterbalance the energy deficit you may have accumulated.

- Remember the excellent animated film *Ratatouille,* featuring Remy, a Parisian rat with a passion for gourmet food? "If you are what you eat," Remy said, "I only want to eat good stuff." What do you think your food choices indicate about how you relate to yourself? Most studies confirm that eating a fresh, balanced, and predominantly plant-based diet improves our health and longevity. So step out of the long lines at your favorite fast-food joint and commit to nourishing your body at least three times per week with the healthy food it craves. And please, don't skip breakfast. After being starved throughout the night, your cells need some fuel in the morning to avoid panicking.

- Other daily self-care improvements include getting seven to eight hours of sleep, moving your body for at least twenty minutes, staying hydrated, and staying away from caffeine, alcohol, nicotine, and other drugs.

- To support your mental and emotional well-being, limit your screen time, especially one hour before you go to bed. Keep at least your bedroom zen and clutter-free, speak kindly with yourself, and make sure to appreciate yourself by engaging your inner cheerleader. Also, consider journaling, meditating, singing in the shower, dancing in the living room, and spending time doing absolutely nothing.

Enjoyable

The sayings "business before pleasure" and "no dessert before dinner" promote the virtue of postponing fun and rewards. Yet having tried this strategy for years, I find nothing honorable about denying yourself the joy of pampering your mind, body, and soul. By devoting just a bit more planning and commitment, you can create a self-care program that's replenishing and enjoyable. Simply incorporate the following suggestions:

- The usual suspects are taking a bath, luxuriating an afternoon in a spa, getting a massage or a mani-pedi, going for a hike, or just spending time in nature.

- You can also meet friends for lunch or dinner, join a cooking class or gym, learn a new creative skill, go for a swim, or take yourself on a date to the movies.

- Take a few days away from your "life" and attend a yoga or meditation retreat, visit friends or family members, or treat yourself to a road trip—drive to a city, national park, or attraction you've always wanted to see. Or take off and follow your nose, with no destination in mind at all.

Expansive

Bad habits thrive in small comfort zones. In other words, to truly outgrow your limitations, you need to venture out of what you've deemed your *safe habitat*. One of the most challenging and most rewarding changes you can make as a helper is learning to receive without feeling the need to pay back or reciprocate.

- As you're getting more into the habit of setting boundaries, you will automatically receive more respect and acknowledgment. To become a better receiver, respond to praise, compliments, rewards, or presents with a simple "Thank you." And call on your inner boundaries to prevent your helper pattern from immediately plotting what you can do or buy in return.
- Practice additional receiving by asking a tall stranger to help you get a bottle of ketchup from the top shelf, request that your beloved give you a foot massage, or telling the friends who invited you for dinner that you would love to eat something meat-free. Remember, it isn't a setback if you get a "no" from those you ask. Everybody has a right to their boundaries. Yet, just by expressing what you need or want, you've already won because you said "yes" to yourself.
- Another form of expanding self-care is to express yourself more. For example, instead of avoiding conflict and keeping the peace, share your opinions and advocate for your preferences. With those who are used to you being their sounding board,

turn the tables on them and make them listen to what's on *your* mind. And rather than postponing indefinitely, get started on the novel or the painting you feel you have inside.

By attending to your needs, asking for what you want, openly receiving from others, and showing more of who you are to the world, you're giving yourself the greatest gift: the commitment to value yourself for who you are and not for what you do for others.

......

Sticking with self-commitment can transform your life. It certainly worked for Mary. After setting clear boundaries with her medical team by refusing to accept their dire prognosis, she dedicated her time and energy to healing the deeper root causes of her autoimmune disease.

Her first big breakthrough came when she could respond to the constantly berating inner voice (that sounded just like her mother) with kindness and compassion. Mary recognized that this inner critic was in fact her helper, who believed it was safer for Mary to feel small and insecure because it would ensure that she continued to please her mom rather than start fighting with her. "Once I stopped putting myself down, I could see so much more clearly that I'm a good person with a caring heart. No matter whether my mom can appreciate me or not, I deserve to take care of myself." With this newfound self-worth, Mary established a previously unthinkable boundary by telling her mother that she wouldn't visit her until she was healthy again. By setting solid inner boundaries, Mary saw her mom from a compassionate distance without the familiar guilt and shame that used to pull her back into the old helper pattern. As we delved deeper into her subconscious mind, Mary developed a warm-hearted dedication to attending to her needs and desires. Caring for her mind and body was no longer just a means to get well and return to who she was before. Self-care became an expression of her growing love and appreciation for herself.

One year after we first met, Mary reported another breakthrough. For the first time in many months, she could once again eat real food: salmon and mashed potatoes. While at first she worried that the meal might have been a one-time event, Mary soon tried other solid food and larger portions without encountering any pain. After another few months, Mary regained all her weight. Today, seven years later, Mary can eat normally and only needs to get the scar tissue of her esophagus stretched once per year. And despite having healed herself, Mary continues to make self-commitment the foundation of her *second* life.

13

THE LOVER PATTERN

Aching for Love

I can't live without your love.

Repeat after me: "I love myself." How did this feel? Solid and accurate or uncomfortable and forced? If you were to gauge your level of self-love on a scale from one to ten, what number would you come up with? The fact is that self-love is a powerful force that leads to exponential change, healing, and success. But most of us are not particularly good at it, because we were never taught how to love ourselves and therefore depend on others to make us feel loveable and worthy. So, we can probably all use some guidance and tools for how to love ourselves more.

Whether we love or reject ourselves as adults is often connected to how much warmth and love we received when we were little. A recent Harvard study showed that filling up a child's love container continues to affect their health and well-being during adulthood significantly. Of the more than three thousand people who contributed to the survey, those who recalled experiencing affection and love from their parents flourished mentally, emotionally, and socially to a significantly greater degree than those who didn't have such memories.[1] Researchers also found that people that didn't receive love and support during their early years were more likely to develop anxiety, depression, obsessive-compulsive behavior, and addictions.[2]

Professor Robert Winston, a world-renowned pioneer in the study of fertility, concluded: "Parents can worry about things that just aren't important to their children's brain development and well-being, such as giving them their own room, buying them toys, and taking them on expensive holidays. Instead, the most valuable gift that a child can receive is free; it's simply a parent's love, time, and support. This is no empty sentiment; science is now showing why babies' brains need love more than anything else."[3]

In my experience, people dealing with the lover survival pattern usually experienced a lack of warmth and love during their upbringing. Yet at the same time, not everyone who entered adulthood without their love container being adequately filled developed this pattern. So what makes our subconscious choose to pivot toward the lover? Unlike the other survival patterns, which aim for a sense of safety and control, the lover pattern seems to have a different mission: to love and be loved. "All You Need Is Love," the famous song by the Beatles, could be its anthem. Lovers feel they matter only when they're in an intimate relationship and thus struggle with the fear of being lonely and unlovable.

This survival pattern is relatively common for people who have gone through traumatic neglect, abandonment, or some form of abuse. We already discussed how being ignored, left, or abused by a parent or trusted family member shatters a child's natural expectation of being sheltered and cared for, and causes profound confusion about the child's worthiness. The lover tries to resolve this confusion by proving those who hurt them wrong. And since lovers question their innate value, they often feel the need to promote themselves through extreme generosity and sexual availability. Like helpers, lovers tend to over-give and overdo. Yet instead of pleasing everybody, they put all their eggs in the basket of one chosen person.

LOST IN LOVE

Judith, an attractive and talented woman in her forties, started working with me to overcome her fear of being unlovable. For many years Judith had been unsuccessfully searching for "the one." Usually, her boyfriends broke up with her after fewer than three months, calling her needy, pushy, and too complicated. Then, while we were in the midst of our work together, Tom came along. He was everything Judith had been looking for—handsome, creative, charismatic, and available. "We're madly in love," she told me. "Our chemistry is off the charts. He makes me feel so beautiful and wanted. For the first time, I know what it is to be adored."

But after a short honeymoon period, things changed, and Tom became increasingly moody. He started to call Judith selfish when she spent too much time at work and narcissistic when she fixed her hair in the mirror. He refused to show her affection in front of his friends, causing Judith to wonder if he kept their relationship a secret. The most challenging change was that Tom went dark for days at a time, neither calling her nor answering his phone. For Judith, waiting for a sign of life from Tom was pure torture. Every time he resurfaced, he was tender and apologetic and explained that he needed to deal with his own stuff and didn't want to let Judith see when he was struggling. But no matter how much Judith pleaded with him to never let her suffer again, he repeated the same behavior, over and over again. "I don't know how to get through the times when he shuts me out," she said. "I can't sleep. I can't think. And I constantly feel like throwing up." Yet as soon as Tom returned with tearful apologies, she forgot how much his disappearance act had upset her. And for at least a couple of weeks, she was in heaven again.

Desperate for answers, one day Judith snooped through Tom's phone. There she discovered text messages and explicit photos of other women with whom Tom had intimate relationships. When

Judith confronted Tom, overwhelmed with shock and anger, he fell on his knees and started sobbing, "I don't know why I do this! These women mean nothing to me. You're the only one who matters. I'm just so afraid of how much I love you that I sometimes need to run away." Whether it was Tom's vulnerability or the declaration of his love, Judith quickly pushed aside the hurtful betrayal and forgave him. Tom later confided in her that he struggled to trust women because he grew up with a highly unpredictable mother with bipolar disorder. But, he assured her, Judith was the first girlfriend he started to feel safe with. Feeling special and chosen, Judith vowed that she would be even more attentive and understanding to help Tom overcome his childhood trauma.

Her devotion to helping Tom didn't stop him from treating her with the usual hot-cold reactivity, mixed with periods of absence. But no matter how harsh, cruel, or neglectful Tom could be, for Judith, these were just the reactions of the hurt and scared little boy inside him, whom she was determined to heal. As all her focus went to making this relationship work, Judith began to treat herself just as Tom treated her, with neglect, lies, and abandonment. Her diet consisted of sweets, nicotine, and alcohol. She had no motivation to exercise, see her friends, or even leave her home.

Judith owned a graphic design company, which through passion and hard work, she'd built up to fifteen employees. As the ups and downs of her relationship occupied most of her energy and time, Judith became less interested in running her company. After she missed crucial deadlines with long-term customers and stopped acquiring new ones, she eventually shut down her business. Tired of hearing me say that she was on the self-destructive path of code-pendency, Judith also stopped our sessions. For Judith, the pain of losing her livelihood—and herself—was insignificant compared to the unimaginable misery of a life without Tom.

One day, everything changed. "In a moment of weakness and boredom," as she described it later, Judith contacted one of the women whose messages and pictures she had found on Tom's phone. She didn't know what she hoped to find out. The woman told Judith that she knew about Tom's affairs, and that he had reassured her that she—and not Judith or any of the others—was the only one who mattered to him. And still, the reality of Tom being a manipulative sociopath didn't sink in for Judith. Denial is a powerful force and Judith chose to believe her boyfriend over her rival. However, Tom became furious when he found out that Judith had reached out to one of his lovers. Calling her crazy and a psychopath, he declared that he never wanted to see or hear from her again.

A few weeks into her confusion and grief, she wrote to me:

I feel paralyzed and depressed. The idea that I need to let go of the hope of a future with Tom sets me into such overwhelm that I cannot function. My mind is racing to make sense of him and to formulate answers I can live with. A story that I can understand. I just don't know what went wrong and what I could have done to prevent him from breaking up with me. I know that he cheated on me several times. I also understand that he could be manipulative and angry, especially when he put me down, telling me that I am selfish and a workaholic. But some part of me doesn't want to believe that he is a sociopath who took advantage of me. There were so many moments of love and kindness between us. This part knows that I was unique to Tom and that he loved me like nobody before. I cannot accept that this wasn't real. I keep on telling myself that he was just too wounded and insecure to embrace my love for him. But if he had just given me a chance, I could have helped him heal. I still feel that I don't know what is true anymore; the loneliness kills me and makes me want to reach out to him. But I know he doesn't want to hear from me, which is even harder to stomach. All I do is overeat, watch TV, and shop online. I somehow want to hold on to the idea that I mattered to Tom and that the last few months were more than just being abused by a manipulator. I can't handle that, even if it is true.

Like a survivor of the sinking *Titanic* trying to clutch on to a piece of wood, Judith's lover pattern desperately held on to her broken relationship, even though it was nothing more than a toothpick that couldn't keep her afloat. When she was forced to move out of her apartment, which she could no longer afford, she finally realized that she had to start focusing on herself again.

Judith's example may sound extreme, and you may have wondered what severe traumas of her childhood could make her so desperate for love. The fact is that Judith didn't experience physical or emotional abuse. She went through what, especially during the '80s, fifty percent of children in the United States experienced—her parents' divorce.[4] Judith remembered that when her father moved out, the world fell apart for her. In contrast to her demanding and somewhat aloof mom, Judith always felt understood and loved by her dad. "I was his little princess. So when he left us, I wanted nothing more than to go with him. But my parents didn't allow that. I remember how often I lay in bed crying, wanting him to come and get me away from this cold place. My dad got a job in a different town, and I saw him less and less often. When he remarried and had two more children with his new wife, it was obvious that he had completely forgotten about me."

WHY FOR THE LOVER FINDING LOVE ISN'T ENOUGH

You could argue that the lover pattern draws on all other avoidance and pleasing survival patterns. It is rooted in past victimization. It makes you hide the most vulnerable aspects from your partner. You procrastinate around career and self-improvement goals to seek instant gratification in the relationship. You fluidly adapt to the interests, preferences, and desires of the special someone to gain closeness, and by focusing on healing your partner's wounds, you achieve the comforting sense of being needed and irreplaceable. Yet as I mentioned before, unlike the other survival patterns, the prime motivation of the lover goes beyond being safe and belonging; it's to be wanted and loved—and not by just anyone, as you will see in a moment.

Here are the most common traits of the lover pattern.

Finding Love Is the Most Important Goal and Focus

For the lover, being in a relationship is the reason to exist. All other aspects of life—education, work, hobbies, and social connections—are approached as necessities without passion or purpose.

Being Alone Is Scary and Must Be Avoided at All Costs

The lover can't bear being alone, which is why, even as singles, they are always with friends, family, colleagues, or acquaintances.

Falling in Love Is Easy

A client who struggled with the lover pattern told me that all it took for her to fall for someone was for that person to show her a little bit of interest. And even if that bit of attention usually turned out to be nothing but a plan for a one-night stand, the desire for "real love" made her quickly dismiss the concern about potentially being taken advantage of.

Constant Insecurity about the Partner's Love and Commitment

Since lovers subconsciously question their lovability, they also question their partner's feelings for them. In response, lovers tend to be clingy and require constant reassurance. Their self-worth depends on the state of their relationship, as they see themselves more through their partner's eyes than their own. As Judith put it, "From one minute to the next, Tom could either lift me up or tear me down. And I never knew which one it would be." The lover's insecurity can also lead to jealousy, oversensitivity, and accusatory behavior. Some lovers *test* their significant other's dedication by frequently provoking conflicts and pointing out "clear signs" that their partner is either unfaithful or ready to leave. Regardless of how much reassurance and how many declarations of love they receive, the lover's nagging need to be wanted is only satisfied for a short time. Lovers continue to push, judge, and nag until they make happen what they always *knew* was just a matter of time—their mates calling it quits.

Eager to Take on Partner's Hobbies, Preferences, and Lifestyle

In chameleon-esque fashion, the lover shows limitless interest in whatever tickles their beloved's fancy. One of my clients told me that he became a fitness nerd with one boyfriend. With the next, he got caught up in fine dining and opera. Only to end up with yet another one where he found himself immersed in the world of fishing and hunting deer. I guess you could say that he broadened his horizons with each relationship. But, as he admitted, he never felt he could tell the men in his life about his interests, mainly because he had never taken the time to develop any on his own.

Ready to Give up Friendships and Personal Interests for the Relationship

Lovers are often loosely attached to their friends and recreational activities. Some admit that the only reason they have a social life is to increase their chances of meeting their mate. While others may see them as flaky, lovers consider themselves focused and motivated by love.

Extreme Loyalty to a Partner, Defending Them to Concerned Friends and Family

For caring bystanders, this is a challenging trait of the lover pattern. No matter how much evidence there is that the relationship is one-sided, dysfunctional, or even abusive as in Judith's case, lovers are unwilling to listen to others' concerns. Common excuses are "You don't know them as well as I do," or "My partner doesn't mean it; they are just in so much pain," or, my favorite, "You're just jealous that we have such a passionate relationship." Many times, lovers end up remorsefully admitting that they should have listened to their friends and families. Yet as soon as they're in another troubling relationship, good intentions to notice and respond appropriately to red flags are replaced by their unwavering dedication to make the relationship work at all costs. Once again, their unwavering dedication to making the relationship work at all costs takes over. When it comes to the lover pattern, love doesn't make us only blind but also deaf, voiceless, and oblivious.

Glorifying the Partner and Positive Times Together as "The Best Ever"

Through the subconscious filters of the lover, their romantic companions appear *golden* and not just rose-colored. Irrespective of the difficulties in the relationship, lovers insist that the person they're with knows and loves them like no one ever before. For the lover, positive aspects of the relationship, whether off-the-charts physical chemistry or the soul-mate-like depth of the emotional connection, justify clinging to the good times no matter how infrequent they become. As a friend who struggled with this pattern explained to me, "It was as if I let my girlfriend continuously run over me with her car, while I told myself, 'It's okay, because she always feels sorry afterward.'"

Self-Blame and the Commitment to "Do Better"

Most lovers are unwilling to admit that their feelings for the other person are kept alive by the hope for a fairy-tale ending rather than a reflection of reality. Some are afraid of being on their own again, others of having been wrong or having wasted valuable time. But most lovers have a staunch belief that *it always takes two to tango,* and that they must have contributed to the difficulties in the relationship. Unfortunately, while taking responsibility is commendable, with the lover, this often leads to unnecessary self-blame and a self-denying willingness to forgive their partner's neglect, insults, and abuse. Many of my clients told me that they became obsessed with the idea that there must be something that they could do differently to make their partner consistently happy and content. (Obviously, the lack of internal and external boundaries is a big issue not only for the helper pattern.) They became more obedient and accommodating, changed their appearances, and tried hard to find the perfect defusing response to criticism or angry outbursts. Nevertheless, usually the only result they achieved was for their partners to become even more disrespectful and demeaning toward them.

Even though this list of somewhat self-destructive traits may suggest that the lover pattern isn't genuinely concerned with survival, for the lover, being loved is like oxygen: an utter necessity they cannot live without. However, if that were the case, wouldn't they settle for anyone ready to commit? Curiously, lovers tend to dismiss potential suitors who show kindness, adoration, and appreciation as needy or uninteresting. A few years before Tom, Judith quickly dumped a lovely young man who was totally into her. At the time, she told herself that they were missing passion. But in one of our sessions, she admitted what many others with similar patterns had also shared with me, "I just thought that there must be something wrong with him that he chose me as his potential mate." So there must be another, even more significant agenda for this pattern than finding love.

The lover pattern shares many similarities with the anxious attachment style of John Bowlby's attachment theory. The British psychologist discovered that experiences during our early childhood, mainly regarding how much and how consistently we received attention and care, influence how we attach to a significant other.[5]

People with an anxious attachment style, roughly 19 percent of the population, often experienced one or both parents as inconsistently attentive and available.[6] The unpredictability of one moment receiving caring attention and the next one being ignored, criticized, or abandoned leaves the child confused and unsure about their lovability and the ability of others to provide them with love. We saw this with Judith, who had never understood how her father could move on and leave his little girl behind.

In general, whenever we're experiencing something hurtful and confusing, we consciously and subconsciously ask ourselves, "Why did this happen? What did I do wrong?" These questions also arise when a parent or somebody we care about neglects, abuses, or leaves us: "Why did those we should have been able to trust let us down? Was there anything we did to cause this?" While it appears incomprehensible that someone could treat us in inconsiderate and hurtful ways, the subconscious protector tries to make sense of it so that we are prepared if something similar should occur again. It assumes four possible explanations:

- Whatever happened is other people's wrong-doing and has nothing to do with me.
- Whatever happened may occur again, which means that trusting others isn't safe.
- Whatever happened could have been prevented by my behaving differently.
- Whatever happened is my fault and a reflection of my being unlovable.

While the healthy and self-affirming response would be assumption #1, our child's mind usually considers the other three. Early in our development, we're simply too dependent on other people's protection and care that we naturally take everything that is or isn't done to us personally. If the inner protector picks #2 and decides that relationships are unsafe and need to be avoided, it activates the invisibility pattern. But if the subconscious assumes that the adults know better than we do, and thus we are to blame, #3 and #4 appear to be the only explanations.

Studies found that individuals with anxious attachment styles show a greater preference for avoidant partners, which confirms this notion.[7] The researchers argued that by choosing avoidant partners, anxiously attached individuals validate their negative concept of being unworthy of love and their expectation that others will remain distant and unavailable, as was the case during their upbringing.

Judith and other clients with similar patterns admitted that they were attracted to partners whose behavior, demeanor, and even looks reminded them of their father or mother. And even though my clients felt unworthy and repeatedly rejected by their aloofness and, at times, abusive behavior, they also experienced unequaled excitement and happiness during the rare moments when the relationships seemed to improve or even thrive. On the other hand, they quickly brushed off potential partners who treated them consistently with respect and adoration as too soft, needy, or uninteresting.

Do we pick unhealthy relationships just because they are more familiar to us? Let's remember that the subconscious mind has two primary missions: (1) to keep us safe and (2) to make us happy, and that the chronic stress caused by living in survival mode is neither safe nor enjoyable. Thus, it is more likely that our subconscious is looking for ways to heal the hurt and confusion of past traumas by collecting evidence that explanations #3 and #4 were false and that we are indeed loveable and can't be faulted. The part of us that didn't feel loved, accepted, and committed to by a parent, our first relationship, or another significant figure during our early years wants to prove to us that this person was wrong and that there's nothing wrong with us. This is why we're subconsciously drawn to the personalities that remind us of those who made us question our lovability in the first place. Unfortunately, similar traits, such as volatility, avoidance of intimacy, or lack of kindness, lead to similar experiences of feeling rejected and unworthy.

Many excellent books on healing childhood trauma, anxious attachment, and co-dependency issues address these topics in much greater depth than the scope of this work allows. But in the end, our healing hinges on our ability to create a healthy and harmonious relationship with ourselves. When it comes to healing the lover pattern and its confusions and insecurities, you've already accomplished a lot through the previous chapters. You have disentangled from those who hurt and victimized you and reclaimed your power by taking self-responsibility to learn and grow from the past. Self-compassion and the reconnection to the innocent self have freed you from the guilt and shame you've projected onto yourself. You've returned to your source and realigned with your essence and thus released any doubt on your worthiness. And you've affirmed your commitment to be the steward of your energy and guardian of your boundaries.

No matter which survival pattern has been the most dominant in your life, to become the empowered leader of your life, the next step is to become your source of love. Because unless you open your heart toward yourself, all your progress will remain like seeds without water, light, or fertile ground. For the lover pattern, this step means resolving the need for love from others by filling the void in your heart. Because wanting to be loved while you reject yourself is asking the other person to give you something you don't believe you deserve. Like shopping with an empty wallet, you dream for a little while before you remember that you can't have what you want. But where do you generate self-love from when your heart feels empty?

14

SELF-LOVE

The Key to Owning Yourself

You can search throughout the entire universe for someone who is more deserving of your love and affection than you are yourself, and that person is not to be found anywhere. You yourself, as much as anybody in the entire universe, deserve your love and affection.

—BUDDHA

Mike was baffled by his relationship issues. Despite his financial success, good looks, charm, and generosity, he couldn't keep women's attention longer than a few months. When we examined his dating history, Mike realized that he had been primarily with beautiful and confident women who saw themselves as somewhat superior to him as they didn't feel the need to put any effort into the relationship. Consequently, Mike had never received a token of appreciation, been given a compliment, or even been asked questions about himself. He knew that, due to his upbringing with a rather self-absorbed mother, he subconsciously didn't believe he deserved to be treated with kindness and empathy. Thus, as soon as an attractive woman gave him a little attention, he felt immediately obligated to do his utmost to make sure he could somehow please her. Yet no matter how hard he tried, his girlfriends quickly became disinterested in him, which crushed his already low self-esteem.

When we met for the first time, Mike told me about his new companion and their turbulent relationship: "She treats me horribly, puts me down, controls me, and makes me feel like I'm crazy. But she loves me like nobody ever has." Through a simple pros and cons list, Mike realized that all he'd held on to was the faint glimmer of hope that one day she would mellow out and their happy times would last longer than just a couple of hours. Shaking his head in disbelief he said, "I'm like a crack addict. I tell myself lies about how much I need my girlfriend and how she's the only one who understands me, while in reality, I'm falling apart more each day. When we first got together, everything was so perfect. What happened?"

It's a common phenomenon of the lover pattern and their anxious attachment style. At the start of a relationship, lovers can confidently display their best traits. But as soon as their feelings are reciprocated, the fear of messing up and losing *the precious one* rears its familiar head. The worries and insecurities about getting rejected again make lovers overly accommodating and needy. As their light becomes muted, smiles forced, their love more wanting than sharing, the lover's partners become confused about these changes. Just as another person's anxiety can make us feel anxious, the lover's lack of confidence can trigger their companion's insecurity and fear of vulnerability. As they pull back, the lover desperately clasps to any sign of hope that they can avoid this relationship slipping away. Like a child fearing abandonment by its parents, the lover's attempts to win back their partner's affection become more desperate and eventually devoid of dignity and self-respect. While their hearts remain open to their partner, through a barrage of shame and self-blame, they become increasingly closed off and disconnected from themselves. Once they are less than a shadow of themselves, they get discarded like a shiny watch that turned out to be just a cheap imitation. The point is that when we are more afraid of losing our partner than losing ourselves, falling in love turns into self-abandonment.

The magic of love is not just about receiving it but sharing it with someone else. Since we can share only what we have, we need to learn to love ourselves. I know, this sounds like a cliché. But imagine inviting someone to your home, hoping they would enjoy being there. The problem is, you haven't spent much time in your house, because you've preferred to go out rather than stay in. So you don't really know where everything is. You don't value your home's charm, and you haven't cleaned up in a while, so it is a bit of a mess. How nervous would you be when your guest shows up at the door? Letting somebody into your heart, while you don't know how to love or even know yourself, is similarly frightening.

I can imagine that you may think, "Loving myself—easier said than done," or "I tried self-love, but it didn't work for me," or "Everybody says I need to love myself first, but nobody tells me how." You may have tried looking in the mirror while repeating "I love myself, I love myself." However, although the words sounded nice, you felt that you were faking it because sadly, the opposite rang truer.

Self-love isn't a switch that you can turn on and off. Like establishing a romantic relationship, self-love is a process that takes openness, focus, energy, and commitment. The good news is that you probably already know a lot about how to love others. And you know what you crave from your beloved; you simply haven't believed that you can give those things to yourself. So let's delve into the four steps to building self-love.

STEP 1: ACCEPT YOURSELF

The first step toward greater self-love is to stop tearing down its foundation—self-acceptance. It's difficult to love somebody when all you can see are their shortcomings. How often do you judge yourself—for your weight, age, hair loss, lack of friends, the state of your bank account, etc.? How often do you compare yourself to others who are *obviously* smarter, better looking, and more successful? And what about the mean ways you put yourself down when you would never dare to speak to anyone else like this? We are born with unconditional self-acceptance. Otherwise, we wouldn't dare as babies to loudly complain when we were hungry, tired, or ready for a diaper change. Even though self-acceptance is a natural force, like an inner source of gravity that keeps us grounded in the understanding that we matter, it often appears easier to reject than to accept ourselves.

As you already know from the invisibility pattern, it all starts with the people who criticized or rejected us, whose judgments we replay over and over until we believe them to be true. Then, to prevent further hurt, our subconscious installs filters that ignore our strengths and positive qualities and instead highlight why we should hide, or at least preemptively criticize ourselves before others can. And somewhere deep inside, we hold on to the fantasy that as long as we beat the drum, announcing that something is wrong with us, we may eventually succeed in whipping ourselves into shape.

Yet insecurity, shame, and self-punishment have a short motivational shelf-life. Just like someone who suffers a minor heart attack can be at first all gung ho about changing their unhealthy habits. But as soon as the pain has worn off, they go back to savoring a couple of cigarettes after a delicious double-cheeseburger with fries. Usually, self-rejection makes us want to distract or numb ourselves rather than work on ourselves.

When you look back on your relationships, how often did you choose to tolerate, absolve, and even defend your partner's poor behavior? I bet that you deserved your acceptance and forgiveness more than they did. Self-acceptance doesn't mean you have to be perfect or that you become complacent, self-centered, or arrogant. Self-acceptance is simply the choice to refuse to live in constant conflict with the person you spend the rest of your life with.

On the journey to becoming my best self, I first tried to make shame and self-doubt my guides. Rather than searching for my strengths, passions, and purpose, I imagined what faults and short-comings others hold against me. But this kept me stuck in the past, running in circles instead of advancing on my path. Once I accepted that, as Benjamin Franklin put it, "I am what I am and that's all that I am," my commitment to overcoming inner obstacles and shortcomings became stronger, yet without the need to measure up to other people's expectations, or prove wrong those who doubted me. I know I have a lot of room for improvement. I still struggle at times with enjoying the present moment, letting go of resistance to things I can't change, and keeping my focus on living up to my name—being a man of peace. But I learned to accept my imperfections and my strengths. Like two sides of the same coin, or the yin and the yang, they are parts of our wholeness. My goal is that when I'm about to take my last breath, my mind will be fulfilled and without regrets, my heart light and overflowing with love, and my spirit ready for the next adventure, whispering gently to me, "Way to go." (But maybe all I'll get is a "Now what?")

STEP 2: APPRECIATE YOURSELF

Deciding to accept rather than fight ourselves is a start. But to learn to love ourselves, we need to dismantle our subconscious distortion filters and obtain a more accurate picture of who we are. Just as we can't settle into a cozy home when all we focus on are the small stains on the carpet, we can't get comfortable with ourselves as long as we focus on our faults and don't appreciate our goodness and strengths. As you already realized from the Self-Reflection chapter, where you took an inventory of your gifts and qualities, you have many more reasons to be your friend than your enemy.

Unfortunately, most of us are more comfortable being appreciative toward others than ourselves. Self-appreciation is a highly underdeveloped skill, often because we may have been discouraged from doing so. My parents frequently popped my balloon of excitement when I came home with a stellar report card. "Don't show off," they cautioned me, "and don't feel too good about yourself. Be humble; otherwise, you may become arrogant, and nobody likes that." I interpreted this message to mean that making yourself smaller and being insecure gets you more friends than being confident. I've already shared with you how I learned the hard way that this isn't true at all.

When lovers fall in love, all they can think of is how their partners have hung the sun and the moon. They ignore their beloved's flaws and weaknesses or embrace them as their quirks and idiosyncrasies. With the lover pattern, their subconscious provides consistent proof that the object of their desire is exactly what they've been waiting for. This form of confirmation bias is how Judith's and Mike's lover patterns convinced them that their dysfunctional partners were indeed the loves of their lives. So you may wonder, if we can fool ourselves with our partners, who is to say that self-appreciation is nothing but bullshitting (excuse my French) ourselves? The difference is that with the lover pattern, the subconscious closes both eyes regarding the shortcomings of our romantic interests, which explains the infamous "love is blind" phenomenon. With ourselves, the lover's subconscious is so used to pointing out our faults that they are all it can see. Through the practice of daily appreciation, all we do is provide it with a more balanced and accurate view of who we are.

In Chapter 12, you've already started with your self-worth journal and met your inner cheerleader, who constantly points out everything you've done well. Now to expand on this, focus mainly on who you are and not just what you did. So every night in your self-worth journal, add to each activity you have listed the specific quality you expressed. Rather than sticking with what you're already used to feeling good about, such as being organized, hard-working, or reliable, pay attention to aspects of yourself that you may have either taken for granted or deemed as "not that unique." Be grateful that you're trustworthy and kind when you refrain from gossiping or judging others. Or that you are committed to staying grounded and present when you turn off the news, because you don't want to immerse yourself in negativity. Embrace that you're solid and self-reliant when you push through procrastination and resistance to your obligations. Acknowledge your multifaceted nature when you make people laugh and brighten their day, when you resolve a problem with a creative solution, or when you respond to another person's anger with compassion. Of course, your inner cheerleader can also learn to sing the praises of your brilliance as a human being—and not just as a human doing.

Since appreciation significantly improves relationships,[1] acknowledging your goodness will bring you closer to yourself and remind you how fortunate you are to be you.

STEP 3: ATTEND TO YOURSELF

Edith Hamilton, the famous educator and author, wrote, "Love cannot live where there is no trust."[2] Trust is critical for a loving relationship; it makes us feel safe and allows us to open up and show our vulnerabilities. When we trust someone, we see them as honest, benevolent, and reliable in how they treat us. And we believe that we can count on them to support us to the best of their abilities. We all know trust doesn't happen overnight but needs to be built and earned. On the other hand, trust can be erased in an instant and thus destroy a relationship.

Let's be completely honest, if you would treat anybody else the way you've been treating yourself, would they be more or less likely to trust you? I mentioned when discussing the procrastinator pattern (Chapters 7 and 8) how detrimental it is to our confidence when we can't rely on our word. A promise without follow-through is a nicely designed gift certificate we can't redeem. Very disappointing. We also undermine self-trust when we spend more time criticizing and comparing ourselves to others than being content and grateful for who we are. But maybe the worst is when we ignore our basic needs—forgetting to eat, rest, or even go to the bathroom, and treat ourselves with even less regard than a clunker car. The only difference is that we can't trade ourselves in for a newer model.

Psychologists John and Julie Gottman, world-renowned experts on marital stability, observed in one of their groundbreaking studies the interactions of 130 newlyweds on a one-day retreat.[3] The Gottmans noticed significant differences in how a spouse responded to their partner's attempts to connect, which they called *bids*. Bids can be verbal or non-verbal, small or large. For example, a bid could be, "Do you want to talk about when we should renovate the kitchen?" or, "Did you read this article in the newspaper?" or, "Can you pass the salt, please?" In response, the bidder's partner could either turn toward the bid and respond with interest, or turn away from it by ignoring or dismissing what the other person said. Although these interactions may appear minor, the Gottmans discovered that the couples divorcing within the next six years had something in common. Only three in ten of their bids for connection received a positive response, while this ratio was at least seven in ten for the pairs that stayed together. The Gottmans found that they could predict with ninety-four percent certainty whether relationships remained intact or broke up just by observing how individuals' needs to connect were received by their partners.

In an interview with *The Atlantic*, John Gottman explained, "There's a habit of mind that the masters have which is this: they are scanning social environments for things they can appreciate and say 'thank you' for. They are building this culture of respect and appreciation very purposefully. Disasters are scanning the social environment for partners' mistakes." Julie Gottman elaborated: "It's scanning the *partner* for what the *partner* is doing right or scanning him for what he's doing wrong and criticizing versus respecting him and expressing appreciation."[4]

We love the people who care for us and are kind, attentive, committed, and safe—those who see, hear, and value us and have our backs. Let's assume that the principles of creating a successful and harmonious relationship also apply to the relationship with ourselves. This means that we need to show up for ourselves to love ourselves. And let's further suppose that our thoughts, emotions, and physical sensations are bids from our mind and body to connect with our conscious selves.

If you struggle in the self-love department, it is likely that your response rate of turning toward the bids of your mind and body is three out of ten or less. You ignore or distract yourself from anxious thoughts. You're annoyed when you feel down and not as upbeat as you should. You override your stomach's pleas to stop eating junk food by popping, chewing, or guzzling heartburn meds and fight against your body's need to rest by downing sugar and caffeine. At times you may even act without integrity, quashing the call of your true self to honor your values. From the perspective of the subconscious, all this unreliable or dismissive behavior proves that you, the conscious adult, don't mean well or at least don't care, and therefore can't be trusted. And as you already know, when your subconscious doesn't trust you, it holds on to the familiar survival patterns that got you through life so far and looks for safety, validation, and love outside yourself.

On the other hand, if you show your subconscious that you are loyal, faithful, and committed to your well-being, you will become the trusted source of safety and love. Here are some examples of how you can create more self-love by responding to the bids of your mind and body.

Mind Bid: "Look, I'm Anxious, Worried, Down . . ."

It's easier to muster love for yourself when you're confident, upbeat, and full of energy. But as soon as your mind starts chiming in with worries, doubts, or sadness, and your emotional landscape becomes dark and dreary, you may try to suppress, disregard, or drown out these unpleasant bids. And if none of these attempts work, you might fuel your negativity by telling yourself all the reasons why these negative thoughts and feelings are correct.

When your mind reaches out, pay attention to whatever thoughts and emotions are coming up without being judgmental or reactionary. Just as you wouldn't block or hang up on a friend or partner in distress, you also wouldn't feed their worries about, let's say, having cancer or losing their job, by suggesting funeral arrangements or the availability of homeless shelters.

Have patience and compassion with the parts of yourself that feel anxious, unsure, or deflated. Respond to the more vulnerable aspects of yourself with encouragement, reassurance, and kindness. Guide your worried mind by offering a perspective focused on positivity and possibilities. Motivate yourself out of paralyzing insecurity by acknowledging your gifts and capabilities. And above all, remind yourself that the best way to take care of your thoughts and emotions is not to identify with them but to care for them.

Mind Bid: "I Need More Safety and Stability."

How would you feel if your partner didn't follow through with their commitments, forgot to do what you asked them to do, didn't show up for date night, or often changed plans at the last minute? You would probably go from confusion to annoyance, then to disappointment and hurt, and finally, to distrust. Most likely, you've experienced a similar range of emotions when you've let yourself down. And after breaking many promises to yourself, your subconscious may now have a difficult time trusting you. But it's never too late to rebuild this trust.

I know I repeat myself, but make your word to yourself count and honor your promises to yourself. Whether you tell yourself that you will clean your kitchen, go to bed early, or be on time to work this week, follow through. Clean up your life and deal with whatever your mind has found stressful and unsettling. This can be paying your bills on time, resolving a conflict with a sibling, or decluttering your basement. Focus only on one or two projects at a time and commit to only what you know for sure you can accomplish. When you want to regain trust in yourself, fulfilling a small commitment is more effective than fulfilling fifty percent of a grand plan. Use your external and internal boundaries to ensure that your decisions to care for yourself don't get overruled by somebody else's needs or demands. And ask for help when you feel overwhelmed or realize you can't manage on your own. Overall, make your mind feel secure and at ease by showing up for yourself, just as you would for a friend who has difficulty believing that anybody cares.

Mind Bid: "I Need to Be Nourished and Supported."

In the same way your body needs a combination of a healthy, well-balanced diet, twenty minutes of exercise each day, and sufficient rest, your mind has the exact requirements to thrive. For some reason, we often treat our mind as an unbreakable computer that can run day and night without needing maintenance. And even when stress, anxiety, brain fog, and exhaustion shake us out of this illusion, we lament our weakness, rush to "fix" the problem, and hope we can get back to how we used to be.

I frequently have to remind my clients that taking care of their mind through meditation, positive inner communication, and tools such as those from earlier chapters isn't a short-term plan to overcome their flaws. If you want to experience life with joy, purpose, and fulfillment, you need to give back to your mind so that it can continue to give to you. Thus, you want to consider your mind a mental-emotional body that needs nourishment, relaxation, and regular workouts to function at the highest level.

Instead of keeping your mind on a "fast food" diet consisting of non-stop exposure to the news, social media, and for dessert, a gruesome crime or zombie TV show, nurture it with anything that feels uplifting, inspirational, and calming. Create an organized, peaceful, and pleasant home environment so your mind doesn't get overstimulated by all the clutter. Clean the mental-emotional jumble through meditation, journaling, or just daydreaming. Give your mind enough rest and space to let it, as one of my friends calls it, "sweetly dangle back and forth, like on a swing set."

Mind-care is also becoming curious to discover and get in touch with those precious hidden or dormant parts of yourself. In one of our sessions, my client Anne told me that she finally realized why she had such a hard time loving herself and attracting love into her life. For as long as she could remember, she only valued herself for being fun, bubbly, and pretty because these were the attributes people seemed to appreciate the most about her. However, there was a deeper and more sensitive side that she neither dared to show to others nor wanted to pay attention to herself. It wasn't until she was dealing with bouts of depression and anxiety that she realized her struggles came from always having suppressed any facet other than a perky bundle of energy. She started to explore and embrace more of her other aspects by doing things she ordinarily would have judged as boring or embarrassing, such as reading a book, spending time in nature, or just hanging out with her parents. Soon Anne noticed how much calmer and more at peace with herself she started to feel.

Help your mind become more expansive and flexible by exposing yourself to new teachings, stimulating experiences, and creative endeavors. Get out of your comfort zone routine and check out a museum, listen to a talk about something random that interests you (like the love life of an octopus), or plan a trip to another country and start learning the basics of their language.

Caring for your mind is a necessity and is most effective when you approach it as an opportunity to gratefully give back to the part of you you probably rely the most on. I know that my anxiety struggles also came from taking my mind for granted, expecting it to behave and perform without giving much attention to its needs. But, just as a foster child or a stray animal can thrive in a warm and loving home, my mind learned to trust me through my consistent and compassionate care and eventually let go of its anxiety.

Body Bid: "I Need to Be Nourished and Cared For."

Most of us treat the body like an annoying stepchild. Studies showed that seventy-five percent of Americans are dissatisfied with their physical appearance.[5] One of the main reasons we as a society are more worried than ever about our looks, is that the omnipresence of media and social media outlets has distorted our beauty concepts and radically narrowed the scope of what we consider attractive and desirable. Only youthful, carefully sculpted bodies have the right to be selfied and presented to the world. This leaves many insecure and with only two options: to work on their physique with drastic diets, blood-sweating workouts, or skilled surgeons, or to hide their frame under layers of shame and self-loathing. Naturally, it's a bit more challenging to love yourself when you reject your outer appearance. Do our bodies genuinely deserve to be the punching bag of our insecurities?

Who takes you everywhere you want to go, joins in with all your activities, and patiently waits while you sit in the office for eight hours or watch TV? Who defends you against invisible forces and makes sure to get vital energy even out of a Twinkie? Who's with you from the first to the last breath of your life? Your body is more than the temple that hosts your soul. It's your most loyal companion who cares and supports you with unceasing commitment.

Since your body, like mine, may not measure up to the unrealistic beauty standards coming at us 24/7, you might have vacillated between bashing it, ignoring it, and taking it for granted. But when you consider the countless ways your body serves you every day—from the unfathomable miracles of keeping you alive, moving you around, and allowing you to connect with others, to providing you with pleasure through your five senses—accepting, appreciating, and eventually loving your physical entity shouldn't be so difficult.

One day, during an early morning run, Danielle remarked how amazingly compliant our bodies are. "We've just been sleeping for eight hours. But as soon as we got up and decided to go for a jog, without any complaints, our bodies were ready to trot through the woods." Since then, I have likened my body to a horse that carries me on its back through the ups and downs of this life's journey. Rather than identifying myself with my physical form, I see it as a separate but closely connected entity. This way, I appreciate more what my body does for me every day. And like the owner of a horse, I'm more aware of my responsibility to care for its needs. Just as I love feeding, brushing, and working with my horses, I enjoy caring for my physical "buddy."

Include your body and how it supports you in your list of daily self-appreciation. Or start your day with a friendly acknowledgment of your body by smiling at your mirror image and then greeting yourself with something like, "Hi, so nice to see you. I'm glad you're here. I'll make sure we have a great day." Then just as with the mind bids, learn to love your physicality by caring for it with kindness and gratitude. On a basic level, this means committing to nourishing your body with a healthy, balanced diet, giving it enough R&R, and keeping it strong and limber. Many of my clients tell me that their days are so packed that they simply forget to eat lunch, drink enough water, or make an appointment for their annual medical checkup. While *being too busy* is a common complaint, if you want to foster a more loving relationship with yourself, there should be nothing more important than noticing and attending to your own basic needs.

Caring also means tuning in to the messages of your body, which go beyond hunger, thirst, and fatigue. As much as you can't blame a luxury car for breaking down when you ignore the blinking light on the dashboard, you can't blame your body for not appearing or performing to your liking when you don't pay attention to it. How often does your body listen to what you ask it to do? And how many times per day do you listen to your body to find out what you can do for it? The sensations you feel throughout the day indicate whether your body is in a healthy balance or under some form of stress. For example, you like to reward yourself on the weekend with a cheese-stuffed pizza or a juicy steak with fries, but always afterward you struggle with gas and difficulty sleeping. Your body is probably telling you that your reward is more of a punishment for it. On the other hand, you may notice how you feel light and energized after having soup and a small salad for lunch, which means that your cells are happy with the fuel they received.

Before each meal, check in with your body and pay attention to how it feels, such as being full of energy, tired, tense, drained, or light. Then just think about what you're planning to eat, the taste and texture, and watch your body's reactions. Notice the sensations that indicate that your cells seem to tolerate, embrace, or reject your choices. To practice this internal communication, eat your meal, and check in with your body during and one to three hours after. It goes without saying that if you want to foster a closer relationship with your physical form, you want to listen and respond to it.

As I paid more attention to this cellular communication, I realized that some of my usual food choices were no longer acceptable to my system. My body didn't hit me over the head with strong discomfort or pain. Its messages were more subtle. You know how the thought of a delicious meal can make your mouth water, and when you think of something you don't like, you may get a knot in your stomach or slight nausea? It appeared my body preferred honey over jam, a vegetarian diet instead of meat, and herbal tea to a glass of wine at night. Since then, I lost twenty pounds, and without even trying, I am back at my ideal weight; my chronic hip pain has disappeared, and I'm sleeping like a kitten.

As you start paying attention to your body's bids, it may surprise you how often your organism tries to communicate what it needs to stay healthy and balanced. For example, you may realize that the tension in your back after three hours of hacking away on your laptop is a call for you to stand up from your desk, stretch, and walk around. Or you may sense that your body isn't always thrilled about your intense midnight runs on the treadmill at the twenty-four-hour gym and would prefer you to go home and unwind. This doesn't mean you're lazy; your batteries may just be running on empty. And when your runny nose and itchy throat tell you that you should stay home to fight off an oncoming cold, just trust your cellular wisdom. Your body has your back and will continue to tell you what's best for you, even if you have been doing the opposite for a long time.

When you commit to listening to and caring for your mind and body, not out of obligation but with an attitude of gratitude and goodwill, your heart will gently reopen and your relationship with yourself will transform.

STEP 4: INDULGE YOURSELF

How do you know that you're loved? And how do you show love? Like most of us, you probably express and experience love with a romantic partner through one or several of the five love languages Gary Chapman described in his groundbreaking bestseller *The Five Love Languages*.[6] They are words of affirmation, acts of service, gift-giving, physical touch, and quality time.

Now, let's apply these love languages to your relationship with yourself. Let's say you covered words of affirmation in Step 2 through self-appreciation. By taking care of your mind and body in Step 3, you gifted yourself with acts of service. However, in most healthy and flourishing relationships, just saying the right things and lending a helping hand aren't enough to make us feel special and adored. So make sure to also spoil yourself with a gift, physical contact, and quality time. Surprise yourself with small tokens of your appreciation that sweeten the present moment and bigger gifts that provide you with lasting joy, because they enhance your life. For example, buy yourself flowers, or treat yourself to the yummy but pricey raspberries you would love to add to your cereal but usually feel too stingy to buy. Or get that new pair of rather expensive headphones with noise-cancellation because it would make your daily commute much more enjoyable. You may wonder, what is the difference between this form of gift-giving to yourself and retail therapy to fill an inner void? One is about showing that you love yourself, and the other is about forgetting that you loathe yourself.

Physical touch can be, of course, a pampering spa treatment or any form of relaxing and rejuvenating bodywork. But expressing self-love through physical touch can also be as simple as taking a bubble bath or applying facial cream or body lotion, not in the usual utilitarian manner, but with much more tenderness and gratitude for each body part. You can also give yourself a foot, face, or belly massage, enjoying that you know best what feels good to you. I often show love to myself by placing my hands on my heart or giving myself a hug. I find that holding myself is the best way to get back in touch with myself. Or in the words of Rumi, "Give yourself a kiss. If you want to hold the beautiful one, hold yourself to yourself."

Spoiling yourself with quality time is more than taking yourself on a trip, a weekend retreat, or dinner and a movie, which are all wonderful, but also too infrequent ways to foster self-love. There are countless daily opportunities for you to spend quality time with yourself. You may change up your morning routine, and instead of rushing out of the door with your coffee mug, get up fifteen minutes earlier and start the day with a real breakfast while listening to uplifting music and telling yourself what you're looking forward to that day. In the evening, rather than killing time watching TV or swiping through social media posts, you could light candles, read a book, or write in your journal. Quality time can also be spent taking a class, starting a new hobby, indulging in an existing one, or strolling through your town, pretending to be a tourist. It doesn't matter what you do or how much time you invest. What matters is your intention for this time: to connect to yourself through experiences that bring more joy and fulfillment to your heart.

• • • • • •
DEEP EXERCISE
SELF-LOVE COMMITMENT MEDITATION

As you've already experienced, good plans and intentions need our subconscious approval and engagement to take hold in our life. The following meditation affirms to your subconscious that you're committed to taking ownership of your body, mind, and heart, caring for all aspects of your being with love and appreciation.

You may want to record this meditation in your voice and then use it daily, until loving yourself becomes second nature to you.

◊ Find a place where you are comfortable and won't get disturbed for the next ten minutes. Then, sit or lie down, relax and take a nice breath in, exhale and let your eyes fall closed. You can put your hands on your heart or keep your arms by your sides. Now with every breath, start sending yourself tender and loving thoughts, as if you were softly stroking your cheeks while whispering, "I see you. I'm here for you. I got you. I love you." With every breath, acknowledge that you are on your side and committed to supporting yourself no matter what life brings you.

◊ Now, welcome your body with love and appreciation. Scan across your physical being and acknowledge every cell and fiber. Maybe you want to thank your senses for helping you connect with the world, your legs for carrying you on this journey, and your arms for holding those you love. Or you want to appreciate your lungs and heart, or your digestive, nervous, and immune systems for their ongoing support in keeping you healthy and alive. Love and appreciate your body like a loyal companion who hosts you until your last breath. Send love and light from your heart to your body and repeat three times, "I see you. I'm here for you. I've got you. I love you."

◊ Then focus on your mind with love and appreciation. Acknowledge all the facets of your conscious mind, such as rationality and intelligence, and the ability to solve problems and bring order to chaos. Thank your subconscious mind's creativity, its fierce commitment to keeping you safe, and its willingness to trust in you to take the lead. Cherish the part of your mind that wants to be free and untethered, and the part that loves structure, predictability, and belonging. The part of your mind that is eager to explore and connect, and the part that loves solitude and stillness. Thank your mind for staying open and willing to learn and grow. Admire the expressions of your mind, like the brilliant facets of a beautiful diamond. Send love and light from your heart to your mind, and repeat three times, "I see you. I'm here for you. I've got you. I love you."

◊ Now, focus on your heart, and love and appreciate your heart in its entirety; for its ability to express love, compassion, and care, for offering you the courage, clarity, and wisdom to stay on your path and believe in your goodness, even when you are met with criticism and rejection. Embrace your heart for staying soft, vulnerable, and open to love. And for reminding you to believe in others' goodness and the light of truth at their core. Send love and light to your heart, and repeat three times, "I see you. I'm here for you. I've got you. I love you."

◊ Then see yourself from the outside—your body, your mind, your heart—and love and appreciate yourself in the present moment. Love who you've been, how you are now, and how far you have come. Still gazing at yourself from the outside, notice the pure light of your essence sparkling from your cells, molecules, atoms, and subatomic particles, and filling the space around you. With its unlimited nature, your essence reminds you that you are neither matter, thought, nor emotion. You are this pure energy of infinite consciousness. And as this light, you can accept, appreciate, care for, and love your body, mind, and heart unconditionally, as they are not your identity but your responsibility—until you leave this earth and move forward to new explorations. From this timeless vantage point loving yourself is easy, as it is your choice to live in peace and harmony with all aspects of your earthly being. A choice that nobody can take away from you. Send this eternal light and love to your body, mind, and heart, and repeat three times, "I see myself. I'm here for myself. I've got myself. I love myself."

◊ And now float back into yourself. Feel your body, your mind, and your heart, lovingly embraced by the light of your essence, just like a baby swaddled in a cozy blanket. Commit to nourishing love for yourself by always appreciating how your body, mind, and heart care for you and providing them with the attention and care they've always deserved.

Then take another deep breath in, exhale, and open your eyes. Welcome back.

......

As Judith learned to love herself, she took responsibility for the trail of painful relationships and breakups without guilt or shame. She understood that the men she was attracted to treated her with the same level of disregard she had become accustomed to since childhood. She also admitted that she had consistently pushed the *good ones* away, judging them as *boring losers* because deep inside, she didn't believe she was worthy of their love. Judith took a break from looking for love outside herself and instead focused on healing the wounds of the past and building a more robust inner relationship. One day I received an email from her: "I cannot begin to tell you how grateful I am. I now live in an entirely different world, a better one, a brighter one. I can see how the lack of self-love has led me to the hardest and most painful places in my life. And I can see now that from here on out being the champion of my light and love will be the reason for everything great in my life. I always knew self-love was fundamentally the answer, but I never believed I would get there."

There are, of course, more steps you can take to open your mind and your heart toward yourself and provide yourself with the attention, kindness, and love you deserve. Self-love takes devotion, dedication, and consistency. But your efforts will be rewarded. Instead of feeling empty and alone, you'll spend the rest of your life in peace and harmony with the one who'll never leave your side.

PART IV

Taking Charge

Integration through Implementation

15

....

THE EMPOWERED LEADER
OF YOUR LIFE

I own my life. I create my reality. I share my gifts
with the world.
And I inspire others to do the same.

Congratulations. You did it. You've arrived at the end of this journey. Off the top of your head, what are the most important lessons you've learned, and what are three changes you've already implemented based on the new insights you've gained?

We all know from our school years that repetition improves retention. So let's recap the six keys of empowerment and how they can impact your life:

- **Self-Responsibility:** Instead of feeling victimized, you accept that even though you can't control all people and circumstances, you always have the power to learn from anything that life brings you. You keep your mind open and flexible and commit to growing and evolving continuously. This way, obstacles become opportunities and limitations become possibilities.

- **Self-Compassion:** Instead of criticizing yourself and comparing or competing with others, you practice patience and compassion. You kindly attend to your vulnerabilities and appreciate your sensitivity. You create space for the gifts of your inner child and provide that innocent self with safety and security.

- **Self-Reliance:** Instead of giving in to the fear of discomfort and failure, you honor your word, follow through with your plans, and trust that you have all the inner resources to create the change, progress, and success you want. You strive for a balance of doing and being, and accept that life isn't about perfection but continuous progress.

- **Self-Reflection:** Instead of morphing yourself to fit the opinions and expectations of others, you align your thoughts, emotions, beliefs, and behaviors with your essence. You commit to discovering and expressing more and more of who you truly are, as being your authentic self is your gift to yourself and the world.

- **Self-Commitment:** Instead of seeking approval through over-giving and over-caring for others, you fill your self-worth account by taking note of the positive ways you show up in life. You take ownership of your energy, balance giving and receiving, establish healthy boundaries, and treat yourself how you want to be treated by others.

- **Self-Love:** Instead of depending on someone else's love, you foster a loving and caring relationship with yourself. You accept and appreciate who you are, attend to the needs of your mind and body, and regularly show affection by indulging yourself. You keep your heart open and commit to providing yourself with the attention, kindness, and love you deserve.

With all these keys at hand, you became the owner of your life and the creator of your reality. Yet, this may not be your first rodeo, and you've attempted to change and outgrow old mindsets, emotional patterns, and self-limiting beliefs before. And while you feel positive and encouraged now, a part of you may wonder whether this is all too good to be true, and whether you can sustain and solidify the ways of the new, empowered self and make them second nature. In short, you may question whether shifting from surviving to thriving once and for all is possible.

Do you know the story of the four-minute mile? For decades it appeared to be an impossible athletic achievement to run one mile in four minutes or less. Many men unsuccessfully chased this holy grail of track and field by optimizing their training and improving the conditions of the competitions. Finally and unexpectedly, in 1954, Roger Bannister broke through the four-minute barrier, with three minutes, fifty-nine, and four-tenths of a second. This achievement in and of itself is truly remarkable, primarily since Bannister didn't abide by strict training recommendations, and the race conditions were anything but ideal. However, what followed was even more astounding. Just six weeks later another runner, Australian John Landy, broke the barrier again with an even faster time. One year after that, three runners achieved a time under four minutes in a single race. Since then, more than a thousand athletes have accomplished the previously unthinkable.

The four-minute mile story shows that what holds us back isn't our lack of capabilities, but our lack of conviction. Sometimes we need someone to show us that our goals are achievable, a leader who transforms the sense of what's possible.

Dr. Edith Eger is a shining example of what it means to transform survival into self-empowerment. When she was sixteen, Edith, her parents, and her older sister Magda were locked in a cattle car and taken to Auschwitz. Edith's parents were sent to the gas chambers on the day they arrived at the camp. Just hours after her parents were killed, Nazi officer Joseph Mengele, the Angel of Death, forced Edith to dance for him—or die. Edith, who studied ballet and gymnastics, danced. Impressed by her performance, Mengele rewarded her with a loaf of bread that she generously shared with her fellow prisoners, despite her tremendous shock and grief. Braving the most atrocious conditions, Edith and her sister Magda helped each other stay alive. In May 1945, after the defeat of Nazi Germany, an American soldier noticed the slight movement of a hand among many dead bodies horrifically piled together in the concentration camp. His alertness saved the young woman's life. Both Edith and Magda survived.

Edith moved to the United States and became friends with Viktor Frankl, an Austrian psychiatrist and neurologist. He also had survived the Holocaust after being imprisoned in four camps in three years. His reflections on choice profoundly influenced Edith. In *Man's Search for Meaning,* Frankl wrote, "Everything can be taken from a man but one thing: the last of the human freedoms—to choose one's attitude in any given set of circumstances, to choose one's own way."[1]

Choosing to take charge of her life, Edith became a doctor of psychology, specializing in helping patients with post-traumatic stress disorder. In her memoir *The Choice: Embrace the Possible,* Dr. Eger reflects on how to live beyond survival:

The choice to accept myself as I am: human, imperfect. And the choice to be responsible for my own happiness. To forgive my flaws and reclaim my innocence. To stop asking why I deserved to survive. To function as well as I can, to commit myself to serve others, to do everything in my power to honor my parents, to see to it that they did not die in vain. To do my best, in my limited capacity, so future generations don't experience what I did. To be useful, to be used up, to survive and to thrive so I can use every moment to make the world a better place. And to finally, finally stop running from the past. To do everything possible to redeem it, and then let it go. I can make the choice that all of us can make. I can't ever change the past. But there is a life I can save: It is mine. The one I am living right now, this precious moment.[2]

Dr. Eger's inspirational story is a testimony to the resilience of the human spirit. And it shows that it's possible for all of us, no matter where we came from and where we are now, to choose to take responsibility for our happiness as the self-empowered leader of our life.

HOW YOU CAN STAY THE LEADER OF YOUR LIFE—FOR LIFE

As I just alluded to, after all your hard work on this journey, your concern may not be so much about *becoming* the leader but *remaining* so. In business, a good leader stays in touch with the company's climate, is an empathetic listener and communicator, is willing to make compromises, has integrity, and is authentic. Let's translate this into the three ways of staying the trusted leader of your life: vigilance, choice, and integrity.

Vigilance

On my podcast, *Empowerment Solutions with Dr. Friedemann,* I had the pleasure to interview Kamla Kapur, an expert on the life and work of the great Persian poet Rumi and the author of *Rumi, Tales to Live By.* During our chat, she talked about how vigilance prevents suffering and how the lack of vigilance can take us into the darkness. "Rumi said that the enemy is within," Kamla explained. "It is our unchecked thoughts that take us into despair, anxiety, and self-flagellation. The thoughts that make us feel very unkind to ourselves are the ones we need to be most aware of."[3]

Although I wouldn't call the source of our anxious or self-critical thoughts, the subconscious mind, our enemy, I agree with Kamla that vigilance—or keen awareness—is crucial for leading our lives. The grooves of old patterns are deep, and the habit of cruising on survival autopilot is too easy to fall back into. Paying attention to what we think, feel, and do is a small price to stay on the self-empowerment track.

Vigilance doesn't mean you have to sit on an inner watchtower of worries and distrust, expecting your subconscious to let you down. You just need to be aware of when your subconscious protector wants to take the wheel and steer you back into survival mode. I know that with a busy life and plenty of external distractions, it can be tricky to stay on top of what's going on in your inner world. Like the beep of a smoke detector or lane-departure warning in your car, stress, anxiety, insecurity, or depression are clear signals that it is time for you to focus inward. Yet a good leader doesn't only show up during emergencies, but is constantly aware of how things stand. Here are some of the more subtle indications that your subconscious needs your attention because it is vying for leadership over your life:

- The people and circumstances of your life—past and present—make you feel small and overwhelmed.
- You overthink the problems you're facing without coming up with a solution.
- Decision-making becomes more difficult.
- You more frequently criticize yourself.
- You become reluctant to say or do what you want.
- You compare yourself with others.
- You feel more sensitive to how people treat or speak to you.
- Assuming that others don't like you makes you want to retreat.
- Gossiping or judging others makes you feel better about yourself.
- You push yourself too hard and ignore your needs.
- Your self-talk is mainly negative and without self-appreciation.
- Your self-care routine is put on hold.
- You feel uneasy in your skin and avoid being alone.
- You rely increasingly on the guidance and approval of others.
- The future appears full of uncertainty and potential disappointments.

- You numb yourself by binging on food, TV shows, and other unhealthy instant gratifications.
- Staying in your comfort zone becomes more important than taking care of your obligations.
- Telling yourself, "I love and appreciate myself," makes you cringe.
- You know that you are better and can do better, but you tell yourself that you have no choice, or that this is who you are and will always be.

Now that you know yourself better, I'm sure you can already foresee other ways your subconscious protector shows you that its trust in your leadership weakened. As a rule of thumb, you can tell that you are about to revert into survival mode when you want to shrink, contract, and protect yourself, when your energy is low, your positivity diminished, and when your peace of mind and love for yourself are nowhere to be found.

While staying vigilant is crucial, how you respond to your subconscious hijacking your life is equally important. Rather than reacting as you used to with feelings of anxiety, annoyance, ignorance, or defeat, take the *observation without interpretation* approach. This means taking note of what you think, feel, and do without judgment or reactivity. Yes, your subconscious may have again presented you with a distorted view of reality and pushed you into self-limiting and disempowering patterns. But as the leader of your life, you're also the leader of your mind. Therefore, don't fear, fight, or fret about your subconscious. Instead, calmly listen to its concerns and complaints, and then take responsibility without blame or shame.

Observation without interpretation is awareness without attachment. You don't need to reject your subconscious for playing old records, and you don't need to join in. You know the road of survival and where it leads. And you know that you've forged an alternate, self-empowering path. All you need to do is invoke your greatest power: the power of choice.

Choice

As you already know, reality is not one truth but mostly a subjective interpretation. And as the creator of your reality, you can choose how you consciously want to perceive yourself and your circumstances.

For Viktor Frankl and Edith Eger, their ability to choose to be generous, caring, and hopeful despite the unimaginable horrors they faced preserved their dignity, humanity, and will to live. Their choice to lead with goodness and compassion while being imprisoned, tortured, and threatened with execution propelled them to transcend their circumstances and become more powerful than their oppressors.

By maintaining awareness and exercising your power of choice, you can change your subconscious's perspective from glass half empty to half full, from how you can avoid getting hurt to how you can achieve happiness. Cognitive reframing, a technique developed by the psychologist Aaron T. Beck, uses the power of choice to shift negative thoughts into a more positive mindset.[4] You've probably used reframing to reshape your reality many times. You accept coming down with a cold as a welcome opportunity to get some rest or catch up on your favorite show. You get stuck in traffic and use the time to call your parents. Your friends stand you up, and rather than feeling rejected, you wonder if they're okay.

Remember the Dynamic Awareness process we learned in the Self-Reflection chapter 10? This advanced form of reframing, which involves the subconscious, allows you to redefine your perception and approach to any situation in your life. Here's a quick summary of its four steps.

1. **Center:** Through a brief meditation, you connect to your essence and affirm the choice to live in alignment with your truth.

2. **Reflect:** Think of the person or event that triggered you to feel small and insecure and thus your subconscious to react with avoidance or pleasing patterns.

3. **Rewrite:** Grounded in your authentic truth and drawing from the wealth of your gifts and qualities, you redefine how you want to think, feel, and respond differently to situations and people who used to activate survival behavior responses.

4. **Rehearse:** Using the language of the subconscious mind—images, feelings, and sensations—you anchor these new, self-affirming responses by visualizing how you will implement and experience them.

Dynamic Awareness reframing is about turning problems into opportunities to grow, failures into feedback leading your way to success, and rejections into reflections on other people's challenges. But as you've probably already experienced, #3 *Rewrite* is often the most challenging step in reframing. How do you gain a new, empowering perspective on people and situations that activate your survival mode?

The following "I wonder..." statements will help you use the six keys you've obtained to turn your reality from focusing on survival to self-empowerment.

- **Victim—Self-Responsibility:** I wonder how I can reclaim my power and let go of the past by appreciating this situation/ person as a catalyst to learn and grow.
- **Invisible—Self-Compassion:** I wonder what my vulnerable self needs to hear from me to feel safe and reassured.
- **Procrastinator—Self-Reliance:** I wonder what action I can take to boost my confidence and trust in myself.
- **Chameleon—Self-Reflection:** I wonder what approach to this situation is in alignment with my authentic self.

- **Helper—Self-Commitment:** I wonder how I can use my time and energy in the most self-caring way right now.
- **Lover—Self-Love:** I wonder how I can lead with self-love.

Beginning your question with I wonder...? has great pedagogical power.[5] Teachers found that encouraging students to ask *wonder questions* led to a more active reflection on the material they learned and better retention of the new knowledge. I wonder...? stimulates our curiosity and motivates us to look for answers, making it a more proactive and empowering method of assessing a situation.

Once you've gained clarity on the new perspective on reality, visualize the positive and empowering shifts with #4 *Rehearse*. Otherwise, the best ideas and intentions remain nothing but gibberish for your subconscious.

But what if you still don't get a positive perspective despite all the great questions and stimulated curiosity? In this case, you want to use one of my favorite tools to directly work with the subconscious. And here is how:

● ● ● ● ● ●

DEEP EXERCISE

CHANGE YOUR PERSPECTIVE TO CHANGE YOUR REALITY

◊ Sit in a comfortable chair, facing a wall that's about six to nine feet away from you. Think about the survival mode–triggering circumstances you want to reframe.

◊ Then, choose to gain a **broader perspective**. Focus on a spot on the wall while you breathe in and out, slowly and deeply. Gently make both hands into fists, but let your index fingers point toward the ceiling. Raise your hands until your extended index fingers are at eye level, about five inches apart. Your index fingers now frame your view of the spot on the wall.

Keep on focusing on the spot in front of you, as you slowly move each fist in a half-circle motion away from your face toward your ears. Breathe. With the focus steady on the dot, watch with your peripheral vision how your index fingers move outward and next to you until they almost disappear from view. As you widen your visual field, you're also moving out of the tunnel vision of subconscious self-protection and can appreciate the situation you reflect on with greater composure. Now calmly assess your options from this broader perspective and let new ideas emerge.

◊ Drop your arms, open your hands, and let them rest next to your body. Close your eyes and set your intention to gain a **higher perspective**. Imagine that you're floating straight up in the air, above this present moment, until you see yourself from a bird's eye view. Looking down on what you're dealing with, you can see that the issue appears relatively small and insignificant and your emotional reactions to it seem far away. Notice your life's path and the connection between the past, where you are now, and the future direction you've chosen. Then spend a few minutes in this higher vantage point and assess your options.

◊ Take a breath and then assume the **infinite perspective**. Imagine you can float along your life's path until the very end, when you've transitioned from the physical form back into your pure consciousness. From this perspective, enjoy peace, unconditional love, and oneness. There is no anxiety, no negativity, and no limitation. And everything that may have appeared to be a matter of survival until this point turns out to be nothing but a small stepping stone on your journey. Be aware of the choices you can make that lead you to grow, evolve, and live without regrets. Spend a few minutes at this infinite vantage point and assess your options.

◊ Deeply inhale and exhale. Now enter into the

heart perspective. Imagine that you float from infinity along a wide arch of light right into the center of your being—into the light of your essence. From the source of your love and kindness, calmly assess your options. Let your truth show you how it wants you to respond to the challenges you've been facing. And then, from your heart, send light to the person or situation you've previously struggled with, and resolve any negative energies with compassion and forgiveness. Take one more deep breath in—and exhale. Welcome back.

......

So far, with vigilance, you've stayed keenly aware of the messages of your subconscious, observing them without attachment. Then, with choice, you calmy respond to your subconscious's survival impulses by providing a positive and empowering perspective. But since you're not just the architect of your reality but also the creator, the new mindset needs to be implemented. Implementation is the linchpin to being the leader of your life. Your subconscious will trust and follow you because you will not just provide lip service but carry on with your plans.

Integrity

Let's be honest, as you are almost at the end of this journey, this book may soon find its place on your bookshelf, next to all the other titles you have previously worked with. And you may already have other publications in mind that you hope will change your life. I appreciate your dedication to self-improvement. The problem is that by quickly moving on, you may miss out on implementing what you have discovered and learned about yourself. Consequently, your hard work and empowering insights won't become integral to your life, which is why integrity is the final step to being the leader of your life.

Leaders with integrity are authentic, honest, and trustworthy.

They align their mission with their core values and commit to reaching these goals with consistency and reliability. Famous examples of leadership with integrity are Abraham Lincoln, Martin Luther King Jr., and Ruth Bader Ginsburg. I know, shoes that we're unlikely to fill. But when you look at your life, you may have come across teachers, relatives, or bosses you admired for how they adhered to their values and beliefs, led by example, and remained true to their word. Leaders with integrity are neither infallible and always in control nor afraid of admitting their mistakes or accepting that they don't know the answers to a problem. They also empower others by giving them the recognition and praise they deserve.

So how does this translate into being the leader of your life? Here are five practical ways to harness the power of integrity so that you can further integrate your growth and empowerment.

1. Create a Mission Statement

A leader without a mission is like a boat without a rudder. A mission statement gives you direction and is a daily reminder of what you stand for, what you want to focus your energy on, and the goal you want to reach. While your overall mission may be to become and remain the authentic, empowered leader of your life, define more precisely the mission you commit to. Here are a few examples. My mission is . . . .

- to learn and grow with all that life brings me.
- to discover, express and embrace my hidden treasures.
- to always keep my word to myself and to always have my back.
- to think, feel, and act with authenticity.
- to commit to taking care of my needs and desires and honor my boundaries.
- to love and embrace all aspects of my being.

You can use your mission statement as a daily affirmation, write it on a sticky note and hang it on your bathroom mirror, or as a client of mine does, make an inspirational song out of it and chant it on the way to work. Inspire yourself daily to live with greater joy, purpose, and authenticity.

2. Set Achievable Intermediate Goals

"Are we there yet?" I don't know about you, but a road trip with my parents wouldn't have been the same without my asking this question when we weren't even one-third into it. As a little boy, the mixture of impatience, susceptibility to car sickness, and a weak bladder made long journeys an unpleasant experience. It would have been tremendously helpful if my parents had opened a map and shown me where we were heading, how far we'd already driven, and where we'd take breaks.

If your mission is to become completely self-reliant, choose tangible goals that prove you're making progress. For example, for the first month, your goal could be always to pay your bills on time or answer all your emails within twenty-four hours. You can cultivate self-compassion by spending a couple of minutes before you get up in the morning and before you fall asleep at night with your little innocent self, the part of your subconscious you have rescued from invisibility in Chapter 6. Or, if you want to become more self-aware and aligned with your authentic self, go to the list of your core qualities, and each week, pick one or two to explore and share with the world. Let's say you choose curiosity and expressiveness. Utilize curiosity by asking your friends deeper questions, picking a new lunch spot every day, or testing a new recipe with completely unknown ingredients. And practice expressiveness by striking up a conversation with a stranger waiting in line at the coffee shop or telling a friend or family member what you appreciate about them.

Intermediate goals keep you motivated and on target, and like tracking your progress on a map, keep your impatience from asking, "Are we there yet?"

3. Be Honest with Yourself

Honesty is a critical component of a leader's integrity. Being honest with yourself means instead of lying to yourself with excuses such as being too busy, too tired, or too deflated, admitting when you're not making enough progress because you're not putting in the effort to achieve your goals. Of course, you can argue that those *excuses* may also be an honest accounting of how you feel. The question is, where do these feelings come from? Is it truly the conscious leader who feels incapable of sticking with the plan, or is it your subconscious fear of failure or need to put others first that creates the resistance? You're not honest with yourself when you pretend that these resisting messages are telling you the truth, when you know that in fact they're just your subconscious's attempt to keep you from doing something it considers terrifying—changing.

4. Accept, Adjust, and Appreciate

This "triple A" concept is another crucial aspect of leading your life with integrity. Accept that you're not always the same, that you have great days, yes, and not-so-great days, and that your limitations may sometimes be stronger than your aspirations. Even if you notice that what you're attempting to achieve takes longer and is much more complicated than you anticipated, empower yourself by making the necessary adjustments to reach your goals. It takes strength and courage to admit your shortcomings, reconfigure your goals, and adjust your approaches to accomplish those goals. Yet creating reasonable expectations leads to reliable results.

A limitation doesn't necessarily mean weakness or a missing quality. An overly cautious and stubbornly dedicated subconscious protector, who keeps on playing tug-of-war with you, can also be a limitation you want to accept and adjust to. It may just take more time, calm inner dialogue, and smaller steps to get this resistant part on board. But by now, you have plenty of tools at your disposal to create a harmonious and collaborative relationship with your subconscious.

The third "A," appreciation, you are already familiar with, so I'll keep the explanation short. Self-appreciation nourishes your confidence, replenishes your self-worth, fills your heart, and fuels your motivation. And for your subconscious to accept you as a leader, you need to not only ask for its compliance but also reward its support. For example, let's say your subconscious wants to hold you back from setting boundaries with your friend, who regularly calls you in the middle of the night with some dating-drama *emergency*. After you've calmly explained to your inner helper that your sleep is sacred and your energy vital, you let your friend know that he can no longer ring you up after 10:00 p.m. Without worrying much about his response, you feel proud of yourself for establishing a clear external and internal boundary. The next day, if all remains calm inside, appreciate your subconscious for trusting you to handle this matter.

In business, the fastest way to lose the loyalty of a team is never to pay them. In life, the fastest way to lose the support of your subconscious is never to show appreciation.

5. Aim for a Bigger Purpose

In a groundbreaking study,[6] eighty healthy adults who described themselves as neither anxious nor depressed were divided into two groups depending on how they were trying to find happiness. One group regularly found joy through self-gratification, such as food, shopping, or fun experiences. The other group found happiness not from consuming but by working on a bigger purpose and contributing. While subjectively, both groups evaluated themselves as equally happy and satisfied, the analysis of their blood cells revealed a very different picture. The members of the first group had elevated levels of inflammation markers and low antiviral and antibody gene response, comparable to people who suffer from chronic stress and depression. The people who found happiness by pursuing a greater good had much lower inflammation marker levels and robust antiviral and antibody gene expressions.

So why is our body more stressed when seeking happiness and wellbeing through purchasable pleasures? It's similar to why you felt more stressed and uneasy as long as you were on survival pattern auto-pilot. No matter how much you consume—and no matter how much you avoid and please—it's never enough for your subconscious. Because when your source of happiness, security, and worthiness is outside of you, you have no guarantee when and how you will be *fed* again. Therefore, you're always living close to the edge of stress and anxiety. But if you're the source of your happiness, safety, and self-worth, and you're generously sharing who you are and the gifts you can offer, you're not only at peace with yourself, but as you find joy by connecting to others, life itself becomes your home.

A journey of self-empowerment could appear as a rather self-indulgent endeavor. Yes, you know you can be of more excellent service when you share your authentic truth, give from the fullness of your heart, and connect from love rather than neediness. But being authentic and empowered, you can also lead by example and thus make an even more significant impact on people's lives.

Model to those who feel powerless what it means to reconnect with oneself and become the empowered leader of one's own life. Inspire with your authenticity. Help others understand the power of choice and how they can be free from the past by claiming its growth opportunities. Show that kindness and compassion are strengths, and that opening your heart and being vulnerable is safer than hiding behind a mask.

Considering the multiple global challenges that demand our attention, we can't afford to let stress, anxiety, and survival consciousness get the best of us. Approaching these challenges from a solid foundation of grounded self-empowerment has become more critical than ever before. After all, the future of our world depends on how we relate to ourselves—and each other. Only when we understand and embrace who we truly are can we learn to appreciate that we are all fellow travelers, sharing the same journey, relying on each other's support.

......

Twenty-five years ago, I showed up as the leader of my life, without even knowing anything about the concept. As I shared with you during the introduction of this book, I was pretty much on autopilot at that time. As a resident in cardiology at a university hospital in Munich, Germany, aiming to become a professor, it was clear that I would have to take a scheduled break from my residency to pursue a two-year postdoctoral research program. All was set. The head of the cardiology department supported me, a scholarship from the German government paid for the two years, and the prestigious Max Planck Institute in Munich had accepted me as a research fellow. But then, as I was about to start my research program, I got a call from the head of the Max Planck laboratory telling me that they, unfortunately, could no longer offer me a position in their group. Completely dumbfounded, I couldn't even listen to his explanations about why they slammed the door in my face. My head spun, my breath accelerated, and I almost fainted. All I could think of was that my career, and consequently my life, was over. All I'd achieved through hard work and long hours was swiped away with one phone call. Looking back, it's evident that my subconscious protector was in overdrive. At a loss about how to respond to this catastrophe, I was spinning through the same cycles of feeling victimized, ashamed, afraid of the future, and unsure about how to get back on track.

Feeling dazed and confused, I did what most people in Munich do when they have to find solutions to insurmountable problems. I went to the next beer garden with my best friend, Sabine. At first, I continued to spew all the complaints about my rotten luck and why my future as a professor in cardiology was kaput. My friend listened patiently but didn't believe a word I said. "I'm sure you'll find another way," she said. "You always do." Since misery loves company, her inappropriately positive attitude made me a little peeved. But listening to her encouraging words also calmed me down. Maybe there was another way, one I'd never thought of. I hadn't even finished my first beer when suddenly a simple question bubbled up from somewhere deep within: "What about finding a research position in the US? You always wanted to live there for a while. Wouldn't that be a great opportunity?" Wherever this inspiration came from, probably my essence, it immediately shifted my entire outlook. I went from feeling deflated and beaten down to hopeful and excited. Of course, my cautious subconscious chimed in with, "What about your girlfriend? Where would you even go? What if nobody there wants you?" But these worries faded once I chose to believe that destiny had thrown me a bone by closing the Max Planck door and opening a whole new adventure for me.

For me, this was one of the most striking examples of the power of choice. A simple inspiration changed my whole perspective, and I went from feeling defeated to seeing the opportunity to fulfill a dream I'd almost forgotten.

Sitting in the beer garden, fantasizing about living in the US for a couple of years, I had no clue that this choice would be just the beginning of a complete transformation of my life. It's breathtaking to realize how one single moment can lead to an endless string of life-changing consequences. I wouldn't have become the leader of my life if I hadn't followed through with pursuing this dream. Without integrity to honor and pursue my choice, despite the many obstacles I faced along the way, I wouldn't have met my wife of twenty years, I wouldn't have changed my career and found my greater purpose, and you wouldn't be reading this book.

I would like to end this book with Dr. Edith Eger's words, which deeply resonate with me because they perfectly describe what the journey to becoming the empowered leader of your life is all about:

To the vast campus of death that consumed my parents and so very many others, to the classroom of horror that still had something sacred to teach me about how to live—that I was victimized but I'm not a victim, that I was hurt but not broken, that the soul never dies, that meaning and purpose can come from deep in the heart of what hurts us the most—I utter my final words. "Goodbye," I say, and, "Thank you." Thank you for life, and for the ability to finally accept the life that is.[7]

ACKNOWLEDGMENTS

This book would not have been possible without my clients, who are my greatest teachers and sources of inspiration. Their transformational changes prove every day that we all have unlimited potential to heal, change, and grow. I feel blessed and privileged to have had the opportunity to support them on their journey from feeling powerless and disconnected to becoming the authentic leaders of their lives. I appreciate their trust and confidence in me and my work and their unshakeable commitment to transcend the darkness to find the light within.

I'm also so grateful for my beloved wife, Danielle Rama Hoffman, and the countless ways she provided me with love and care. Whether I needed a little push to keep on writing, some cheerleading to boost my confidence when I was doubting, or a gentle reminder that it was time for some self-care, Danielle's patience and support were instrumental for this book to come into existence.

Much appreciation goes to my friend and personal editor, Kelly Malone, who right from the beginning assured me that this is timely and much-needed work. As with my first book, *The Fear and Anxiety Solution,* Kelly's editorial support was a safety net, making writing exciting, fun, and risk-free. Her skillful corrections, suggestions, questions, and funny and uplifting comments gave this book more structure, clarity, and eloquence.

A special thanks to everyone at Bear & Company, especially Jon Graham and Emilia Cataldo, for believing in this work and making it available to the world.

Our four-legged family members and their unconditional love and acceptance have been invaluable anchors in my life. Whenever I spent too many hours on the computer, all I needed to do was feed our horses or play with our cats to quickly get grounded and recentered in the now. I'm so grateful for them showing me every day what it means to be present, authentic, and filled with unconditional love and acceptance.

It is with love and appreciation that I honor my mind—conscious and subconscious—my body, and my heart, whose loyal support allowed me to stay sane and healthy even during the most demanding times of completing the manuscript.

Last but not least, thank you to my essence and guides. Their input and inspiration kept this book in alignment with its higher purpose: to reconnect us with our truth and open our hearts to love and compassion so that we can transcend the self-protective patterns that separate us from ourselves, one another, and our sacred responsibility, to become the caring stewards of this planet.

Notes

INTRODUCTION

1. Arianne Cohen, "How to Quit Your Job in the Great Post-Pandemic Resignation Boom," *Bloomberg Businessweek* website, May 10, 2021.
2. "Economic News Release," U.S. Bureau of Labor Statistics, Accessed October 30, 2010.
3. Bryan Lufkin, "What We're Getting Wrong about the 'Great Resignation,'" *BBC Worklife* website, October 28, 2021.

CHAPTER I. SURVIVAL AND THE SLOW LOSS OF SELF

1. Emma E. McGinty, *et al.,* "Psychological Distress and Loneliness Reported by US Adults in 2018 and April 2020," *Journal of American Medical Association* 324, no. 1 (2020): 93–94.
2. American Psychological Association. "Stress in America 2020: Stress in the Time of COVID-19," PsycEXTRA Dataset, vol. 1(May 2020).
3. Jagdish Khubchandani and James H. Price, "Short Sleep Duration in Working American Adults, 2010–2018," *Journal of Community Health* 45 (2020): 219–227.

CHAPTER 2. THE SUBCONSCIOUS MIND: YOUR AGENT OF CHANGE

1. Chun Siong Soon, *et al.,* "Unconscious Determinants of Free Decisions in the Human Brain," *Nature Neuroscience* 11 (2008): 543–545.
2. J. M. Richards and J. J. Gross, "Emotion Regulation and Memory: The

Cognitive Costs of Keeping One's Cool," *Journal of Personality and Social Psychology* 79, no. 3 (2000): 410–424.

3. Susanne Erk, *et al.,* "Emotional context modulates subsequent memory effect," *Neuroimage* 18 (2003): 439–447.

CHAPTER 4. SELF-RESPONSIBILITY: THE KEY TO OWNING YOUR PAST

1. Donna J. Bridge and Ken A. Paller, "Neural Correlates of Reactivation and Retrieval-Induced Distortion," *Journal of Neuroscience* 32, no. 35 (August 29, 2012): 12144–12151.

2. Eleanor Roosevelt, *You Learn by Living* (1960), 152.

3. "Interview to the Press" in Karachi about the execution of Bhagat Singh (23 March 1931), published in *Young India,* 2 April 1931.

4. *Wisdom for the Soul: Five Millennia of Prescriptions for Spiritual Healing,* compiled by Larry Chang. (Gnosophia, 2006), 321.

5. Britta A. Larsen, *et al.,* "The immediate and delayed cardiovascular benefits of forgiving," *Psychosomatic Medicine* 74, no. 7 (October 2012): 745–750; and Kelly S Flanagan, et al., "The potential of forgiveness as a response for coping with negative peer experiences," *Journal of Adolescence* 35, no. 5 (2002).

CHAPTER 6. SELF-COMPASSION: THE KEY TO OWNING YOUR HIDDEN GIFTS

1. Inbal Ben-Ami Bartal, "Empathy and Pro-Social Behavior in Rats," *Science* 334, no. 6061 (2011):1427–1430.

2. F. Warneken and M. Tomasello, "Altruistic helping in human infants and young chimpanzees," *Science* 311, no. 5765 (March 3, 2006): 1301–3.

3. Helen Keller, *Let Us Have Faith* (Garden City, NY: Doubleday & Co., 1940), 50–51.

4. Karl Pillemer, *30 Lessons for Living: Tried and True Advice from the Wisest Americans*, (New York: Hudson Street Press) 252.

5. Jasper H.B. de Groot, Monique A.M. Smeets, *et al.,* "Chemosignals Communicate Human Emotions," *Psychological Science* 23, no. 11, 1417–1424.

CHAPTER 7. THE PROCRASTINATOR PATTERN: WAITING FOR TOMORROW

1. Cari Romm, "One in Five People Are Chronic Procrastinators," *The Cut,* July 24 2017, The Cut website.

2. Piers Steel, "The nature of procrastination: a meta-analytic and theoretical review of quintessential self-regulatory failure," *Psychological Bulletin* 133, no. 1 (2007): 65–94.

3. Manfred E. Beutel, *et al.*, "Procrastination, Distress and Life Satisfaction across the Age Range—A German Representative Community Study," *PLOS One* (2016).

4. Diane Tice and Roy Baumeister, "Longitudinal Study of Procrastination, Performance, Stress, and Health: The Costs and Benefits of Dawdling," *Psychological Science* 8, no. 6 (2012):454–458.

CHAPTER 8. SELF-RELIANCE: THE KEY TO OWNING YOUR ACTIONS

1. Daniel T. Gilbert, "How mental systems believe," *American Psychologist* 46, no. 2 (1991): 107–119.

2. Timothy J. Buschman and Earl K. Miller, "Shifting the spotlight of attention: evidence for discrete computations in cognition," *Frontiers in Human Neuroscience* 4 (November 2, 2010).

3. Vicki G. Morwitz, *et al.*, "Does Measuring Intent Change Behavior?" *Journal of Consumer Research* 20 (February 1993): 46–61.

4. Anthony G. Greenwald and Catherine G. Carnot, "Increasing voting behavior by asking people if they expect to vote," *Journal of Applied Psychology* 72, no. 2 (1987): 315–318.

5. Gaston Godin, *et al.*, "The effect of mere-measurement of cognitions on physical activity behavior: a randomized controlled trial among overweight and obese individuals," *International Journal of Behavioral Health and Human Activity* 8, no. 2 (2011).

6. Godin G, *et al.*, "Asking questions changes behavior: mere measurement effects on frequency of blood donation," *Health Psychology* 27, no. 2 (March 2008): 179–84.

7. Jonathan Levav and Gavin J. Fitzsimons, "When questions change behavior: the role of ease of representation," *Psychological Science* 17, no. 3 (2006): 2017–2013.

8. Neil Garrett, *et al.*, "The brain adapts to dishonesty," *Nature Neuroscience* 19 (2016): 1727–1732.

9. Amy N. Dalton and Stephen A. Spiller, "Too Much of a Good Thing: The Benefits of Implementation Intentions Depend on the Number of Goals," *Journal of Consumer Research* 39, no. 3 (October 2012): 600–614.

10. K. L. Milkman, *et al.,* "Harnessing Our Inner Angels and Demons: What We Have Learned About Want/Should Conflicts and How That Knowledge Can Help Us Reduce Short-Sighted Decision Making," *Perspectives on Psychological Science* 3, no. 4 (2008): 324–338.

11. Peter M. Gollwitzer, "Implementation Intentions: Strong Effects of Simple Plans," *The American Psychologist* 54, no. 7 (1999): 493–503.

12. Todd Rogers, *et al.,* "Beyond Good Intentions: Prompting People to Make Plans Improves Follow-through on Important Tasks," *Behavioral Science & Policy* 1, no. 2 (2015): 33–41.

13. Floor M. Kroese, *et al.,* "Bedtime procrastination: introducing a new area of procrastination," *Frontiers in Psychology* (June 19, 2014).

14. B.A. Kamphorst, *et al.,* "Too Depleted to Turn In: The Relevance of End-of-the-Day Resource Depletion for Reducing Bedtime Procrastination," *Frontiers in Psychology* (March 14, 2018).

CHAPTER 9. THE CHAMELEON PATTERN: FITTING IN AT ALL COSTS

1. Richard Bandler & John Grinder (1975a). *The Structure of Magic I: A Book About Language and Therapy.* Palo Alto, CA: Science & Behavior Books.

2. Susie, Demarinis, "Loneliness at epidemic levels in America," Science Direct 16, no. 5 (September-October 2020): 278-279.

3. Bansal A, Garg C, Pakhare A, Gupta S. "Selfies: A boon or bane?" *J Family Med Prim Care.* 2018 Jul–Aug 7(4): 828–831.

4. "Number of Social Network Users from 2017 to 2025," *Statistica* website, Accessed December 29, 2021.

5. "Percentage of U.S. population who currently use any social media from 2008 to 2021," *Statistica* website, Accessed December 30, 2021.

6. Mustafa Koc and Seval Gulyagci, "Facebook addiction among Turkish college students: the role of psychological health, demographic, and usage characteristics," *Cyberpsychology, Behavior, and Social Networking* 16, no. 4 (April 16, 2013): 279–84.

7. Tracii Ryan, *et al.,* "The uses and abuses of Facebook: A review of Facebook addiction," *Journal of Behavioral Addiction* 3, no. 3 (September 2014): 133–148.

8. Melissa G. Hunt, *et al.,* "No More FOMO: Limiting Social Media Decreases Loneliness and Depression," *Journal of Social and Clinical Psychology* 37, no. 10 (December 2018) 751–768

CHAPTER 10. SELF-REFLECTION:
THE KEY TO OWNING YOUR TRUTH

1. Tolle, Eckhart. *Oneness with All Life: Inspirational Selections from A New Earth.* London: Penguin, 2008.

2. G.A. Bonanno, *et al.,* "The importance of being flexible: the ability to both enhance and suppress emotional expression predicts long-term adjustment," *Psychological Science* 15, no. 7 (July 2004), 482–7.

3. Steven C. Hayes, *et al., Mindfulness and Acceptance: Expanding the Cognitive Behavioral Tradition* (New York: Guilford Press, 2004).

4. Todd B. Kashdan, "Psychological Flexibility as a Fundamental Aspect of Health," *Clinical Psychology Review* 30, no. 7 (November 1, 2010): 865–78.

5. Steven C. Hayes, *et al., Acceptance and Commitment Therapy: The Process and Practice of Mindful Change* (New York: Guilford Press, 2011), 96.

6. Hayes *et al., Mindfulness and Acceptance.*

7. Shane J. Lopez and C.R. Snyder, editors, *Oxford Handbook of Positive Psychology, 2nd Ed* (New York: 2009), 367–374.

8. R. Hogan, *et al.,* editors, *Handbook of Personality Psychology* (San Diego: Academic Press, 1997), 825–847.

9. B.L. Fredrickson, "What Good Are Positive Emotions?" *Review of General Psychology* 2, no. 3 (September 1998): 300–319.

10. Christopher Peterson, *et al.,* "Strengths of character, orientations to happiness, and life satisfaction," *Journal of Positive Psychology* 2 (2007): 149–156.

CHAPTER 11. THE HELPER PATTERN:
OVER-EXTENDED AND UNDERAPPRECIATED

1. Elizabeth W. Dunn, Lara B. Aknin, *et al.,* "Spending money on others promotes happiness," *Science* 319, no. 5870 (March 21, 2008): 1687–8; and Francesca Borgonovi, "Doing well by doing good. The relationship between formal volunteering and self-reported health and happiness," *Social Science Medicine* 66, no. 11 (June 2008): 2321–34.

2. Pierre Gérain and Emmanuelle Zech, "Do informal caregivers experience more burnout? A meta-analytic study," *Psychological Health Medicine* 26, no. 2 (February 2021): 145–161.

3. Angelou, Maya. *Wouldn't Take Nothing for My Journey Now.* London: Bantam, 2011.

4. The Dalai Lama, *The Art of Happiness, 10th Anniversary Edition, A*

Handbook for Daily Living (New York: Riverhead Books, 2009), 207.

5. Charlotte Grosse Wiesmann, *et al.,* "White matter maturation is associated with the emergence of Theory of Mind in early childhood," *Nature Communications* 8, no. 14692 (March 21, 2017).

6. V. Gallese, *et al.,* "Action recognition in the premotor cortex," *Brain* 119 (1996): 593–609.

7. Daniel Goleman and Richard E. Boyatzis, "Social intelligence and the biology of leadership," *Harvard Business Review* 86, no. 9 (September 2008), 74–81, Harvard Business Review website.

8. Bianca P. Acevedo, *et al.,* "The highly sensitive brain: an fMRI study of sensory processing sensitivity and response to others' emotions," *Brain Behavior* 4, no. 4 (July 2014): 580–94.

9. Yuan Cao, *et al.,* "Low Mood Leads to Increased Empathic Distress at Seeing Others' Pain," *Frontiers in Psychology* 8, no. 2024 (November 20, 2017).

10. Barbara Oakley, *et al.,* editors, *Pathological Altruism* (Cary, NC: Oxford University Press, 2012), 10–30.

11. Tobias Esch and George B. Stefano, "The neurobiological link between compassion and love," *Medical Science Monitor* 17, no. 3 (February 25, 2011).

12. James A Coan, *et al.,* "Lending a hand: social regulation of the neural response to threat," *Psychological Science* 17, no. 12 (December 1, 2006): 1032–9.

CHAPTER 12. SELF-COMMITMENT: THE KEY TO OWNING YOUR ENERGY

1. May, Rollo. *The Courage to Create.* New York: W.W. Norton Company, 1994.

2. Paulo Coelho, "If you think adventure is dangerous, try routine—it's lethal," Twitter, November 14, 2011.

CHAPTER 13. THE LOVER PATTERN: ACHING FOR LOVE

1. Ying Chen, *et al.,* "Parental warmth and flourishing in mid-life," *Social Science & Medicine* 220 (January 2019): 65–72.

2. Pino Alonso, *et al.,* "Perceived parental rearing style in obsessive-compulsive disorder: relation to symptom dimensions," *Psychiatry Research* 127, no. 3, (July 15, 2004): 267–78; and R.M. Rapee, "Potential role of childrearing practices in the development of anxiety and depression," *Clinical Psychology Review* 17, no. 1 (1997): 47–67.

3. Robert Winston and Rebecca Chicot, "The importance of early bonding on

the long-term mental health and resilience of children," *London Journal of Primary Care* 8, no. 1 (2016): 12–14.

4. Sheela Kennedy and Steven Ruggles, "Breaking up is hard to count: the rise of divorce in the United States, 1980–2010," *Demography* 51, no. 2 (April 2014): 587–598.

5. John Bowlby, *Attachment: Attachment and Loss,* Volume One (New York: Basic Books, 1969).

6. Cindy Hazan and Phillip Shaver, "Romantic love conceptualized as an attachment process," *Journal of Personality and Social Psychology* 52, no. 3 (1987): 511–52.

7. Bjarne M. Holmes and Kimberly R. Johnson, "Adult attachment and romantic partner preference: A review," *Journal of Social and Personal Relationships* 26, no. 6–7 (December 2009): 833–852.

CHAPTER 14. SELF-LOVE: THE KEY TO OWNING YOURSELF

1. Sara B. Algoe, Laura E. Kurtz, and Nicole M. Hilaire, "Putting the 'You' in 'Thank You': Examining Other-Praising Behavior as the Active Relational Ingredient in Expressed Gratitude," *Social Psychology and Personality Science* 7, no. 7 (2016): 658–666.

2. Hamilton, Edith. *Mythology: Timeless Tales of Gods and Heroes.* Boston: Little, Brown and Company, 1942.

3. John M. Gottman, *et al.,* "Predicting Marital Happiness and Stability from Newlywed Interactions," *Journal of Marriage and Family* 60 (1998): 5–22.

4. E. E. Smith, "The Secret to Love is Kindness, *The Atlantic* (June 12, 2014), The Atlantic website.

5. David A. Frederick, *et al.,* "Correlates of appearance and weight satisfaction in a U.S. National Sample: Personality, attachment style, television viewing, self-esteem, and life satisfaction," *Body Image* 17 (June 17, 2016): 191–203.

6. Gary Chapman, *The Five Love Languages: How to Express Heartfelt Commitment to Your Mate* (Chicago: Northfield Publishing, 1992).

CHAPTER 15. THE EMPOWERED LEADER OF YOUR LIFE

1. Viktor E. Frankl, *Man's Search for Meaning* (Boston: Beacon Press, 2006), 66.

2. Edith Eva Eger, *The Choice: Embrace the Possible* (New York: Scribner, 2017), 155–156.

3. Dr. Friedemann Schaub, "How vigilance prevents suffering; with Kamla Kapur: Empowerment Radio 065 Part 3," YouTube video, 0:20, November 27, 2019, Accessed December 29, 2021.

4. Aaron T. Beck, "The past and the future of cognitive therapy," *Journal of Psychotherapy Practice and Research* 6, no. 4 (Fall, 1997): 276–284, National Library of Medicine website.

5. Christine Lindstrom, "The Pedagogical Power of Wonder Questions," *The Physics Teacher* 59, no. 4 (March 31, 2021): 275–277.

6. BL Fredrickson, KM Grewen, KA Coffey, SB Algoe, AM Firestine, JM Arevalo, J Ma, SW Cole. A functional genomic perspective on human well-being. Proc Natl Acad Sci U S A. 2013 Aug 13;110(33):13684-9.

7. Edith Eva Eger, *The Choice*, 232–233.

INDEX

ABOUT THE AUTHOR
AND RESOURCES

Friedemann Schaub, M.D., Ph.D., is a physician, researcher, personal development coach, and the author of the multiple award-winning book *The Fear and Anxiety Solution: A Breakthrough Process for Healing and Empowerment with Your Subconscious Mind. The Fear and Anxiety Solution* was the 2012 Independent Publisher Award Gold Medal winner and the USA Best-Book Award winner in the category best new self-help book. Dr. Schaub's Breakthrough and Empowerment Program has helped thousands of his clients worldwide to overcome fear, anxiety, and self-limiting patterns by addressing the deeper, subconscious root causes of these mental and emotional challenges. Dr. Schaub's research and advice have been featured in *Oprah Magazine, Huffington Post, Reader's Digest, Teen Vogue,* and *Shape.* He is also the host of the podcast *Get Real—Empowering Solutions for Anxiety-Free Living* and a sought-after speaker and expert on fear, anxiety, and human potential.

Dr. Schaub holds a medical degree from the University of Munich in Germany and a Ph.D. in molecular biology from the University of Washington in Seattle. He practiced as a physician in the cardiology department at the University of Munich and was a research scientist at the University of Washington. Dr. Schaub's medical research has been published and featured in highly prestigious medical and science journals, including *Nature Medicine* and *Circulation*.

> "Medicine and research taught me the power of the mind-body connection and how our thoughts, emotions, and beliefs strongly impact health and illness."

Dr. Schaub recognizes that our abundant self-healing abilities can only function effectively when mind, body, and spirit are in alignment; in particular, the subconscious mind holds the keys to accelerated healing, change, and growth.

Realizing the enormous potential of conscious-subconscious collaboration, he extensively studied mind-activating modalities and became a certified master practitioner in Neuro-Linguistic Programming (NLP) as well as Time Line Therapy, and a certified trainer in clinical hypnotherapy. Based on this wealth of knowledge and experience, Dr. Schaub created a Breakthrough and Empowerment Program specifically designed to eliminate deep-seated emotional baggage, self-sabotaging patterns, and limiting beliefs that prevent us from leading productive, fulfilling, and balanced lives.

Dr. Schaub lives with his wife, Danielle Rama Hoffman (author of *The Temples of Light, The Council of Light,* and *The Tablets of Light*), and their cats and horses in the South of France.

RESOURCES

Please refer to the programs and products on the following page to support and enhance your personal growth and empowerment.

And visit www.drfriedemann.com for self-empowering tools, video-seminars on how to break through fear, guided meditations, blog articles, and more.

You can also follow Dr. Schaub on Instagram
www.instagram.com/dailyempowermentsolutions
and Facebook
www.facebook.com/Dr.FriedemannSchaub.

Re-align with Your Essence Meditation

This guided meditation is based on the exercise with the same name in Chapter 10 of *The Empowerment Solution* (see page 202). With this process, you will be able to remove those protective layers that have obscured the awareness of your authenticity so that you can freely reconnect with your authentic truth.

https://drfriedemann.com/essence/

Personal Breakthrough Program

What holds us back is not who we are but who we think we are. This is why we are capable of much more than we may have believed—and were made to believe by others. The Accelerated Breakthrough Program is a proven solution that has helped thousands of Dr. Schaub's clients overcome fear, anxiety, depression, low self-esteem, and self-sabotaging behavior. This step-by-step process consists of one-on-one coaching, conscious-subconscious mind integrative processes, and practical, self-empowering tools tailored to your needs.

Empowerment Solutions Podcast

In this weekly podcast, Dr. Friedemann Schaub and his expert guests share proven tips, tools, and strategies for overcoming mental, emotional, and behavioral challenges that hold you back from enjoying your best life. You can watch *Empowerment Solutions* on https://www.youtube.com/user/drfriedemannschaub